Winnie Lightner

HOLLYWOOD LEGENDS SERIES
CARL ROLLYSON, GENERAL EDITOR

Winnie Lightner

TOMBOY OF THE TALKIES

DAVID L. LIGHTNER

UNIVERSITY PRESS OF MISSISSIPPI • JACKSON

www.upress.state.ms.us

Designed by Peter D. Halverson

The University Press of Mississippi is a member of the
Association of American University Presses.

Frontispiece: Publicity still from *Gold Diggers of Broadway* (1929).
(Courtesy Ron Hutchinson/The Vitaphone Project.)

Photographs not credited otherwise are from the collection of the author.

First printing 2017
∞
Library of Congress Cataloging-in-Publication Data

Names: Lightner, David L., 1942– author.
Title: Winnie Lightner : tomboy of the talkies / David L. Lightner.
Description: Jackson : University Press of Mississippi, 2016. | Series:
Hollywood legends series | Includes bibliographical references and index.
| Includes filmography.
Identifiers: LCCN 2016019163 (print) | LCCN 2016024280 (ebook) | ISBN
9781496809834 (hardcover : alk. paper) | ISBN 9781496809841 (epub single)
| ISBN 9781496809858 (epub institutional) | ISBN 9781496809865 (pdf
single) | ISBN 9781496809872 (pdf institutional)
Subjects: LCSH: Lightner, Winnie, 1899–1971. | Actors—United
States—Biography.
Classification: LCC PN2287.L448 L55 2016 (print) | LCC PN2287.L448 (ebook) |
DDC 791.4302/8092 [B] —dc23
LC record available at https://lccn.loc.gov/2016019163

British Library Cataloging-in-Publication Data available

CONTENTS

Winnie Lightner

Introduction

FROM STAGE RIGHT SHE BOUNDS INTO VIEW AND BURSTS INTO SONG. It's a ribald number about a tropical island where the natives frolic in blissful nakedness, and if a missionary shows up and gives them any bother, they eat him. "Never mind their morals," the singer cries. "Say, what have they to hide? The women dress in corals, and the men seem satisfied."

It is a typical blast of mirth and gusto from wild and wonderful Winnie Lightner, the first great female comedian of the talkies. In 1929 she stole the show in *Gold Diggers of Broadway*, one of the earliest and best of Hollywood's magnificent musical comedies. She went on to head the cast in seven other Warner Bros. features. Her co-stars included Chester Morris, Joe E. Brown, and the comedy teams of both Olsen and Johnson and Smith and Dale. After that Winnie played supporting roles in four more movies, acting the part of worldly-wise, loudmouthed best friend to Loretta Young, Joan Crawford, or Mona Barrie. Winnie was renowned for her ability to belt out song after song in rapid succession, her bold and brassy acting style, and her gleeful mockery and subversion of conventional morality and gender roles. All of those attributes led to her being called the tomboy of the talkies.

Born on the eve of the twentieth century and reared amid the cacophony and grime of West Side Manhattan, Winnie began performing in big-time vaudeville at age fifteen. She was blessed with a resonant singing voice that carried easily to the far reaches of the second balcony. Soon she discovered that her musical gift was matched by a knack for delivering spot-on wisecracks coupled with facial mugging and bodily contortions. Together with two partners, she toured from coast to coast on the Keith and Orpheum circuits, and their act reached the pinnacle of vaudeville success by playing the fabled Palace Theater on a regular basis.

In the 1920s Winnie deserted vaudeville for Broadway, where lavish revues like Florenz Ziegfeld's *Follies* and its many competitors were in their heyday. Winnie starred in three annual editions of George White's *Scandals*, two of the Shubert Brothers' *Gay Paree*, and one of Harry Delmar's *Revels*. In those shows she introduced many songs that became popular hits nationwide. Some of them are heard even now, notably the two George Gershwin classics "I'll Build a Stairway to Paradise" and "Somebody Loves Me." She also appeared in numerous comedy skits, which included everything from voicing a heartfelt musical plea, "Give Me the Rain," whereupon Eddie Conrad drenched her with a bucket of water, to badgering W. C. Fields as he struggled with a collapsing automobile.

When the movies began to talk and to sing, Winnie joined them. When she delivered some spicy lyrics in a one-reel short subject, she acquired a permanent place in motion picture history as the first performer to be censored for spoken words rather than visual images. In the feature films that followed, she delighted audiences, and especially their female component, with her boisterous and aggressive behavior. In her best film roles she was the comic epitome of a fire-breathing feminist, who abused men and spurned their advances—unless they were filthy rich, in which case she latched onto the suckers as potential meal tickets.

When a regressive social climate rendered audiences unreceptive to feminism, Warner Bros. tried to reposition Winnie as glamorous and sexy, assigning her contradictory roles in which she played a top dog in the workplace who was meekly subservient at home. The new image did not go over at the box office, however, and Winnie's stardom came to an end. In her final pictures she reverted to the noisy feminist of old, a role that was acceptable because as a secondary player, she merely served as comic contrast to female stars who conformed to societal expectations.

Winnie Lightner deserves recognition as a significant figure both in show-business history and in women's history. She was a feminist icon, a terrific singer, a brilliant comedian, and a headline act in vaudeville, Broadway, and the talkies. So why have you never heard of her? That is a good question. It is surprising that an entertainer once so famous could now be so forgotten. One of the aims of this book is to explain how that public amnesia came about. It is a curious story with some surprising twists. Much of Winnie's best work was presented live on stage and was thus ephemeral, yet even her motion picture performances proved less permanent than might be supposed. When a fickle public tired of musicals, songs were cut from Winnie's films, and her wonderful singing voice all but silenced. Technological changes in the movie industry resulted in her films being mutilated or even lost. Feminism withered as the era of the carefree flapper gave way to a time of unprecedented economic collapse and social malaise. Then a pall of prissiness descended over Hollywood with the introduction of the Motion Picture Code. Finally, Winnie decided to retire at age thirty-five and thereafter refused all entreaties to return to the spotlight.

This book takes the reader to a vanished world. Winnie's career spanned the First World War, the Roaring Twenties, and the grimmest years of the Great Depression. During that time American society underwent wrenching change, and so did show business. When Winnie first dashed onto the stage, thousands of vaudeville theaters blanketed all but the most desolate regions of North America. Yet even as Winnie entered that flourishing realm of popular entertainment, it was being challenged by an upstart rival consisting of flickering images projected onto a glorified bed sheet.

At first the lowly nickelodeon, with its hodgepodge program of short, silent, and fuzzy reels, posed no serious threat to vaudeville's color, noise, and musicality. But the quality of motion pictures improved apace, and soon filmmakers began turning out multi-reel features with captivating plots and extended story lines. Once that happened, the lower cost of providing popular entertainment via filmed rather than live performance began to eat away at the viability of vaudeville. Whether by luck or design, Winnie left for the Great White Way just as big-time vaudeville was faltering but Broadway revues were flying high, thanks to their urbane and affluent clientele. Then, in a second stroke of either good fortune or good judgment, Winnie joined the exodus from New York to Hollywood just as the coming of the sound revolution ensured that both then and for decades to come, it was in the darkness of the cinema that the glittering stars came out.

Some of the bright and shining stars of the early talkies are still remembered, but many are not. Winnie Lightner is among the forgotten. She should not be. This is her story.

CHAPTER 1

A Tomboy in Pigtails

PEOPLE SCREAMED AND SCATTERED IN TERROR AS A HORSE CAREENED
through the heart of town. Astride the beast, clinging on somehow, were
four drunken men. They drove the poor animal at full gallop until at
last it collapsed, spilling its riders in all directions. As the horse struggled
to get up, a local teenager dashed into the street and grabbed its bridle,
only to be set upon by one of the drunks. The teenager returned punch
for punch and knocked the man down. But the attacker leaped to his
feet, pulled out a knife, and rushed at the youth a second time. The
youth dodged the blade and again trounced his assailant. The other three
drunks then joined the fray. Fortunately for the outnumbered young
man, a town constable appeared. Weighing in with his billy club, the
constable whacked the skulls of one drunk after another. Soon all four
were splayed on the ground, unconscious.

These stirring events took place 2 December 1893 in Greenport, a
coastal village on the north fork of Long Island ninety-five miles east
of New York City. Greenport usually was a more tranquil place. Most
days the loudest noise was the squawking of seagulls, and the biggest
nuisance the odor of fish being made into fertilizer at a local plant. The
brave youngster who tried to seize control of the horse was Chauncey Reeves, who was just shy of his nineteenth birthday. The constable
who arrived in the nick of time was Chauncey's father. Chauncey would
eventually follow in his father's footsteps and become a policeman. For
now, though, he had other ideas. He had already worked in a traveling
minstrel company, learning the ropes and developing his talents. Now
he sought engagements as a "blackface single" in vaudeville. Chauncey
may have been as adept at singing, dancing, and rubbing his face with
burnt cork as he was at swinging his fists; nobody knows for sure. The
only surviving evidence of his show-business career is a mention in an

obituary published after he died at age seventy-three. Apparently he was one of the legions of young men and women who dreamed of climbing the ladder to stardom but never managed to get a firm foothold on the first rung.

Less than a year after his encounter with the drunks and their runaway horse, Chauncey Reeves married. His bride was eighteen-year-old Winifred Touhey, an immigrant from Ireland. Probably the marriage was hastily arranged, for Winifred soon gave birth to the couple's first child, a boy. They named him Joseph. It may have been that event that persuaded Chauncey to give up his show-business ambitions and settle down in Greenport, where he could support his young family more reliably. Two years later Winifred gave birth to a second son. They named him Frederick. Finally, on 17 September 1899, Winifred bore a third child, this time a girl. What should have been another joyful occasion turned to tragedy, however, for Winifred died in childbirth. Suddenly Chauncey Reeves became a bereaved single parent faced with the daunting responsibility of caring for two little boys and a newborn girl.

Chauncey now made three decisions, each of them harrowing but understandable given his circumstances. First, he named the newborn baby Winifred Josephine Reeves, preserving the memory of the wife he had just lost by giving his newborn daughter the same first name. Second, he moved back into his parents' home. Third, and most agonizing of all, he entrusted the care of two of his children to others. By moving in with his parents, Chauncey could continue to provide a home for the younger of his two boys: Little Freddie could be looked after by his grandmother while Chauncey went to work on the fishing boats. But rather than burden his mother additionally with the care of the other two children, Chauncey decided to place them with relatives who would raise Joseph and Winifred as their own. Chauncey's late wife was survived by a brother and a sister. Joseph was given to the brother and his wife. Winifred was entrusted to the sister and her husband. So it came to be that Winifred was, from infancy, brought up by her aunt and uncle.

Winifred would grow up to become Winnie Lightner, star of stage and screen. The name Lightner did not come from her foster parents, however, or from any of the four men Winnie would eventually marry. Just how Winnie became a Lightner will be explained, but not just now, for that development marked the end rather than the beginning of her childhood.

Winnie's foster parents were Margaret and Andrew Hansen. Both were thirty-four years old when Winnie entered their lives. The Hansens resided on the Upper West Side of Manhattan, where they rented accommodations in a five-story tenement on the south side of Sixty-Sixth Street just west of Broadway. Their building and its neighbors were packed closely together, each occupying a lot one hundred feet long and twenty-five feet wide, with narrow airshafts providing a modicum of light and ventilation to the interior rooms. The immediate neighborhood was decidedly a working-class area, although not as insalubrious as the notorious Hell's Kitchen, which lay a little way to the south, from Fifty-Ninth Street on down to Thirty-Fourth. Some of the Hansens' male neighbors were day laborers, but many were skilled craftsmen. They included a carpenter, a cobbler, a barber, a baker, and a candy maker. Most married women did not work outside the home, but the widowed and single were employed as laundresses and cleaners.

Andrew Hansen was a stationary engineer, a tradesman skilled in the operation of heavy equipment like boilers and steam engines. He probably walked to work. Only a block west of his home stood a cluster of big storage tanks operated by the Consolidated Gas Company. Just beyond them sprawled the switching yards of the New York Central Railroad. Then a series of piers poked like the teeth of a comb into the Hudson River. At the piers a procession of steam-powered lighters arrived and departed, ferrying railway freight cars to and from New Jersey and throughout the busy harbor. Such an industrial environment offered many employment prospects for a man with Andrew's training. Indeed, among the railroad sidings just west of his home stood an engine and boiler house, an ideal workplace for a stationary engineer.

The tragic circumstances of her birth left no mark upon Winnie, whose earliest memories were of the security and stability of life in the Hansen household. She naturally formed her primary emotional connection with her foster parents. It was to Andrew Hansen she turned when in need, as on the occasion when (according to a newspaper account) she broke open a hotel room door, "aided by her foster father and a crowbar," in order to catch her philandering husband and a chorus girl *in flagrante delicto*. But we are getting ahead of our story.

The Hansen family lived in modest comfort, and Winnie had a happy childhood. Unlike some of the other performers she would come to know during her years in vaudeville, she never went hungry or suffered abuse. She spent carefree days playing with the other children on her street, joining in their sports and mischief. A favorite sport was "one-old-cat," a game of stick and ball in which a batter ran to the pitcher's position and back again. The mischief included such delights as roasting "mickies" (pilfered potatoes) over an open fire. Also, she later recollected, "I used to jump on the back of ice wagons with the boys. I even fought it out with bare fists in an empty lot on Columbus Avenue with a local bully—and won." Looking back from the perspective of an adult, Winnie realized that she had been a classic example of a little tomboy in pigtails. "I was just as much a member of the gang as any dirty-faced boy in the whole crowd," she recalled. "I could run from a cop as fast as any other kid."

Winnie believed that her tomboy childhood served her well. "I have never had trouble with men," she observed. "The free-and-easy spirit of comradeship developed through playing with the kids some years ago has resulted in the most complete protection a girl could want. . . . Every man appreciates what he calls the 'regular fellow' among women. He never tries making undue or improper advances to the girl or woman he knows is a 'regular fellow.' Usually she is both pretty and pretty strong, and her care-free manner is her greatest protection." Winnie liked men and was pleased when they found her attractive, but she was never deferential to them or emotionally dependent on their approval. Confident that she was both pretty and pretty strong, she thought for herself and made her own decisions. In that respect the woman they came to call the tomboy of the talkies had been a tomboy virtually all her life.

Winnie's childhood world gradually expanded beyond the confines of her immediate neighborhood. Decades later she still remembered the impressive landmarks that ranged eastwards from her home. Almost across the street, she recalled, the Hotel Marie Antoinette stood at the northwest corner of Sixty-Sixth and Broadway, extending along the latter for an entire block northward. The older part of the hotel rose eight stories, while its more northerly addition reached twelve. The building's vastness impressed little Winnie, who would have been even more impressed had she known that it contained no fewer than five hundred guestrooms and even more impressively (by early twentieth-century norms), three hundred bathrooms. Walking east from the Marie Antoinette, Winnie would pass the Sixty-Sixth Street entrance to the subway line that had opened along Broadway in 1904, touching off a frenzy of real estate development, but not reducing the traffic congestion that plagued the great thoroughfare.

Once she had negotiated her way across the no-man's-land of carts, carriages, and a few sputtering automobiles that was Broadway, Winnie could continue on along Sixty-Sixth Street. Almost immediately she would pass beneath the massive steel supports for the elevated train that ran up Columbus Avenue, and then she could gaze in wonder through the plate glass windows of Thomas Healy's lavish restaurant and night club, situated on the northeast corner of Sixty-Sixth and Columbus. The sea of tables, each covered with a crisp white cloth and sparkling place settings, the soaring columns ornamented with elaborate plasterwork, and the lofty ceiling studded with chandeliers were a far cry from the humble kitchen where Winnie and her foster parents ate their meals. Healy's was popular with the so-called sporting crowd, its airy dining and ballrooms accommodating upwards of a thousand patrons, often including theatrical celebrities and, occasionally, notables such as Theodore Roosevelt and King Albert of Belgium. Private parties wishing to dine more intimately at Healy's could book the Silver Grill Room, the Log Cabin Room, the African Jungle Room, or the Beefsteak Dungeon.

Winnie probably would have been a tad too young to join in the merriment when a great crowd of rubberneckers gathered in the wee hours of 13 August 1913 to watch a squad of policemen raid Healy's for violating the city's curfew law. Tables were overturned and crockery smashed as the officers clubbed, shoved, and dragged outside the several hundred customers who defied an order to exit the premises. Twenty-four hours later, Healy's was back in business, partly because the district attorney sided with the proprietor, who argued that the curfew required him to shut down only his bar, but mainly because the police commissioner thought better of enforcing the law in the face of public ridicule. When he had enforced the curfew, the commissioner had ignored the well-known fact that Healy's was frequented by prostitutes. The latter were always elegantly dressed and accompanied by male escorts. So long as both courtesans and clients behaved with discretion, nobody cared.

Next door to Healy's loomed another impressive landmark, the St. Nicholas Rink. Fronted by a series of eleven neoclassical arches with flagpoles in between, the St. Nicholas was an indoor ice-skating rink, one of the first to be equipped with a mechanically frozen surface. Erected in 1896 by a consortium of investors that included John Jacob Astor and Cornelius Vanderbilt, the building also served as a venue for prizefights. When describing her childhood, Winnie gave no hint that she had ever gone skating at the St. Nicholas, but she did vigorously defend the sport of boxing, suggesting that she and her playmates may have attended some of the prizefights. "It is far healthier for a woman or a young girl to watch a clever exhibition of the art of self defense," she declared, "than to sit in a stuffy theater watching some vampire-type actress show them a few tricks as to how to use their physical charms on men. It is far safer for a group of girls and boys to sit at ringside watching a clean bout than for a group of girls to gather in the ladies room of a smart hotel and exchange some of the stories such girls usually boast of knowing and telling."

East of the St. Nicholas Rink stood another remarkable edifice, Durland's Riding Academy. This complex, which extended through the block to Sixty-Seventh Street, housed a huge arena, stables for hundreds of horses, and an assortment of lounges and clubrooms. People came here to saddle up for canters along the four-mile bridle path in Central Park. Those who wished to enjoy the fresh air in a more sedate manner could hire a carriage as well as a horse. Riding lessons were given in the arena, and every afternoon there was a "music ride" for those who preferred to do their cantering indoors accompanied by forty musicians. Because the arena had a balcony with seats for six hundred, all sorts of other activities took place there, ranging from at least one meeting of suffragettes, to games of "horseketball," in which young men played an equestrian version of basketball, attempting slam-dunks while keeping a firm grip on the reins. Even if Winnie never got to see any of the wonders inside Durland's arena, she could at least enjoy the spectacle of the horses and carriages entering and exiting the stables in a steady stream.

Even more memorable than the grand buildings in Winnie's purview was the leafy paradise that stretched beyond them. Central Park, a vast oasis of greenery only a two-block stroll from Winnie's home, was an almost entirely artificial creation sprung from the genius of architects Calvert Vaux and Frederick Law Olmsted. But in the eyes of a child like Winnie the park seemed a miraculous vestige of primeval nature within the heart of the metropolis. Here were mysterious rocky outcrops to climb, ponds to splash about in, birds and squirrels to feed, and paths to explore amid labyrinths of flowering shrubs and trees. Winnie remembered especially the great Sheep Meadow due east of Sixty-Sixth Street, where John Conway, the Central Park shepherd, tended his flock. Winnie was among the three generations of children that Conway befriended, allowing them to carefully hold the newborn lambs in their own small arms. It was perhaps from him that Winnie acquired a life-long love of animals, which she would later indulge by keeping a series of pets, beginning with little lapdogs that could be carried about in hotels and Pullman cars, and ending, at her Hollywood mansion, with enormous St. Bernards that could well have carried her.

Besides visiting Conway at his usual outpost in the park, Winnie may have seen him nearer her home. On 18 May 1913, the city of New York held a grand civic pageant in which twelve thousand municipal employees paraded up Broadway as half a million spectators looked on. Clerks, cleaners, gardeners, street sweepers, and policemen were all applauded. The firemen and the mighty draft horses that pulled their engines were greeted with special enthusiasm. Another favorite with the crowd was Winnie's friend John Conway, clad in a kilt and accompanied by his two faithful collies and a dozen of his prettiest sheep.

While the streets of New York provided an education in themselves, Winnie also received more systematic instruction. When she reached the appropriate age, the Hansens enrolled her at a Catholic parochial school operated by the Church of the Blessed Sacrament on West Seventy-First Street between Broadway and Columbus. Established by the founder of the parish, Matthew A. Taylor, and commonly known as Father Taylor's School, the institution was opened in 1903 and staffed by the Sisters of Charity of Mount St. Vincent. The school offered classes through the eighth grade, and Winnie completed the whole program. By the standards of the day, she received a good education, one far superior to that of most vaudevillians, many of whom had little or no formal schooling.

Winnie remembered one more important edifice from her childhood. She once told an interviewer that the back of her home had faced the rear wall of a vaudeville theater. Sometimes when the theater was empty and its emergency exit doors propped open for ventilation, she would sneak inside and climb up onto the stage. There she would perform childish stunts and pretend that she was entertaining a vast audience. One day a janitor caught her in the act, gave her a clout on the ear with his dustless mop, and ordered her to leave. "I told him I'd go," Winnie recalled, "but someday he'd pay admission to see me on that stage. And he did, too."

If the story is true, then its setting was the Lincoln Square Theater, which was indeed situated so that its rear exits opened just opposite the tenements that lined the south side of Sixty-Sixth Street. The front entrance to the theater was on Sixty-Fifth Street, but it could also be reached from Broadway by walking through an arcade that transected a block-long, six-story building containing a warren of shops, offices, and furnished rooms, the last named being inhabited by a motley collection of starving artists, bohemians, alcoholics, and eccentrics. The Lincoln Square Theater was erected in 1906 on what had been an empty lot. It had seating for sixteen hundred and claimed to be the safest theater in existence, having not just the only steel and asbestos safety curtain in the city, but also the only water curtain in the world (the latter an artificial cascade that would flow from sprinklers above the proscenium in the event of a fire).

At first a stock company put on plays in the new theater, but in September 1908 the prominent theatrical agent and entrepreneur William Morris began using it as a venue for high-class vaudeville. Morris did not prosper in that location, however, and so fourteen months later the theater was taken over by Marcus Loew, who was pioneering a new form of entertainment that combined a multi-reel motion picture with a relatively small number of minor vaudeville acts. Loew repeated his complete program several times daily, in contrast to the "two-a-day" (a matinee and then a single evening performance) that was the norm among the "big-time," all-vaudeville shows staged by people like William Morris. Because his low costs enabled him to charge exceptionally low admission prices, Loew hit upon a formula that would enable him to build an empire. The Lincoln Square was one of the earliest of what eventually totaled some two hundred Loew's theaters, peppering New York City but also ranging as far as Chicago and Dallas. Loew's formula would continue to prosper long after big-time vaudeville had disappeared.

From this little potted history of the Lincoln Square Theater, it can be deduced that Winnie larked about in its empty auditorium during the fourteen months when William Morris was in charge, for then the house routinely stood empty for around three hours each day between matinee and evening shows. Once Marcus Loew took over, there would have been no opportunity for a little girl to sneak inside and play at being a star. Winnie was therefore about nine years old when she first set foot on a vaudeville stage—and was rewarded with a vigorous smack from a mop.

Six years later Winnie again cavorted on a vaudeville stage, but this time she was appearing as a full-fledged professional. She had come out of nowhere right into the big time. That was extraordinary. Many vaude-villians had to toil for years at exhausting, low-paid work in places like dime museums, medicine shows, or carnivals before they managed to gain entry into even small-time vaudeville. Then nearly everybody had to spend a decade or so eking out a living on the lesser vaudeville circuits before they at last succeeded in advancing to the big time, if indeed they ever got there at all.

Winnie's shortcut to the big time came about because she was taken under the wings of two established performers, both twice her age, who decided to take a chance on a fifteen-year-old unknown. Their names were Newton Alexander and Theodora Lightner. This stroke of luck explains how the girl who had been born Winifred Reeves and then spent her childhood as Winifred Hansen became Winnie Lightner. A vaudeville act named "Newton Alexander, Theo Lightner, and Winnie Hansen" was too big a mouthful. Better to call it "The Lightner Sisters and Newton Alexander," with Winnie adopting Lightner as her stage name and posing as Theodora's sibling.

The next two chapters will trace the careers of Winnie's vaudeville partners through their long, lean years of struggle up to the time they brought Winnie into their act. Winnie was spared a similar ordeal because her partners had cleared the way for her. Winnie had it easy, because Newton and Theo had paid their dues.

CHAPTER 2

The Exposition Four

WHEN WINNIE LIGHTNER WAS BORN, THE MAN WHO WOULD BECOME her senior partner in vaudeville was already a show-business veteran. Newton Alexander was the youngest of three brothers, all of them talented and versatile musicians. They could play all sorts of string, reed, and brass instruments but were particularly adept at the last. Where and how they acquired their musical skills is unknown. All three were born in the 1870s at various locations west of the Mississippi. Their father was named James W. Alexander. According to a newspaper report, James at one time managed a circus as a business partner of Samuel A. Scribner, who later became a key figure in the burlesque industry. Another report says that James toured with his young sons in a musical act. James eventually left show business, however, and settled in Pittsburgh, where he ran a photographic studio.

The first conclusive evidence of the three Alexander brothers at work as entertainers appears in 1896, when the *New York Clipper*, a show-business trade paper, published some brief items about a tent show called G. W. Belford's Carnival of Novelties. The Belford troupe consisted of five officers and twenty-three others. Among the latter were Woodruff Alexander, Russell Alexander, and Newton Alexander. Woodruff was then twenty-two, Russell nineteen, and Newton seventeen. Young as they were at that time, they may well have worked even earlier, not just with their father, but also on their own in places like dime museums or medicine shows, which ranked even lower than carnivals and circuses in the show-business pecking order. In February the *Clipper* noted that the Belford outfit was getting ready to start touring that spring by sprucing up its wagons with a new paint job in white and gold, and that Mr. Belford had acquired some fine new horses. Also, he intended to add a new balancing act to the show, and his sister Katie would perform on the flying rings. The company would include a twelve-piece band headed by O. V. Burr, with Mrs. Belford as cornet soloist. In August the *Clipper* named everyone in the company and added, "The show has been laboring under continued stress of wet weather and bad roads, but is holding its own."

Soon after his stint with the carnival, Russell Alexander parted company with his brothers. He composed a piece of band music called "The Darlington March" and succeeded in placing it with the C. L. Barnhouse Company, a major publisher of such material. Then, perhaps as a result of that accomplishment, he landed a position with the famous Barnum and Bailey Circus for a tour of Europe that lasted from 1897 to 1902. During the tour he not only played the brass instrument known as the euphonium, he also arranged all of the music for the Barnum and Bailey Band. He also somehow found time to create many of the works that would make him one of America's most distinguished composers of band music. Many of his marches are still part of standard band repertoire. They include both "Belford's Carnival" (1897), in which he saluted the humble outfit that had launched his and his brothers' careers, and "Colossus of Columbia" (1901), the most famous of all of his marches. When the Spanish-American War came along in 1898, he honored the valor of American infantrymen by composing "The Storming of El Caney," a galop that captured the fury of a battle charge with a tumult of cornets, tubas, and trombones.

While Russell was overseas making a name for himself, his brothers were scrounging whatever work they could find. Like Russell, Newton got a lift from the war with Spain, for the spring of 1898 found him touring the Northeast with the Sawtelle Dramatic Company, which staged tableaux showing the Goddess of Liberty defending starving Cuba from villainous Spain, "Old Glory and the Cuban colors predominating." The Sawtelle company also featured "The Imperial Orchestra" (of just which empire was left unspecified), in which Newton no doubt played. Meanwhile, his brother Woodruff signed on as tuba soloist with a traveling comedy show called "In Old Maine," which centered on an eccentric Yankee and featured music by the "Grassville Centre Band."

After their respective engagements ended, Newton and Woodruff placed a classified ad in the *Clipper* announcing that "Newton Alexander, Cornetist" and "Woodruff Alexander, Tuba and Double Bass," both "thoroughly experienced," were "at liberty." When the ad brought no result, the two brothers decided that if they were going to get anywhere in show business, they needed to do more than just blow their horns.

They needed an act. Together with two other young musicians, William Patton and James B. Brady, they created one. They called themselves the Exposition Four, and they worked up a routine in which they not only played their various instruments, they also sang, danced, and told jokes.

Success came quickly. In the winter of 1898–99 the Exposition Four was a featured act with the Al G. Field Greater Minstrels, then the biggest and most famous minstrel company in America. It had fifty performers on its roster and traveled in its own private train. Although the heyday of minstrelsy belonged to an earlier time, it was still a major form of popular entertainment. Its appeal was fading not because white audiences had become any less receptive to its often demeaning portrayal of African Americans, but simply because vaudeville had eclipsed minstrelsy. In fact, the Field show had adapted to changing popular tastes by morphing into something quite different from old-time minstrelsy. It still had an all-male cast, and it still had the traditional three-part structure, but there the similarity ended. Whereas the classic minstrel show had begun with all of the players seated in a semi-circle listening to jokes and banter between the blackfaced Mr. Interlocutor and the two end men, Mr. Tambo and Mr. Bones, the Field show started off with an elaborate production titled "Gathering of the Nations," "a panoramic glimpse of notable places and faces." The middle part of the Field show, although still consisting of the traditional "olio" of variety acts, was greatly expanded. Where the old-time olio had been staged in front of the main curtain merely as a way of keeping the audience entertained while the stage was reset, the Field show presented numerous specialty acts, including the Exposition Four. Finally, the classic minstrel show had ended with a musical afterpiece staged in a plantation setting. The Field show ended with a playlet entitled "In Cuba," featuring Theodore Roosevelt and his Rough Riders, along with their horses and a Saint Bernard dog. One of the human roles, that of Spanish general Ramón Blanco, was played by Willie Patton. It is likely that the other members of the Exposition Four also assumed roles in parts one and three of the Field show, in addition to performing their specialty act in the intervening olio.

The next step up for Newton Alexander and his three partners was to try their hand at burlesque and vaudeville. At the time there was no clear-cut distinction between the two, but vaudeville was generally more sedate and catered to a broader audience. Children did not attend burlesque shows. Nor did "ladies," although some working-class women did. Vaudeville, on the other hand, appealed to all classes: from the toffs in evening dress down in the front row orchestra seats, to the working stiffs way up in the gallery, but most especially to the middle class. Burlesque was aimed squarely at the working class, although of course some middle and upper class people enjoyed thumbing their noses at social convention by joining in the merriment. Burlesque still featured the element from which its name derives: a comical play that was either an original creation or a travesty version of an established work, for example *Julius Sneezer* and *Cleopotroast*. The striptease, which later became the defining feature of burlesque, was not commonplace until the 1920s. That is not to say that sex was not central from the beginning. Any burlesque company worth its salt included a chorus of voluptuous young women, fully clothed from neck to ankles as required by law, but jammed into strangulating corsets and skin-tight body stockings. Sex was certainly not absent from vaudeville, either; it was just less blatant. Many a vaudeville bill included a display of "living statues," in which men and (mostly) women assumed classical poses. Respectable middle-class people happily viewed this display of "art," unconcerned that the garb of the posers was every bit as revealing as that of the chorus girls in a burlesque show. Vaudeville promoters walked a thin line, always promising to provide good, clean entertainment suitable for the whole family, but trying also to smuggle in enough sex appeal to keep their adult clientele coming back for more.

If they had a choice, performers usually opted for vaudeville over burlesque because vaudeville was more prestigious and generally paid better. But for those at the lower end of the pay scale, burlesque did possess one advantage: The whole show traveled as a unit, with the employer making all of the necessary arrangements and picking up the tab. In vaudeville, except out west where population was sparse and theaters widely dispersed, a constellation of acts usually joined together to form the bill for a particular week at a particular theater, but then everyone went their separate ways. Consequently, performers traveled individually and had to cover their own costs. This was no small consideration for an act like the Exposition Four, who not only would have to buy train tickets and meals for themselves, but also pay the cost of hauling heavy trunks packed with fragile musical instruments as well as props and costumes. Although the Four were good enough to obtain repeated bookings during the summer of 1900 on vaudeville bills at a seaside venue called Doyle's Pavilion in Atlantic City, New Jersey, expenses probably dictated that their next tour was with a burlesque company. Tony Stanford was both author and star of the company's original two-act play, *The Queen of the Orient*. As a reviewer helpfully pointed out to potential customers, "The scene of the play is laid in Turkey and the women of the harem are often paraded before the audience in a pleasing but inoffensive manner." All thirty-five members of the Stanford troupe participated in the play, which was divided into two parts, spelled by an olio of six variety acts, one of which was "The Exposition Four, musical wonders and triple tongue cornetists."

The Queen of the Orient first played for a week at Bergen Beach, a summer resort on Jamaica Bay operated by Percy G. Williams. On a good day, up to twenty-five thousand people from New York City, Brooklyn, and nearby communities went to Bergen Beach to enjoy its amusement park, theater, and beer hall. Tony Stanford's company next moved on to engagements in Washington, DC, and other cities. In December it played the Theatre Comique at Broadway and Twenty-Ninth Street in Manhattan, but with unfortunate results. In the midst of a performance, Tony Stanford announced that the remainder of the show had been cancelled because the theater manager had absconded with the box office receipts. That abrupt and rather rash announcement touched off a riot. A squad of policemen wielding truncheons arrived just barely in time to stop the people in the gallery from ripping out the seats. Fortunately, the Exposition Four left the Stanford company well before that debacle.

The Four had returned to vaudeville. In late September they appeared for a week at the Wonderland Theater in New Haven, Connecticut. Installed on the cheap in what had been a church, the Wonderland was operated by Sylvester Z. Poli, who had a well-deserved reputation among vaudevillians as a promoter who was friendly and honest, but who watched his pennies with extraordinary care. Poli was happy to book an act if it was tolerably competent, but he was even happier if it was cheap. The Exposition Four qualified on both counts. After their stay at the Wonderland, the Four were booked for successive weeks at two small-time theaters in Brooklyn, the Novelty and the Brooklyn Music Hall, both owned by the same Percy Williams who ran Bergen Beach. Then they played a "split week" divided between theaters in Worcester and Springfield, Massachusetts. All of those dates were arranged by William Morris, who handled the bookings for both Poli and Williams, as well as many other theater owners.

In all of the Exposition Four's early appearances, the other acts on the bill were just as obscure as they were. Unlike the Four, most of these other acts never did make it to the big time. There were, however, two notable exceptions. When the Four played the Novelty in Brooklyn, the bill was headed by John and James Russell, performing their sketch "The

Irish Servant Girls." The Russell Brothers were already famous for their comic portrayal of two Irish biddies. Both men were big and burly, making their female impersonation especially funny. But even though they were hugely popular, the Russells came under increasing criticism from Irish American organizations, which condemned their act as demeaning to Irish women. The Russells eventually gave in to the pressure and transformed themselves into *Swedish* servant girls. Then, when the Exposition Four played the Brooklyn Music Hall, the headliner was Horace Goldin, a magician who performed such feats as stuffing a bunch of ducks into a bucket on one side of the stage, whereupon they emerged from a tub on the other side. Goldin presented his entire routine in silence, for the simple reason that as a recent immigrant from Poland he had not yet mastered the English language. In 1900 Goldin was no better known than the Exposition Four, but by 1910 he would rank as one of the foremost illusionists in show business.

After sharing the bill at the Brooklyn Music Hall with Goldin and his waterfowl wizardry, the Exposition Four played Tony Pastor's Theater in lower Manhattan. Tony Pastor is widely regarded as the founding father of vaudeville. Vaudeville evolved out of the earlier institution known as the music hall, where variety acts performed amid thick clouds of cigar smoke before an all-male audience usually more interested in getting drunk and chatting up the waitresses than in watching the show. (Percy Williams's Brooklyn Music Hall retained the old music hall name, but not its original character). When Tony Pastor opened his little theater on Fourteenth Street in 1881, he was one of the first entrepreneurs to set out to attract entire families to his variety show by banning alcohol and promising to stage only wholesome entertainment. He thrived for a time, but by 1900 he was losing out to Benjamin Franklin Keith, whose Union Square Theater had opened nearby in 1893. Keith presented a similar program of "polite" vaudeville, but in a much larger venue, where economy of scale gave him a competitive edge. B. F. Keith and his partner, Edward F. Albee, were on their way to becoming the oligarchs of American vaudeville. They had opened their first theater in Boston in the 1880s and then expanded to Providence, Philadelphia, and New York. The driving genius of their enterprise was Albee. It was he who had the vision to realize that vaudeville could be consolidated and rationalized like any other industry.

Just as John D. Rockefeller, Andrew Carnegie, and J. Pierpont Morgan dominated and transformed oil, steel, and railroads, Edward Albee dominated and transformed big time vaudeville. He built a chain of theaters that by 1915 numbered more than thirty and extended throughout most of the eastern and midwestern states, reaching northward to Toronto and southward to New Orleans. More importantly, beginning in 1900 he persuaded the owners of other theaters and theater chains to join in an arrangement whereby they all agreed to book acts through a central agency run by Keith-Albee, originally named the Association of Vaudeville Managers (AVM).

For performers, the emergence of this cartel was both good news and bad. On the plus side, the new agency represented so many venues it could offer the best acts in the business a contract that guaranteed a full season of work along a route that minimized idle days and long "jumps" between cities. But on the negative side, the AVM charged performers a hefty 5 percent of their salaries as an agency commission, as well as helping itself to half of the additional 5 percent the performers paid to their personal agents. Moreover, Albee strove zealously to keep a lid on the performers' salaries, which was easier to do now that managers were not bidding against one another for acts.

While many owners happily joined the AVM, which promised to drive down costs and ensure quality, others resisted. Albee eventually vanquished most of the resisters by strong-arm tactics such as threatening to open rival theaters in their territories. Sylvester Poli and Percy Williams were among the most prominent holdouts, but both were beaten into submission by 1907. The staunchest resister of all, booking agent William Morris, never did surrender, despite his loss of major clients like Poli and Williams. More and more performers reluctantly stopped working through the Morris agency, however, because those who stayed loyal to him were blacklisted by Albee, meaning they could not work in any of the theaters that belonged to the AVM. Morris fought back by creating his own chain of theaters, but by 1911 he was in dire financial straits. Even then, he did not surrender to Albee. Instead, he sold his theaters to Marcus Loew. That Loew's chain of "combination" (small-time vaudeville plus film) houses was thriving and expanding is a good illustration that Albee's cartel never came close to controlling the whole vaudeville industry. The cartel did dominate the big time, which eventually was swallowed up almost entirely by two giant chains, Keith-Albee in the East and Orpheum in the West, both of which belonged to the AVM. But in small time there remained a score of chains plus many hundreds of independent houses that were not affiliated with the AVM.

Long after the demise of vaudeville, retired artists spoke warmly of men like Tony Pastor, William Morris, Percy Williams, and even old cheapskate Sylvester Poli. They were remembered fondly as responsible businessmen who appreciated and took a genuine personal interest in their performers. Nobody ever spoke in such terms about Edward Albee. Few performers ever met him. When they did, they usually were kept waiting in an anteroom well past the appointed hour. Then, when at last they stood before him, Albee coldly looked up from behind his desk and told them what their salaries would be, take it or leave it. Most took it.

It would be a while before the Exposition Four entered the orbit of Keith-Albee and the cartel. In fact at the time Albee began organizing the AVM, the Four made a professional sidestep into a wholly different theatrical format. For thirty weeks in 1900–1901, they toured with Robert Fitzsimmons and company in a play called *The Honest Blacksmith*, "a Comedy Drama of Home and Sporting Life." Robert Fitzsimmons was the reigning boxing world champion, having famously knocked out Gentleman Jim Corbett in the fourteenth round of a match held in March 1897. Like Corbett (as well as the champion before him, John L. Sullivan) Fitzsimmons capitalized on his success in the boxing ring by undertaking a theatrical tour. Champions in all sorts of sports often appeared in vaudeville and on other stages, but they seldom fared well. While at first they would attract audiences curious to see them in person, their lack of theatrical training and talent soon became apparent, and ticket sales shrivelled. Fitzsimmons proved a surprising exception to the norm.

Born in Cornwall in 1863, Fitzsimmons immigrated as a boy to New Zealand. There he trained as a blacksmith and practised the trade for several years before taking up boxing. The first act of *The Honest Blacksmith* reprised that true story, with Fitzsimmons actually manufacturing horseshoes at a real forge, shoeing a live horse, and then handing out shoes as souvenirs to the audience to take home. Then the play morphed into an entirely fictional melodrama, wherein Fitzsimmons's character, a man of spotless virtue, struggles against the machinations of an oily villain. By the time the final curtain falls, the villain has been vanquished, of course, and our hero ends up winning $30,000 in a prizefight. Along the way, he lectures his wayward younger brother on the danger of that newfangled evil, the cigarette. "Look at me," he declaims, "I never smoked one of those things in my life, and you have one in your mouth all the time. I have a good liver, heart, wind, and conscience. And you—your heart is on the bum; you haven't enough wind to inflate a 5-cent balloon, your liver is like a lump of lead, and your conscience is dead to the world."

Fitzsimmons's wife played the wife of his character in the play. The third leading role belonged to Edward Dunkhorst ("The Human Freight

Car"), who was Fitzsimmons's real-life sparring partner. Audiences flocked to the show, especially in places where prizefighting was illegal. People who had no opportunity to see a real bout particularly enjoyed watching the world champion work out with a punching bag and demonstrate his moves in the ring with the help of Dunkhorst. Fitzsimmons had a natural gift for acting. Critics remarked that he delivered his lines clearly and with feeling. He could even sing. His wife, critics said, was even better.

Just where the Exposition Four fit into all of this is uncertain. Possibly they had roles in the play. If so, it is unlikely that four young men bearing cornets and trombones could have slipped comfortably into the setting of either a smithy or a boxing ring, so they must have either divested themselves of their instruments or maybe just performed in the background. Perhaps they also did an olio turn between the two scenes. No critic mentioned an olio, but it could have provided a useful interlude while stagehands dismantled the forge and set up the ring. At any rate, critics praised the Exposition Four for their contributions, whatever they were. When the show played Utica, New York, a reviewer there said that Fitzsimmons's rendition "of a topical song, with the Exposition Four as a chorus, was in its way inimitable." The critic added that while Mrs. Fitzsimmons was the best actor in the play, "the quartet made the second hit of the evening, its musical exhibition being enthusiastically applauded." The reviewer for another newspaper in the same town was even more complimentary, declaring that "the best feature of the evening from an artistic point of view was the entertainment furnished by the Exposition Four. . . . They not only sing well, but they play the various instruments used on such occasion with great skill. The encores were numerous, and the feature was really worthy of all the applause it received."

When *The Honest Blacksmith* finished its season, William Morris booked the boys for a week on the vaudeville bill at Percy Williams's Orpheum Theater in Brooklyn. This was another upward step for them, for the Orpheum was the leading vaudeville house in Brooklyn. Performers loved playing the Orpheum because its interior was tall and narrow, creating a sense of intimacy despite its seating capacity of seventeen hundred. Then Morris placed the Four in a musical comedy, *The Pan American Girl*, which ran all summer at Williams's Bergen Beach resort. In that production, Willie Patton got laughs playing a country hick, while Newton Alexander took on the role of a bellboy and later got to show off his remarkable ability to play two cornets simultaneously.

In the 1901–2 season, the Exposition Four toured the Columbia burlesque circuit (the "eastern wheel") with a unit called Weber's Dainty Duchess Company. They played roles in the company's farcical playlet, *Raz-Ma-Taz*, and did their own specialty act in the olio. While no doubt many in the audience had come mainly to see the twenty lovelies in the chorus, the Exposition Four attracted favorable comment. Indeed, when toward the close of the season the show played the Kernan Theater in the nation's capital, a reviewer described their act as far superior to anything else in the olio. One of their instrumental numbers featured one of them manipulating a trombone slide with his right foot, while another (Newton, no doubt) played two different cornet parts at once. Also, said the reviewer, "they sing solos, ensemble numbers, dance, and do everything imaginable, and they do it all remarkably well." The audience liked them so much it demanded two encores. The stage manager's refusal to allow a third caused such uproar that the succeeding act was entirely drowned out by continuing calls to bring back the Exposition Four. "It was a scene the like of which has not been witnessed at Kernan's for seasons," wrote the reviewer, "and goes to prove that the average burlesque audience recognizes an unusually good act of any kind when it comes along—a very infrequent happening, by the way, though, in the burlesque business."

In the summer of 1902 the Four advanced another big step when, following several seaside engagements, they appeared on the vaudeville bill for the week beginning 11 August at Keith's Theater in Boston. That is significant in two respects. First, it meant the Four had joined the exodus from the William Morris agency in order to enjoy the wider opportunities available through Edward Albee's cartel. Second, they had cracked the big time. True, they probably were a last-minute addition to a rather lackluster bill put on during the summer doldrums. Still, Keith's in Boston was unquestionably a first-class, two-a-day house, one of the most prestigious in the country.

Despite having made their big-time debut, the Four were not ready to embrace vaudeville exclusively and permanently. Instead, they toured for two full seasons in Gus Hill's production *McFadden's Row of Flats*. Derived in part from the famous *Yellow Kid* comic strip, the *McFadden's* show had toured annually since 1897. It was so well known that one reviewer referred to it as "the 'Uncle Tom's Cabin' of musical farce." Its plot revolved around the rivalry between two immigrant saloonkeepers, one Irish and the other German, who were running against each other for alderman in the notorious Five Points neighborhood of New York City.

The developing story was interspersed with slapstick comedy, musical numbers, and variety acts. Audiences returned year after year, confident that there would be enough new material to keep the show fresh. During their two seasons with *McFadden's*, the Exposition Four put on their own musical turn, joined in song and dance numbers with the women of the chorus, and assumed acting roles in the unfolding story. James Brady played police officer Kerrigan, Woodruff Alexander was a character called Sure Money (as well as another one named Weary Willie), and Newton Alexander was Bill Cheatem.

It was the Exposition Four's bad luck to be with the *McFadden's* show when, after having toured for five successive years without any problem, it met active resistance from Irish Americans. It is easy to see why they took offense. The lead character in the play, Tim McFadden, was a grotesque stereotype of an Irishman, made up so as to look rather like an ape with red whiskers. Even more objectionable was another major character, Mrs. Murphy, a slatternly widow usually seen smoking a clay pipe and carrying a bucket of beer. Mrs. Murphy makes her first appearance in a wheelbarrow pushed onstage by James Brady in his role as Kerrigan the policeman. He promptly dumps her out of the barrow, explaining, "I found her down in the alley and this was the only way I could get her home."

When *McFadden's Row of Flats* played Denver in October 1902, it was vociferously condemned by local chapters of both the Ancient Order of Hibernians and the Gaelic League. Things escalated from there, as Irish nationalists in one city after another made it a point of pride to demonstrate that they, too, would not tolerate the show's abusive stereotypes. The climax came at the New Star Theater in upper Manhattan on 27 March 1903, when at a signal two hundred men rose from their seats and pelted the performers with rotten eggs and vegetables. One of the principal targets was "a red-headed Irish policeman with green whiskers"—that is, James Brady of the Exposition Four. The disturbance did not end until the actual police arrived and made several arrests. Much the same thing happened a few days later when the show was presented at the People's Theater in Philadelphia. The production continued touring, however, until it finished its regular season in May.

After a summer playing vaudeville dates in New York City and at nearby seaside resorts, the Exposition Four rejoined *McFadden's* for another annual tour. At that point, Russell Alexander, having completed his long engagement overseas with Barnum and Bailey, rejoined his brothers, replacing Willie Patton in the act. In *McFadden's* Russell played a character named Dooley. From here on, the Exposition Four consisted of the three Alexander brothers plus James Brady. Russell and Newton celebrated their reunion by jointly composing a march entitled "The Exposition Four," which was published in 1903.

In their second season with *McFadden's* the Four were featured much more prominently in the advertising for the show, being accorded first place among the olio acts. Evidently they had made such a good impression the previous year that Gus Hill was confident they would be a drawing card this time around. Although Irish protests had proliferated a year earlier, there were no major demonstrations against the show in 1903 or 1904. Indeed, a new edition of *McFadden's* would continue to appear without significant opposition every year for the rest of the decade. Many years later there would even be two movie versions of the venerable *McFadden's Row of Flats* title: first a silent released in 1927 and then a talkie in 1935, although neither of them embodied the original storyline.

Because the *McFadden's* company ended its 1903–4 tour out on the West Coast, the Exposition Four afterwards played some small-time vaudeville dates in places like Portland, Oregon, and Butte, Montana. Then they worked their way back east. By late June they had begun a long series of bookings in the Keith-Albee houses and other theaters affiliated with the cartel formerly called the AVM, but now known as the United Booking Office (UBO). From that point until the dissolution of the Exposition Four more than a decade later, the group was never without work. In 1905–6 they made another burlesque tour, this time with a troupe called the Merrymakers Extravaganza Company, on the Empire circuit or "western wheel." Despite its nickname, that circuit included theaters coast to coast, and the Exposition Four accompanied the Merrymakers all the way from San Francisco to New York. The troupe presented a conventional three-part show that began with a musical comedy, followed by an olio and then an afterpiece. The company included the obligatory chorus of young women, and many reviewers noted that they were unusually adept at singing and dancing. One critic also noted approvingly, "The girls are for the most part good looking without being heavy enough to be too much of a good thing." The opening portion of the show was entitled "Running for Mayor" and involved election shenanigans reminiscent of those in *McFadden's Flats*. The afterpiece was called "The Mayor's Vacation" and was a pure farce. The Exposition Four participated actively in all three parts of the production and received much favorable comment. Their musical act during the olio won praise almost everywhere, and one critic also lauded both Newton and Russell for their excellent portrayals of "rustic characters" in the afterpiece.

When the Exposition Four then returned to vaudeville, they were regarded as a standard act, meaning one with a solid reputation making it welcome on virtually any bill. Occasionally, when appearing at small-time venues, the Four were even the headliners. If there was any doubt that they had "arrived" it evaporated when they appeared the week of 23 September 1907 at Hammerstein's Victoria Theater in Manhattan on a bill headed by the mercurial singer and dancer Eva Tanguay, the biggest female star in all vaudeville. Hammerstein's Victoria was then the foremost vaudeville house in the United States. For the next eight years, the Exposition Four made at least one appearance annually at Hammerstein's, sharing bills with such greats as W. C. Fields, Al Jolson, and Will Rogers. Some of their engagements took place in the summer months when owner-manager William Hammerstein moved his evening shows to a roof garden on top of the theater. There the patrons could not only enjoy the splendid vaudeville show, they could also visit a miniature farm, complete with ducks and a cow and presided over by Farmer Wilke, whose beard was said to be ten feet long. The roof garden was a wonderfully cool place to spend an evening in the summertime—or at any rate that was the impression customers got when they stepped out of the elevator that had carried them up from street level. They did not know that whatever its actual temperature, the roof garden was bound to seem cool because Willie Hammerstein heated the lift.

Between 1907 and 1915 the Exposition Four spent most of its time performing at Keith-Albee and other UBO houses, but the group still accepted occasional bookings on other vaudeville circuits or with burlesque companies. In 1912, the Four spent several months with an outfit called Neil O'Brien's Great American Minstrels in what proved to be an ambitious but unsuccessful attempt to revive a fading genre. Accepting employment outside the UBO could be tricky, because anybody who worked for what Keith-Albee branded as "opposition" risked being blacklisted by the UBO. The peril was compounded because it was not always clear whether a particular employer would be viewed as opposition, and because there was not much consistency in the application of the UBO blacklist. Whereas a minor act might find itself proscribed without knowing why, a megastar like Eva Tanguay was never blacklisted no matter what she did (and she did plenty).

In 1910 the Exposition Four had to pay damages to a theatrical agent who sued them after they refused to sign a contract the agent had negotiated for the group with the William Morris circuit. The contract would have given them a twenty-five-week route at a salary of $360 a week. That was good money by vaudeville standards, although it must be remembered that the Four had to pay all of their travel costs and other expenses and then split the remainder four ways. Apparently the Four had reneged on signing the Morris contract because they feared, probably with good reason, that doing so would get them blacklisted by Keith-Albee and the UBO. Early in 1913 the Four had another brush with disaster when they rashly consented to appear on a Sunday vaudeville program put on by the Shubert brothers at their Winter Garden Theater in Manhattan. The UBO cancelled the contracts of several other acts that had done the same, but the Four went unpunished, apparently because the Albee organization decided their one-time lapse was not important enough to bother about. "Why borrow trouble?" UBO manager John J. Murdock retorted when asked why the Four had escaped his wrath.

In these their glory years, the Exposition Four had a repertoire so remarkably varied that it is easy to imagine an entire vaudeville bill made up of elements that featured in their act. The act's core, of course, was the Four's virtuoso playing of musical instruments. Cornets and trombones were the main ones, but one reviewer counted fourteen others. Hand-bells, chimes, xylophone, piano, organ, and cello all received mention from critics. In their most straightforward presentations the Four stood abreast in front of a special drop bearing their monogram that they carried with them. At first the drop was made of a shimmery pigeon-gray material; in later years it was pale blue velvet. But besides just standing and playing their assorted instruments in a conventional manner, the Four offered many novelties. One of their numbers began as a display of butter churning, but then the churns turned out to be musical instruments. Another selection imitated the noise of a sawmill, including the peculiar screech of a circular saw working its way through a knotty plank. Frequently the act finished with the Four mimicking a circus band marching through the streets of a town, just as Russell Alexander had actually done during his years in England with Barnum and Bailey.

Often the act included a "church" segment, with one of the Four posing as a choirboy soloist while the others supplied instrumental accompaniment for a pious tune like "The Holy City" or "The Palms." Reviewers in the show-business press often deprecated that scene as incompatible with the rest of the act, but the Four kept it in anyway. They even included it when they toured with the Merrymakers Extravaganza Company, despite the rather understandable observation of one critic that "the music is good, though they do not want choir boys in burlesque houses." Additional singing, mostly of ragtime and popular love songs, was offered both by individuals and by the entire quartet vocalizing in harmony. Some of their songs were originals composed by Newton Alexander. Several of his better ones were published and thereafter incorporated into the acts of other vaudeville professionals. Clog dancing and other fancy footwork also had an important place in the Exposition Four act.

Another feature was supplied by Woodruff Alexander, who put on blackface to sing and crack jokes. He was accused of imitating Ernest Tenny, of an act called The Waterbury Brothers and Tenny, but in fact there were legions of vaudevillians who performed similarly. While "corking up" obviously resulted in gross caricaturization of African American appearance, performers' behavior varied from affectionately sentimental to viciously racist stereotyping of blacks. Reviewers' praise for Woodruff's version as "not overdone" may indicate that it was at least not among the most offensive. Sometimes the act included a whole minstrel segment featuring typical minstrel tunes like "My Dusky Moon," which was closely associated with the famous George Primrose minstrel company, and Newton Alexander's own compositions "Honey, Don't Go Out the Gate" and "New Orleans."

Beginning about 1906 the Four added yet another dimension to their routine by becoming quick-change artists. They would perform a number in matching costumes, then pass behind some scenery and emerge a few seconds later wearing completely different apparel. They got so good at this maneuver that some viewers could scarcely believe their eyes. Once, when the Four were appearing in Fort Wayne, Indiana, two young men in the audience got into an argument after the show. One of them was convinced that the Four really were changing their costumes in a matter of seconds, while the other insisted that the quartet was actually an octet, and that the four men who emerged from behind the scenery were not the same four who had stepped behind it. The two young men made a wager and then approached the theater manager, who permitted them to watch from the wings at the next show. They saw how pulling a couple of strings caused one layer of clothing to fall off, revealing another in its place. The loser of the bet remarked that it had been worth losing just to see how the miracle was accomplished. Russell Alexander joked that the only item of apparel the Four did not change was their collars, but that he was working on that. He added that once he had figured out how to transform the collars, he would work on the collar buttons.

On 26 April 1915 Hammerstein's Victoria Theater put on one final gala performance, then closed its doors forever. It was to be demolished and its prime site taken over by the first big motion picture house to be constructed in the Times Square area. William Hammerstein had died two years earlier, and without his guiding genius at the helm the Victoria's fortunes had declined, bringing to an end its reign as the acknowledged queen of American vaudeville venues. The Palace Theater, which had opened in 1913 five blocks up Broadway at Forty-Seventh Street, had seized the crown. The final bill at the Victoria was a grand tribute to Willie Hammerstein, bringing together a collection of acts he had especially liked that had sustained the reputation of his theater during its decade of supremacy. Reading over the program for that last performance is today a melancholy experience, for nearly all of the once famous names that appear on it are now forgotten. The only exception is the entry for "Will Rogers, The Lassoer of the Bull. Who Always Made Willie Laugh On and Off Stage." The name Will Rogers still resonates with a good many Americans. But no ordinary person nowadays has heard of "Harry Breen, Colonel of the Nuts," or "Princess Radjah, The Originator of Oriental Dances." One other now forgotten act on that final program was "Exposition Four, Comedy and Music. Who Willie Always Depended Upon To Make Good."

Indeed they had made good. From their earliest days plodding along the muddy roads with Belford's Carnival, and throughout the arduous years of toil in minstrelsy, melodrama, burlesque, and small-time vaudeville, the Four had clawed their way up the show-business ladder, constantly grasping new opportunities and adding new enhancements to their repertoire, until they made it to the big time. At the apex of the vaudeville pyramid, at theaters like Hammerstein's Victoria and the most prestigious of the Keith-Albee houses, they appeared on many bills. They never became headliners in the big time, but they did become a standard act. In that career trajectory, they were typical of thousands of talented, dedicated artists who once entertained hundreds of thousands of Americans each week during the golden age of vaudeville. Long after the demise of the big time, the extraordinary versatility of the Exposition Four would still be remembered with admiration by the group's professional peers. In 1938 actor Roger Imhof, looking back on the golden age, said, "I can name many outstanding acts but my most liked act was The Exposition Four. . . . They sang great. Played every instrument. Were dancers. . . . They did everything, and did it well."

Sadly, that final show at Hammerstein's Victoria was also the final appearance by the Exposition Four, not just there but anywhere. Following that performance, the act ceased to exist. It vanished because of a terrible illness that was sapping the strength of two of the three Alexander brothers. Russell and Woodruff both had struggled for years with tuberculosis. Infectious and incurable, the "white plague" was all too common in the general population, but it seems to have been even more prevalent among vaudevillians, perhaps because they spent so much time sharing close quarters in crowded railroad cars, stuffy theaters, and seedy hotels. For several years whenever either Russell or Woodruff had been too ill to perform, the act had either laid off for a short time or else the ailing member's place was taken for a longer interval by a substitute who had been hired for the duration. In May 1911, for example, the Four had cancelled a scheduled appearance at Keith's, Boston, because Russell had "gone to the Adirondack Mountains to recover his health." And in July 1913 when they headlined at the Empress in San Francisco, their act was said to consist of "the Alexander brothers and Willing and Cooper."

Russell Alexander died in a sanatorium in Liberty, New York, on 1 October 1915. In a poignant letter to the publisher of Russell's band music, Newton Alexander conveyed the sad news. "You never knew Russell very well other than through correspondence," Newton wrote. "I will tell you though that he was one of the best boys that ever lived and his death was a terrible shock to us. The Exposition Four now is a thing of the past." The surviving brothers parted company. Woodruff began working as a blackface single. His solo career was short-lived, however, for on 4 May 1918 he, too, died of tuberculosis. Newton Alexander escaped the deadly affliction that felled his brothers, but without them he faced the daunting task of building an entirely new act. Fortunately, he was already well acquainted with an experienced performer who now became not only his new vaudeville partner, but also his spouse. Her name was Theodora Lightner.

CHAPTER 3

Newton and Theo

THE EXPOSITION FOUR SPENT THE SPRING AND SUMMER OF 1913 ON the Sullivan and Considine circuit. Often called Empress time because many of its theaters bore that name, Sullivan and Considine was then the largest chain in small-time vaudeville. Within a few years it would begin to crumble and lose out to its archrival, the Pantages circuit, but for now it was riding high. Sullivan and Considine had spread east from the West Coast as far as Kentucky. On their tour, the Exposition Four played Detroit, Cincinnati, Chicago, Milwaukee, Minneapolis, St. Paul, Winnipeg, Butte, Spokane, Seattle, Vancouver, Victoria, Tacoma, Portland, San Francisco, Sacramento, Los Angeles, San Diego, Salt Lake City, Denver, and many smaller communities. Most of the time they shared bills with three other acts that followed the same route. One of these acts was Marcou the Shadowgrapher, who stood between a light projector and a screen and used his nimble fingers to create amusing silhouettes of animals and people. Another was the Booth Trio, three young daredevil bicyclists whose best stunt was riding up a fifteen-foot staircase and then jumping off sideways to the floor. Finally there was a sister act (vaudeville jargon for any two women working as a team), Lightner and Jordan, who offered an assortment of songs.

Giving three or more shows a day, the performers spent most of their waking hours either inside or very near the theater. Sharing the same bills week after week, making the same tedious railroad journeys, and lodging at the same malodorous hotels and boarding houses, they had ample opportunity to get to know one another. Camaraderie among the acts developed to the point that the Alexander brothers once played a practical joke on Marcou, the man of the magical shadows. They happened to be playing the Empress Theater in Fort Wayne, Indiana, on April Fools' Day. The Alexanders honored the occasion by sending Marcou a spurious fan letter allegedly written by a young lady named Flossie, who declared herself passionately eager to make his acquaintance and suggested that they meet at a certain street corner. Although Flossie did not mention it, the corner in question was clearly visible from the stage door of the Empress. Of course the Alexanders told everyone except Marcou about their scheme, and they all gathered at the stage door to see if he would keep the rendezvous with his admirer. Sure enough, they soon spotted him waiting at the designated corner. Amidst the onlookers' laughter and giggles, Dave Booth, one of the three bicycling experts, had a brainstorm. He proposed that he himself should become the amorous Flossie. Everybody else enthusiastically agreed and quickly set about equipping him with makeup and clothing. Soon the little band peeking out the stage door watched with delight as an extraordinarily ungainly and aggressive woman approached Marcou. He hesitantly shook hands with her, but moments later, after she had forcefully gripped his arm, he ran off down the street yelling, "I don't want to know you!" Flossie tried to give chase but was hampered by her unfamiliar skirt and footwear.

Flossie's attire had been supplied by the two young women of the sister act, Theo Lightner and Dolly Jordan. In their act Theo played the piano while one of them, more often Dolly, sang solo, or else the two harmonized. Their repertoire consisted of sentimental numbers like "Next Sunday At Nine (or Dearie Won't You Call Me Dearie)," "The Trail of the Lonesome Pine," and "Floating Down the River ('Cause It's Midnight Now in Dixieland)." They were a minor act on the bill, which was headlined by the Exposition Four.

The 1900 federal census reported that Theodora Lightner had been born in Pennsylvania in 1883 and now resided in Harrisburg, the state capital, along with her widowed mother, Ann, and her brother, Charles. Her mother was a dressmaker, her brother a bookkeeper, and she herself a pianist in a department store. In 1903 she married a man with the surname Dammon, but by 1910 she evidently had separated from him, as she was again living with her mother. Just when or how she began her stage career is uncertain. Possibly she spent several years on the lowest rungs of the show-business ladder, but no record survives. At any rate, during the week of 18 October 1909 Theo Lightner appeared in New Britain, Connecticut, at a theater that was part of a little chain of small-time houses operated by Frank A. Keeney. The following week she played Keeney's Third Avenue Theater at Thirty-First Street in Manhattan. Her act was billed as a pianologue, meaning she played the piano and accompanied herself by speaking rather than singing. *Variety* published a brief review of her New York City debut. "If Theo. is a beginner as a pianologist she is doing exceedingly well," declared the reviewer. "If, on the other hand, Miss Lightner is experienced," then "she might just as well give it up." Her piano playing was fine, but her speaking voice lacked musicality. Still, the reviewer said the audience liked her and "for the present the smaller time can use her nicely."

Another bit of evidence dating from the dawn of Theo's career is a piece of sheet music for the song "Next to Your Mother, Who Do You Love?," copyright 1909. This relic is interesting both because the song's lyrics are by a then utterly unknown young man named Irving Berlin, and also because the cover has a little inset photograph of a then equally unknown performer named Theo Lightner. The cover is mostly purple and orange, but the inset is black and white. Sheet music often was produced that way, with the whole print run done in one or more colors, and then separate little batches run through the press so as to add monochrome pictures of first one performer and then another. Perhaps Theo performed the number in her act and then tried to augment her meager income by inviting audience members to buy the sheet music after the show.

Actually, the sheet music gives her name not as Theo but as Thea. What apparently happened is that for professional purposes Theodora shortened her given name to Theo, but then music publishers and newspaper editors decided that Theo could not be a woman's name and "corrected" it to Thea. Theodora evidently decided that the matter was not worth fighting about. Although surviving records more frequently refer to her as Thea, this book will call her Theo, because that was her own preference, at least at the outset of her career.

In 1911 Theo teamed up with another young woman, Elvia Bates, in a sister act. Elvia was a vaudeville veteran, having starred in a comic sketch entitled "Her Last Rehearsal," in which she played the part of a hapless would-be actress who botches the role of Juliet while being wooed by an equally clumsy Romeo in the balcony scene from Shakespeare. Evidently this comic turn was a great success, as it toured for at least three seasons, 1903 through 1905, and on one occasion it played Keith's famous theater at Union Square. While it appears that neither Elvia nor Theo had done any singing before they became partners, their act together included songs as well as humorous dialogue. They specialized in lively numbers like "Maggie Magee," "Mammy's Shuffling Dance," and "The Madhouse Rag." They played small-time houses in secondary cities like Lowell, Massachusetts, and Auburn, New York. One of their more unusual appearances was in Worcester, Massachusetts, in May 1912, when they participated in a benefit for a local woman whose husband and three sons had perished the month before with the sinking of the *Titanic*.

Later that year Elvia and Theo split up, and Theo took on a new partner named Dolly Jordan. Jordan was another seasoned veteran, having sung solo in burlesque and vaudeville since 1901. As partners, Theo and Dolly played such metropolises as Portland, Rockland, and Brunswick in Maine. When they played Fitchburg in Massachusetts, they shared the bill with just three other acts and an assortment of short films. Thus it was a big step up for them when they landed a contract to tour the Sullivan-Considine circuit from March through October of 1913. That commitment gave them a thirty-week stretch of employment security the like of which neither of them had ever before experienced. Proudly, they placed an advertisement in *Variety* declaring that "those two classy girls," Lightner and Jordan, were "booked solid" on Sullivan-Considine time. On the tour, they polished their performance skills, probably with some helpful coaching from the Exposition Four, with whom they shared bills most of the time. Evidently their stint on Sullivan-Considine was highly beneficial, for afterwards they received increasingly favorable notices. When they played Cedar Rapids, Iowa, in November, the local theater manager claimed Theo and Dolly were practically stopping the show wherever they appeared, and that it had become necessary "for one of the girls to give a little talk of appreciation at each performance."

Their reputation grew to the point that they were able to take a giant step, making their first appearance in big-time vaudeville. They made their debut the first week of March 1914 at the opulent Keith's Theater in Boston. They were a minor act on the bill, but their presence loomed a bit larger on opening night because what was supposed to be the headline act, Miss Oxford's Elephants, was snowbound in New Jersey. A reviewer commented that despite the absence of Oxford and her pachyderms, the show was a good, well-balanced one, adding, "Lightner and Jordan, attractive young women, sang and danced acceptably." While not effusive praise, these words indicate that Theo and Dolly had held their own in one of vaudeville's most prestigious venues.

They fared even better a few weeks later when they appeared in New York City at Hammerstein's Victoria. This time their performance was a good deal better than merely acceptable. A reviewer in the *Clipper* singled them out as having scored one of the biggest hits among the nineteen acts that made up the bill, characterizing them as "two exceptionally clever young ladies with a world of looks, magnetism, and personality, besides possessing voices that they know how to use." The act began with Theo accompanying herself on the piano as she sang what the critic referred to as a "rube" song. Then she provided piano accompaniment while Dolly put over a number entitled "I'm Saving All My Lovin' For You." Finally, Theo continued to play as the two women harmonized in three more songs: "Down in Shenandoah Valley," "Bring Back My Lovin' Honey Boy," and "Oh! That Lovey Rag." The reviewer opined confidence that "their little piano and singing offering is bound to be welcomed on any bill, and as a standard sister act their success is assured." A reviewer in another trade paper, the *Billboard*, was similarly enthusiastic, saying that Theo was "a good pianist," Dolly was "full of ginger" (the contemporary euphemism for sexy), and the two of them were "on the big-time to stay." The only dissent came from *Variety*, whose editor, Sime Silverman, did not care for their selection of songs. He also suggested that both women could improve their singing voices, and that "too much practice by the pianiste who recites will not injure her speaking tones."

What might have been the duo's biggest break of all came on the third of August, when Lightner and Jordan played the Palace, which was in the process of displacing Hammerstein's as the greatest big-time venue of them all. Theirs was a last-minute, unadvertised booking that came about because one of the scheduled acts was unable to appear. Unfortunately, on this occasion they did not impress the critics. The only reviewer who took any notice of them was Silverman, who merely reported that they sang several songs, with Theo at the piano. "As it must have been an emergency call," he said, "let it go at that." Theo and Dolly subsequently played major big-time venues only occasionally. But they did receive a steady supply of routings via the United Booking Office, which means they had become a standard UBO act.

On their way up, Theo and her partner had passed by countless other acts that never made it to the big time. Performers who were not doing well often envied others' success and sometimes accused them of improper conduct. The UBO tried to police such matters, but with limited success. The most frequent allegation was that an act had copied some bit of business that another act had originated. Theo and Dolly became embroiled in one such dispute. The incident began in mid-January 1915 when *Variety* reviewed a new act that had played the Orpheum in Brooklyn. It was a sister act in which Irene and Bobbie Smith entertained with songs and comedy. The reviewer mentioned that the Smiths had rendered one song "in the usual style, with the two seated on a piano bench." In response to that comment, *Variety* published a letter from a performer named Billie Cullen, who worked with a partner named Jane Ward. Cullen claimed that the Smiths and other performers had copied the use of a piano bench from his own act, and he singled out Theo and Dolly as the worst offenders. "The idea of using a piano bench lengthwise with both seated, while doing double numbers, was first used by us as a detail to make our act a trifle different from other piano turns," wrote Cullen. "The first ones to 'lift' it were Lightner and Jordan, two women with a piano (the former a supposed friend of my wife and who, after seeing our act, remarked what a novel idea it was.)" Cullen's letter prompted an indignant reply from Theo Lightner: "I met you on Broadway last August, and you said you had trouble with the booking office, and to get reinstated you were doing a new act with a piano. Had you mentioned at this time your 'original idea,' I would have told you we had been using the piano bench over two years. When I saw your act you did not use a piano or bench. We have always had a piano act with a bench." *Variety* published no further correspondence on the matter, so Theo had the last word and seems to have got the better of the argument.

At the time of the catfight over who first thought of sitting lengthwise on a piano bench, Theo and Dolly were making a swing through the South on UBO time. The Exposition Four were doing the same, and the two acts appeared on bills together in Charleston, Savannah, Jacksonville, Tampa, Atlanta, and Charlotte. Relations between the two troupes evidently were cordial, for both featured some of the same songs (although not, of course, when appearing on the same bill). The shared numbers included the previously-mentioned "I'm Saving All My Lovin' For You" and "Oh! That Lovey Rag," both composed by Newton Alexander. Moreover, the sheet music for the latter states that it was "written especially for Lightner and Jordan," and its cover is dominated by a large color portrait of the two women.

It is, then, no great surprise that when illness caused the dissolution of the Exposition Four, Newton Alexander asked Theo Lightner to partner with him in a new act. It is somewhat puzzling, however, that Newton and Theo did not include Dolly Jordan in their plans. It would have made sense to do so, for she was the strongest vocalist of the three. Not that Newton and Theo could not sing reasonably well, especially when harmonizing with others, but they really shone as instrumentalists, Theo with her ragtime piano and Newton with almost any instrument he picked up, capped off by his amazing ability to play two cornets at once. The answer to the puzzle is that Newton and Theo had decided to become partners in life as well as in vaudeville, and Jordan had decided to do the same with a partner of her own. Dolly's new soul mate was Frank Willing, whom she had gotten to know when he substituted for an ailing Alexander brother in the Exposition Four. Willing and Jordan, a song-and-piano act, soon became a vaudeville staple and remained so into the late 1920s.

The Lightner and Jordan partnership ended abruptly. Although the Exposition Four performed for the last time in late April, Theo and Dolly continued to tour together for another two months. They were announced for several further bookings that had to be cancelled. Their final appearance was at Keith's Theater in Washington, DC, the week beginning 21 June 1915. Astonishingly, Theo Lightner and Newton Alexander debuted their brand new act only two weeks later. No doubt Newton had been preparing for it ever since the demise of the Exposition Four. At first it was announced that Theo and Newton would appear as a twosome, but before their first engagement they decided to form a trio by taking on a third partner. The newcomer was a teenage girl named Winifred Hansen. She was fifteen years old and had no professional experience. That veterans like Theo and Newton would take a chance on such an ingénue was remarkable. Evidently they had spotted Winnie's talent and potential, but where and how they made that discovery is uncertain.

As noted earlier, Winnie's father, Chauncey Reeves, had worked in minstrelsy and vaudeville. But he had done so only briefly and as a youthful lark, years before Winnie was born. The possibility that Chauncey retained show-business connections and used them to help launch Winnie on her career cannot be ruled out entirely, but it appears more probable that Winnie on her own initiative took the necessary steps to bring herself to the attention of show-business professionals like Newton and Theo. She could do so with relative ease, because she had the good fortune to reside in Manhattan, the epicenter of the entertainment industry.

In 1930 Winnie told an interviewer that she took her first tentative step into show business when a cousin heard her singing at home and suggested she try to get a job at a cabaret down near the docks. Winnie took that advice and got hired for a week at a dollar a day. "I must have been good," Winnie remembered, because in the course of her performance one evening a group of sailors tossed her a total of seven nickels. Before the week was up, she had an even better stroke of luck. An uncle who worked as a porter at a hotel frequented by theater people persuaded one of them to give his talented niece an audition. "My uncle pushed me into the room," Winnie recalled. "The first thing I saw was a girl sitting in a negligee smoking a cigarette. I took one look at her and turned green. I thought I'd been captured by white slavers and would never see my mother again." Winnie's apprehension subsided somewhat when a man who was also present in the room asked her if she could sing. Winnie replied that she could. Then her apprehension returned when he asked her if she had pretty legs. Winnie was not entirely sure about the answer to that question, so she raised her skirt a bit and let him judge for himself. He said her legs were all right. Then he asked her to sing. When she had finished, he said her voice was all right, too. Finally, he asked her to model an evening gown. It was the first time in her life Winnie had donned such a garment, but again the result was pronounced satisfactory. The man now said that his name was Newton Alexander, the woman in the negligee was his partner, Theo Lightner, and he would pay Winnie ten dollars a week if she would join their act.

A summary of Winnie's career published in 1967 (which may have been derived from an interview with her at that time) repeated the story that her uncle landed her the audition. But this summary gave a different and more complicated account of prior events. According to the 1967 article Winnie got her start in show business by singing in an amateur contest and winning a trip to Coney Island. Then she got a job with a music publisher, and soon afterward performed in one of Gus Edwards's kiddie acts, a vaudeville staple since 1907. Unfortunately, little Winnie's debut with the Edwards show ended in disaster. She sat among a group of children clustered in front of a trunk. A comedian concealed inside the trunk was to surprise the audience by throwing open its lid and leaping out. Winnie, hands behind her back, fiddled nervously with the trunk latch and somehow managed to lock it shut. When the comedian tried to jump out on cue, he slammed his head against the trunk lid and fell back inside, ruining what was supposed to be the climax of the scene. The curtain came down, and Winnie was summarily fired. This mishap would have been the end of her career, had her uncle not come to the rescue.

Obviously the 1930 and the 1967 accounts conflict, and even where they agree it is by no means certain they are correct. All that can usefully be said is that some assertions in the two accounts seem more plausible than others. For example, the claim that Winnie first sang in a cabaret near the docks appears doubtful. The piers to the west of Winnie's home serviced only lighters ferrying freight cars to a vast railroad yard. It was an unlikely location for a cabaret, especially one patronized by sailors. On the other hand, given that both shores of the island of Manhattan fairly bristled with piers, no doubt there were some cabarets in close proximity to docks where ocean-going vessels tied up. Still, one has to wonder how likely it is that Winnie's cousin would have known about any such place, or that Winnie would have sought her first job any great distance from her own neighborhood.

The story of Winnie's accidently locking the trunk in a Gus Edwards kiddie show is perhaps too good to be true, but the assertion that she once performed in such a show is at least somewhat plausible. In the many such shows he produced over the years, Edwards employed hundreds of youngsters, and some of them grew up to become stars: Groucho Marx, George Jessel, Ray Bolger, Eleanor Powell, and Lillian Roth, to name just a few. It is possible that Winnie should be added to the list. It is even more plausible that Winnie did indeed win an amateur contest, and also that she did indeed land her first job with a music publisher. Those were in fact the two most common ways for a young person to gain a foothold in vaudeville.

Many vaudevillians got their start by competing as amateurs, and New York City was the best place to do so. Scores of theaters featured a weekly amateur show in which virtually anybody could take to the stage. The performers often received a coin or two from the management just for participating. Almost as often they received a rough reception from the audience, for whom it was great fun to jeer and boo any acts that were not up to snuff. And, yes, there really were some theaters in which a giant hook emerged from the wings to drag off any act that proved particularly inept. The show always ended with the manager gesturing toward each act in turn, so that audience members could vote by applauding their favorite. The winner then took home a prize, often just a paper certificate or a cheesy little trophy, but sometimes an item of real value, perhaps even a half-eagle gold piece. There were so many amateur shows in the New York City area that there were even "professional amateurs" who eked out a living solely by appearing in them. Most of the participants, though, were there because they hoped to be noticed by somebody who would help launch their careers. Perhaps the theater manager presiding over the contest would be sufficiently impressed to offer them a paid spot on an upcoming bill, or maybe a theatrical insider in the audience would recognize their talent and recommend them for a booking elsewhere. It could happen. Stars as illustrious as Fred Allen, Pearl Bailey, Fanny Brice, Eddie Cantor, and Mae West all got their start that way.

The theater most renowned for its amateur nights was the Circle, lo-cated at Sixtieth Street, just a skip down Broadway from Winnie's child-hood home. Audiences at the Circle could be enthusiastic about acts that excelled, but were legendarily brutal toward the untalented. Bad acts were not hauled off with a hook, but sometimes the manager walked out on stage with a big sign reading "Beat It!" Anyone with a burning desire to make it in vaudeville had to be brave enough to endure such trials by fire. It is easy to picture Winnie rounding up her foster parents, neighbors, and schoolmates to cheer her on as she entered a contest at the Circle. But there is no surviving evidence that it ever happened. Once Winnie had become a film star, a story did circulate that she made her vaudeville debut in an amateur contest. But according to that story, Winnie grew up in Buffalo and made her amateur appearance there. Be-cause Winnie was in fact raised by her foster parents on West Sixty-Sixth Street in Manhattan, this story clearly is a fabrication.

For those aspiring vaudevillians who could sing, there was an alter-native approach to breaking into the business. New York City was the center not only of vaudeville, but also of the music publishing industry. Before the introduction in the 1920s of electrically recorded phonograph records and nationwide radio networks, sheet music was the principal means by which popular melodies were disseminated. With sheet music in hand, families and friends would gather around a piano and enter-tain themselves at home. To stimulate sales, music publishers employed "pluggers," who sang and peddled a company's latest offerings on street corners or anywhere else they were not shooed away. Saloons and coffee shops sometimes allowed a plugger to come in and entertain the custom-ers with a song or two and perhaps collect a few tips. Some bottom-end vaudeville theaters let a plugger sing while a slide of the lyrics was pro-jected onto a screen. Publishers also employed pluggers at their retail shops, so that potential customers could listen to a song before buying the music for it, and also at their business offices, where they happily gave away copies of the music to vaudeville professionals who wanted to use it in their acts.

Jack Haley, an actor who had long worked with Winnie, wrote in his memoirs that she got her big break when Theo and Newton heard her sing at a music publisher's and hired her on the spot. That scenario is less colorful but perhaps more plausible than the story that Winnie's uncle arranged for her to have an audition in a hotel room. Pluggers generally were young and paid a pittance. For example, singer and comedian Billy

Glason started off at age fourteen at a publisher's office where, he later recalled, "They even paid me a little to introduce songs." The following year, he became a full-time plugger, singing both at a sheet music store and, during the summer, outside ice cream parlors along seaside boardwalks. Winnie was fifteen when Theo and Newton hired her. It seems quite possible that Haley's account, although uncorroborated, is correct. Presumably Theo and Newton dropped by a publisher in search of tunes to use in their new act, heard a young plugger at work, and were bowled over by Winnie's ability to belt 'em out like nobody's business.

Whose idea it was that Theo Lightner and Winnie Hansen pass themselves off as sisters is unknown. It was a fib they clung to from 1915 to the end of their careers. (The previously mentioned 1930 interview was an exception, in that Winnie did tell that interviewer that her real surname was Hansen and that she became a Lightner when she joined the act.) It must have occurred to either Winnie or Theo, or else to Newton Alexander, that "The Lightner Sisters and Newton Alexander" would be a succinct and catchy name for the new act. Theo and Winnie could easily pass for sisters, as their facial features happened to be remarkably similar. Moreover, Theo looked only slightly older than Winnie, even though she was actually twice Winnie's age. Unlike her new partners, Winnie had no established professional identity, so there was no reason for her to balk at adopting Lightner as her stage name. Indeed, she might benefit from becoming known as the sister of an established vaudeville professional who had played the big time. That reputation might have come in handy if she ever had to go it alone. But she did not have to go it alone. The new act was a success from the start, and Newton, Theo, and Winnie would remain together as a team for many years to come.

CHAPTER 4

A Jolly Trio

IN JULY 1915 THE THEATRICAL SCENE IN BUFFALO, NEW YORK, SLIPPED into its annual dog days torpor. Two of the local stock companies gave final performances on 2 July and then closed pending the arrival of less oppressive temperatures. Vaudeville soldiered on, however, with a new weekly bill debuting as usual every Monday at Shea's Theater on Court Street. Because the Fourth of July fell on a Sunday that year, many people did not work the following day. Consequently, the matinee on Monday was well attended, even though Mike Shea, the theater's canny owner-manager, had announced that evening prices would be charged. Gallery seats went for fifteen cents rather than the usual dime, and orchestra seats topped out at seventy-five cents instead of the usual fifty cents. For that price, customers received between two and three hours of entertainment from a total of eight different acts.

The order in which the acts appeared went unrecorded but probably went something like this. Following an overture by the house orchestra, the show kicked off with an exhibition of fancy bicycle riding by a young man who, among other things, wheeled around the stage on a five-seater while playing a mandolin and carrying his female partner on his shoulders. Next up was a song and dance routine by two women and a man. Then came a comedy sketch that featured a whole family of actors and revolved around the misfortunes of a rotund and rather dim rural lad named Reuben Plump. The last act before intermission consisted of five men wearing Mexican outfits and wielding a mélange of musical instruments with which they performed tunes ranging from ragtime to *Rigoletto*. Once the patrons had returned to their seats following the break, they were treated to a routine featuring a man and his trained dog. Next came a husband and wife who danced and sang. The penultimate act was a monologue delivered by a portly gentleman satirizing Theodore Roosevelt. The live entertainment was brought to a close by some shapely young women posing as classical statues within a giant upended clamshell illuminated in brilliant colors. Finally, any customers not already heading for the exits could watch a short film.

The program was briskly paced and decidedly varied, with something for everyone. Children loved the bicycle riding and the dog act, ladies admired the fashionable gowns worn by the several women who danced and sang, and gentlemen quietly relished the curvaceous young beauties in the clamshell. Just about everybody found something to savor among the many musical selections, and most people laughed at the antics of both the hapless farm boy and the ersatz Teddy Roosevelt. It was a typical two-a-day vaudeville program. While the specific acts on view at Shea's appeared nowhere else, there were thousands of other theaters from coast to coast whose bills that day were just as briskly paced, just as varied, and just as pleasing to the audience.

It was no coincidence that vaudeville emerged in the late nineteenth century as the nation's foremost mode of popular entertainment, just as big business came to dominate both industrial production and retail distribution, passing on to consumers the lower prices made possible by efficiency and standardization. Vaudeville brought that same efficiency and standardization to the theater business, providing entertainment to the masses in exchange for a modest admission price. Putting on a conventional stage production like a drama or a comedy had always been a gamble, for if the show flopped the theater would remain dark, generating no revenue until another show could be mounted. Vaudeville was far less risky because every bill included such a wide assortment of acts that customers could be counted on to return week after week, confident there would always be something they would like. Also, the various vaudeville circuits—and most especially the United Booking Office (UBO) operating under the steely eye of Edward Albee—contained costs through efficient organization. A vaudeville act could tour for years presenting essentially the same routine before one audience after another.

Yet vaudeville never became as standardized as the motion picture industry that eventually supplanted it. Vaudeville was an intermediate step between the traditional and the modern, analogous to the canals that revolutionized transport in their day, but then gave way to the railroads. Unlike a film, a vaudeville act could evolve over time, and most performers made at least some effort to cater to the tastes and preferences of local audiences. The manager of every theater was in charge of the crucial business of determining the order of acts, and the sequence that prevailed at the first performance would be altered later on if the manager decided that rearrangement would improve the audience experience. Performers squabbled over who deserved the choicer positions on the bill, but they all knew that in the end the manager had the last word. Besides striving for contrast between each act and the one that succeeded it, the manager had to be mindful that some acts required more space and equipment than others. If a troupe of acrobats required that the stage be filled with guy wires and apparatus, then the next act would have to be performed "in one," meaning in front of either the main curtain or a drop just behind it. That consideration, along with certain other conventions that nearly always were observed, makes it likely that the ordering of the bill at Shea's theater on 5 July 1915 was similar to the sequence outlined above.

A closer look at each act that appeared at Shea's in Buffalo on 5 July 1915 can provide a richer sense of what it must have been like to witness a reasonably representative vaudeville program. It also demonstrates the link between vaudeville, which in retrospect seems to have been at its zenith, and the rising motion picture business that would soon surpass it in popular appeal.

American audiences, unlike their more courteous British counterparts, were notorious for arriving late. That meant people already in their seats by curtain time had to contend with the noise and commotion of tardy folk, who continued to drift in throughout the first and sometimes even the second act on the bill. Consequently, the show almost always began with something that did not have to be seen very distinctly and did not have to be heard at all. The first act to appear at Shea's on 5 July was the Dunedins, Jimmy and Myrtle. Even if latecomers were obstructing the view, everyone seated could at least catch glimpses of Jimmy whizzing around on his bike, and nobody had to hear what he said because he said nothing. As an opening act, the Dunedins were a bit unusual in that they started off with Myrtle performing a brief song and dance "in one" before the drop behind her rose to reveal Jimmy already in motion. No doubt many missed out on Myrtle's initial effort, but they likely could catch her later as she balanced on a wire while Jimmy circled around her. It must have been somewhat disheartening to performers like the Dunedins to know they were fated to be an opening act and seldom, if ever, receive a better position on the bill. Still, it was a living, and Jimmy Dunedin could still be seen wheeling around on vaudeville stages as late as 1938.

Performers hated being placed in the second position on a bill because they found it difficult to command the attention of an audience still getting settled. Which act, then, landed that dreaded number two spot at Shea's on 5 July 1915? It was the Lightner Sisters and Newton Alexander. Described as "A Jolly Trio," theirs was just the sort of light musical turn that suited second place. Moreover, they were a new and untried commodity, while every other act had previous experience and would have felt aggrieved if Mike Shea had placed them, rather than the newcomers, in the number two slot. To be sure, both Theo Lightner and Newton Alexander were old hands in vaudeville. In years past both had appeared at Shea's with previous partners, Theo at least once and Newton several times. Winnie Lightner, though, was an utter novice, just fifteen years old and appearing professionally for the first time. Yet it comes as no surprise that Mike Shea took a chance on Winnie. Of all the theater managers, vaudevillians liked Mike best. He took a genuine personal interest in the performers, and he always gave everybody a break. Sometimes he even paid people more than the amount specified in their UBO contracts. When he did that, Edward Albee seethed with rage but was powerless to interfere.

Exactly what the Jolly Trio did at Shea's went unrecorded. The advance billing said merely that "their comedy is up-to-date and they have good material," which sounds more like an expression of hope than a statement of fact. But from descriptions later that year of what was presumably pretty much the same act, it appears that it consisted chiefly of singing several songs, garnished with dancing and light banter. When the trio made a return appearance at Shea's in November, the billing that time claimed that Theo and Winnie were "dainty" and "attractively costumed," and that the Jolly Trio demonstrated that "refined songs, cleverly and delicately sung, invariably win out." One of those refined songs likely was Newton Alexander's composition "I Wonder What You're Thinking About," published that year. From other comments about the act, it appears that Theo played piano, all three members of the trio participated in the singing and dancing, and Newton showed off his prowess with brass instruments by playing two trombones at once. In their debut at Shea's, Winnie and her partners probably performed "in one" (at the front of the stage) or possibly "in two" (in front of a drop located halfway back). Meanwhile, stagehands invisible to the audience removed the Dunedins' bicycles and other equipment, and then brought in the props that set the scene for the third act on the bill, a sketch titled "The Lost Boy."

Edward Blondell, a former circus acrobat and clown, along with his wife Kathryn, first performed "The Lost Boy" in 1905. When Kathryn subsequently gave birth to the couple's two children, daughter Joan in 1906 and son Edward Jr. in 1909, they, too, were given roles in the skit as soon as they could possibly handle them. Joan was three when she officially joined the Ed Blondell and Company entourage while it was touring Australia, and she was eight when she appeared along with the rest of the family at Shea's in 1915. If not literally born in a theatrical trunk, Joan almost certainly did spend her infancy there rather than in a bassinet. A classic example of a vaudeville baby, Joan Blondell would grow up to become a prominent actress in motion pictures. Winnie Lightner was not the only future movie star on stage at Shea's.

The last act before intermission was the Five Musical Byrons, five real-life brothers, originally from St. Louis, who played a variety of instruments, including piano, harp, clarinet, saxophone, cornet, and trombone—plus the "Byrondolin," a device of their own invention that was played by four of them at once. (Why they did not go all the way and make it a five-man instrument is unclear; maybe Byron number five had to steady the thing while the others played it.) The Byrons had been in vaudeville since at least 1906. They had toured the Orpheum circuit out west, and at one time they leased and operated their own little theater in Chicago. The Byrons somewhat resembled the recently disbanded Exposition Four, but whereas the Exposition Four had included one performer made up in blackface, all five of the Musical Byrons had black faces, not because of makeup, but because they actually were African Americans. Their presence at Shea's demonstrates that vaudeville bills, except in certain southern locales, often were racially integrated decades before other forms of entertainment, like major-league baseball, breached the color line.

Because they were constantly on the move, vaudevillians had little opportunity to form connections with any community other than their own. Spending most of their leisure as well as working hours in close proximity to one another, they generally learned to put aside their prejudices and respect talent wherever it appeared. Racial minorities of every hue, Catholics and Jews, and even gay men and lesbians, encountered relatively little hostility from fellow performers. It would not be at all surprising if the Byron brothers were among the volunteer babysitters Ed and Kathryn Blondell relied upon to look after their children when they themselves were busy with such chores as unpacking costumes and props, providing their "sides" (musical charts for each instrument) to the house orchestra, and discussing stage settings and lighting cues with the appropriate personnel.

Out in the wider society, though, prejudice was rampant. Local folk were suspicious of strangers, especially those associated with theatrical entertainment, which still seemed morally suspect to many people, perhaps because it was so much fun. Only a minority of hotels and boarding houses welcomed vaudevillians, and artists who had no time to remove their stage makeup before they dashed out to grab a meal in between shows counted themselves fortunate if they knew of even one nearby bar or beanery where their unusual appearance would not cause difficulties. For those performers who belonged to a visible minority, the situation was far worse. Most white people were quite happy to watch from the other side of the footlights while African Americans performed on stage, but did not want to get any closer than that. Most theaters, if they admitted black customers at all, confined them to the gallery. When the Byron Brothers headed the bill at the Lafayette Theater in Harlem during Christmas week 1914 they played the only house in New York City at which black patrons could buy orchestra seats. In touting that Christmas bill, a local newspaper addressed to the black community declared the Byron Brothers the best musical act in all vaudeville. But on the same page the paper printed a lengthy article describing the endless rebuffs that black vaudevillians encountered endeavoring merely to purchase food and shelter. This hardship prevailed not just in the South, but even in northern states like Maine, where proprietors invariably explained that they themselves had nothing against Negroes, but that white customers would complain if blacks were allowed in. How the Byron Brothers managed to eat and put a roof over their heads while they played Shea's in Buffalo is unknown. But they managed, and their rousing performance brought a lively climax to the first half of the bill.

Following intermission, the audience quickly got caught up in the antics of Ed Vinton and his dog Buster, widely regarded as one of the best trained dog acts in the business. Ed would make a move, and then Buster would immediately replicate it. But for being particular favorites in Buffalo (because they made it their home base and resided there in the off season), Ed and Buster might well have been the opening act. They had toured nationally for years and would continue to do so until 23 April 1917, when Ed suddenly dropped dead from a heart attack just as a Detroit audience applauded the end of his and Buster's turn.

Dogs were the most common vaudeville animal act, but there were many others, involving everything from apes to zebras. Although such acts were popular with audiences, they were less favored by vaudevillians, who could not help noticing that many of the animals were mistreated. At best, the animals spent most of their lives chained up in dank theater basements, or being jostled about in cramped cages as they rumbled along inside railway baggage cars. A few vaudeville stars had both the conscience and the clout to refuse to appear on any bill with an animal act, not because they feared being upstaged but because they refused to be associated with cruelty. One can hope that Ed Vinton treated Buster as a beloved companion, but many trainers believed animals were unreliable unless they lived in constant terror of receiving yet another beating should they miss a cue or botch a trick.

The sixth act on the bill at Shea's was Keno and Green, a song and dance act. Although Joe Keno and Rosie Green performed in the same light-hearted style displayed earlier by the Lightner Sisters and Alexander, they of course had their own distinctive repertoire. Their act further illustrates the continuity between vaudeville and the movies. In 1920 Joe and Rosie had a daughter they named Mitzi. Adopting her mother's surname, Mitzi Green became a child actress for the Paramount and RKO studios, and as an adult she appeared in films as well as on Broadway and television. Yet another link between vaudeville and film is manifested by Keno and Green's last-minute substitution for yet another song and dance act, Burns and Fulton, which had been advertised but did not appear. Why the latter cancelled is unknown, but it may have been because at around this time Sammy Burns abandoned his vaudeville partner Alice Fulton in order to break into pictures as a comedian. He appeared in a 1915 two-reeler called *Sammy's Scandalous Scheme*, in which he played a fellow frustrated that his girl had a crush on Charlie Chaplin. Burns made only a few films before his movie career petered out. By the early 1930s he was running a dancing school in New York City.

The next-to-closing slot on a vaudeville bill normally went to the headline act, the one most people in the audience had come to see. Not infrequently it was the only one they had heard of. In this case the headliner was Lew Dockstader, a name that certainly rang a bell for most people at the time. For decades Dockstader had reigned as one of the greatest of minstrel men, touring with his own large company when he had the money, and with others when he did not. With the decline of minstrelsy, he had branched out into other venues, appearing in a film as early as 1906 and in vaudeville by 1910. While primarily remembered for his appearances as a blackface minstrel, he was a versatile comedian, as evidenced by his affectionate spoof of ex-president Theodore Roosevelt, a role he first performed back when Roosevelt was in the White House.

In his monologue "My Policies," Dockstader satirized Teddy's penchant for demanding progressive reform at home, carrying a big stick abroad, and slaughtering wild animals in Africa. Dockstader's impersonation was abetted by the fact that he and Roosevelt both were in their late fifties, had portly builds, and sported impressive soup-strainer moustaches.

The final live act, which may have caused some people to begin filing out, but probably induced a good many others to stay in their seats and pay close attention, was called "The Aurora of Light." It consisted of tableaux in which attractive young women, each of them "A Living Venus Clothed in Rainbows," stood like classical statues within an upended clamshell contraption bathed in colored lights. This was one of dozens of acts sent on the road by promoter Jesse Lasky in partnership with his sister Blanche. Besides his vaudeville activity, Lasky was involved with film production, in which he soon became a major participant. In 1916 his Jesse L. Lasky Feature Play Company merged with Adolph Zukor's Famous Players to form Paramount Pictures. Then, after Zukor elbowed him aside at Paramount, Lasky independently produced numerous movies.

The program at Shea's ended with a short film, which sent the audience a clear signal that the show was drawing to a close. That is not to say that Mike Shea did not consider the film to be a worthwhile part of his program. There is an old legend that vaudeville managers were contemptuous of films and used them only as "chasers" to empty their theaters. That analysis may have been true of some small-time houses where there were multiple shows a day. But in a big-time house like Shea's there was no need for a chaser, because the matinee and the single evening performance were scheduled hours apart. Reports from within the Keith-Albee organization make clear that theater managers took films seriously and complained if they were not of good quality. Oftentimes they did place films at the end of the program, mostly because the live performers liked being able to quit work a bit early instead of trying to hold an audience that was getting fidgety.

How the audience responded to the Lightner Sisters and Newton Alexander debut at Shea's went unrecorded, so it is impossible to say if anybody present would have predicted that Winnie Lightner had just taken her first step toward stardom in vaudeville, Broadway shows, and motion pictures. The Jolly Trio must have been at least reasonably successful, however, because its appearance at Shea's was followed by a steady stream of other UBO engagements. Those began humbly with a split-week booking divided between Wilkes Barre, Pennsylvania, and

Troy, New York. After that came a three-day run at Proctor's in Schenectady on a bill that included only five live acts, the remainder of the program consisting of a four-reel photoplay, plus two additional one-reelers.
Film had already begun to cannibalize vaudeville, as that arrangement
illustrates. A Schenectady newspaper reported that the Jolly Trio "made
a big hit" with the "capacity house" that attended the opening performance, although that may have been mere puffery, as all of the other
acts on the bill also received favorable comment, and a paid advertisement for the show appeared right next to the article.

Still, it is evident that the Lightners and Alexander quickly hit their
stride. In mid-October they advertised in the trade press that through
their agent, Edward S. Keller, they were "Booked Solid UBO." By the
close of 1915 their engagements had included many of the most prominent big-time houses in the eastern states: the Maryland Theater in
Baltimore, the Orpheum in Brooklyn, the Colonial in Manhattan, the
Grand in Pittsburgh, and the B. F. Keith Theaters in Washington, DC,
Philadelphia, Boston, and Providence. Best of all, during the week of 4
October 1915 they played the Palace, the preeminent venue not only
in New York City but in all of vaudeville. Jack Haley, who seven years
later made his own Palace debut as a minor participant in Winnie's act,
wrote in his memoirs that only those vaudevillians who had experienced
it could appreciate "the anxieties, the joys, the anticipation, and the ex-
altation" that performers felt the first time they passed through the iron
gate at Forty-Seventh Street and crossed the courtyard to the stage door.
"A feeling of ecstasy," he said, "came with the knowledge that *this was
the Palace*, the epitome of the more than 15,000 vaudeville theaters in
America, and the realization that you have been selected to play it. Of all
the thousands upon thousands of vaudeville performers in the business,
you are there. This was a dream fulfilled; this was the pinnacle of variety
success."

At the Palace Winnie and her partners occupied the lowly number
two spot and performed "in one" for fifteen minutes. Reviews in the
trade press were mixed. The briefest but also the most favorable evalu-
ation came from *Billboard's* critic, who wrote, "The Misses Lightner and
Alexander present a high-class musical and singing act. The smaller girl
comedies throughout the act with excellent results. The songs are well
selected and the trio were an early hit." *Variety's* reviewer was less enthusiastic, describing the trio as a "conventional three act" that had achieved
"a limited degree of success" with one Lightner girl playing the piano and
the other "leaning toward comedy." The group fared better as singers. As

a novelty, they offered one number in three different versions: British, Italian, and "straight." Another of their songs, "Tennessee," sung as a duet, was "a round hit." The reviewer judged that overall they "did satisfactorily" and concluded, "The big-time should find room for this trio, especially since similar acts that can pass the big-time test are decidedly scarce." Finally, the reviewer for the *Dramatic Mirror* described the act rather differently and was less complimentary about the singing. He said, "The Misses Lightner and Newton Alexander advance upon a baby grand and capture it during a bombardment of songs. . . . Mr. Alexander plays upon the cornet briefly, too. The sisters seem entirely too aggressive in their methods. This may come from too much confidence—or a lack of it. They should subdue their style and use better taste in selecting their song material." The reviewer took particular exception to a song that included the lyrics "I wonder why I married such a good for nothing man. Down on my knees, I hope the Lord will make him freeze."

While the Jolly Trio was only moderately successful at the Palace, the wonder is that the group had been there at all. It was highly unusual for a new act to play the Palace so soon after being formed, and it was unheard of for a neophyte like Winnie to play there a scant three months after launching her career. For their agent to have landed them the booking was a remarkable feat. No doubt this was possible only because reports on the act's earlier appearances had become increasingly favorable, and because Winnie's partners both had solid reputations that outweighed her own lack of credentials. After all, both Newton and Theo had previously been in standard acts that might well have played the Palace had these acts not been dissolved just as the Palace was displacing Hammerstein's Victoria as the nation's premier vaudeville house. During her partnership with Dolly Jordan, Theo had actually made a fluke appearance at the Palace as an emergency substitute, and it seems all but certain that the Exposition Four would eventually have secured a Palace booking had they not vanished along with Hammerstein's Victoria. In playing the Palace at the dawn of her career, Winnie was riding on her partners' coattails. But it is notable that none of the reviewers regarded her performance as inferior. Newton and Theo had experience and maturity, but Winnie's natural talent could not be denied.

The week following their Palace debut, the Jolly Trio played the Orpheum in Brooklyn. Recently acquired by the Keith-Albee chain, the Orpheum had been completely refurbished, its interior now glowing with Italian marble, bronze sculptures, luxurious carpets, and silk draperies. The Orpheum ranked second only to the Palace as a venue for vaudeville in the New York City area. When the Jolly Trio played the Orpheum, a reviewer declared that the entire bill had displayed "an undeviating measure of merit." It was, the reviewer said, difficult to pin down what made a particular vaudeville bill successful, "aside from the merely general requirements of action, verve, coloring and sparkle." But at the Orpheum that week there was "just 'something' that" caused "all the acts to please," and "Thea and Winnie Lightner and Newton Alexander fitted in well with the standard."

While no doubt happy to have done well at the Orpheum, Winnie probably was even happier to play the Colonial, where the Jolly Trio was on the bill for the week of 22 November, following a tour that had taken the act to UBO houses in Pittsburgh, Montreal, Erie, Buffalo, and Toronto. The Colonial was located at Sixty-Second Street and Broadway in Manhattan, just a few minutes stroll from Winnie's childhood home on Sixty-Sixth Street. Surely her foster parents Margaret and Andrew Hansen watched proudly as she strutted her stuff on stage, and there would have been ample opportunity in between the two-a-day shows to visit with the Hansens at home. Nothing was said publicly about any such encounters, however, because doing so would have contradicted the fiction that Winnie was Theo's sister and shared Theo's surname.

Winnie had launched her career at a fortuitous time, although it did not seem so at first. The national economy had stalled in 1913 and remained sluggish all through 1914 and well into 1915. Conditions were still so poor in August 1915 the United Booking Office announced that in the coming season UBO acts would be paid their full salaries only when they played one of eleven top houses. Everywhere else, they would have to accept pay cuts. Fortunately, by the close of 1915 the Jolly Trio's bookings had included eight of the eleven full-salary venues. Even more fortunately, the salary reductions elsewhere soon were rescinded because the economy began to soar. When the booming guns of August 1914 heralded the beginning of the First World War, most people expected the fighting to be over within a matter of months. But when the war developed into a stalemate, the belligerents turned to the United States as a source of desperately needed foodstuff and other supplies. In America, a rising tide of exports meant an economic bonanza for farms, mines, and factories that lasted throughout the war.

While happy about the return of good times, most Americans wanted no involvement in the contest for supremacy that raged among the European empires. Most agreed with their president that they should endeavor to remain neutral in both thought and deed. That a flood of exports from the United States reached the Allies, while only a trickle went to the Central Powers, was the result not of any decision to favor the former but simply because the Allied blockade of Germany choked off access to her markets. As the war dragged on, however, public opinion changed. Americans were appalled by the many civilian deaths, especially American deaths, that resulted from Germany's use of a vicious new weapon, the submarine, which torpedoed helpless passenger and merchant vessels without warning and made no attempt to rescue survivors. Consequently, American sympathies increasingly favored the Allies. Even among those Americans who remained firmly wedded to neutrality, there was a growing realization that the United States might be drawn into the conflict and must prepare for that eventuality. At last, in April 1917 amid a crescendo of patriotic fervor the United States entered the war on the side of the Allies.

Vaudeville reflected Americans' evolving attitudes. Early on, when most people wanted nothing to do with Europe's horrific slaughter, vaudeville reflected this disapproval and disengagement. When Winnie and her partners appeared at Proctor's, Schenectady, in July 1915, the advertised headliner was a one-act play entitled *War Brides*. It starred Alla Nazimova as a heroine who organizes a movement of women who refuse to bear children who will serve as cannon fodder for future wars. The play, with its powerful pacifist message, was well received. Its popularity waned later on, however, and it disappeared entirely once the United States joined the war.

The week America entered the conflict, Winnie and company were playing Pittsburgh. Their bill included a film, *America Prepared*, which was loudly cheered. Five months later, when they played the New Brighton Theater in Brooklyn, one reviewer remarked that the program there left him with the "guilty feeling" that he ought to enlist in the army. The show began not with the customary dumb act of animals or acrobats, but with an illustrated lecture from a local alderman on the topic "Uncle Sam's fighting forces." One of the later acts consisted of a detachment of men from the Seventy-First Infantry Regiment, who first gave a snappy demonstration of military drill. Then three former show-business professionals who now served in the regiment led the men in such musical hits as "Good-by Broadway, Hello France," "We're on Our Way to Berlin and We'll Get There, By Heck," and "When I'm Through with the Arms of the Army, I'll Come Back to the Arms of You." The headliner was good old Lew Dockstader with another of his comic monologues, this time an impersonation of a big city political boss. One reviewer noted approvingly that besides satirizing Tammany Hall style politics, Dockstader worked in several digs at "slackers and pacifists."

Winnie and her partners did not incorporate such blatant war propaganda into their own act, either then or later on. They did not lack patriotism, for they gave benefit performances that raised relief funds and promoted the sale of war bonds. Once, when a collection was taken up for the Red Cross, Winnie won enthusiastic approval from a Brooklyn audience when she spontaneously climbed down from the stage and personally helped pass the collection plates. Perhaps the Jolly Trio did not adapt their own act to the exigencies of war because they shared bills with so many acts that already provided a surfeit of such material. One such act was Howard's Animals, an opening act that ended with a parade of terriers carrying flags of the Allied nations. Another was Liberty Aflame, a headline act described as "a gorgeous patriotic spectacle" featuring Miss Olive Oliver as the Goddess of Liberty. Something of a record in the war-mania department was set when the Lightner Sisters and Alexander appeared at the Palace in July 1918 on a bill headed by Trixie Friganza, one of the biggest vaudeville stars, in terms of both fame and corpulence. Friganza strode onto the stage wearing a big white coat and carrying an armload of rubber balls. She tossed the balls in all directions, reaching people seated in all parts of the house. Next she opened her coat to display a previously concealed portrait covering her ample torso. Finally, she invited the audience to "pelt the Kaiser," which brought on a storm of both rubber balls and applause.

In 1916 the Jolly Trio toured the Keith circuit and other UBO affiliates on routes that took them as far west as Indiana and as far south as Alabama. Then, for seven months beginning in August, they played Interstate (an independent circuit centered on Texas) and Orpheum time, starting off in Omaha, working their way down to Houston and back again, then heading for the Pacific coast along what vaudevillians called the "death trail," with long jumps between the Canadian outposts of Winnipeg, Calgary, and Vancouver. After a six-week sojourn in the more hospitable environs of California, the trio headed eastward via Salt Lake City, Denver, Lincoln, Kansas City, Des Moines, and Minneapolis, then southward to New Orleans, and finally back to the Northeast and the familiar routine of playing UBO time in theaters great and small.

During the Orpheum tour out west, the Trio continued to deliver its song repertoire, which now included two new sentimental numbers by Newton Alexander, "You Never Can Tell" and "There's a Rose in the World for Us All," both published in 1916. Once they were back east, however, the act increasingly reflected Winnie's emergence as a comic talent. Not that her comedic gifts had previously passed unnoticed. Although some early commentators either singled out Newton Alexander as providing most of the humor in the act, or else gave equal credit to all three participants, as early as December 1915 one prescient observer said that one of the Lightner Sisters displayed "a comedy vein that produces laughs whenever she chooses to make you laugh. A rare gift say we." As time went on, similar comments cropped up more and more frequently. In Pittsburgh in April 1917 a local critic remarked that Winnie, "a comedy cut-up and a busy worker all the time she is on the stage, is one of the hits of the bill." In Utica, New York, the following month, a reviewer described her as "about the funniest young person" that had ever appeared there.

For a long time, many commentators did not know which Lightner sister was which, and so they simply talked about the "younger Miss Lightner," the "slighter of the two girls," "the more sprightly girl," or the "snappier and more gingery of the Lightners." Eventually they learned to name Winnie as the one with the special knack for clowning around and making faces. Reviewers sometimes tried to convey the scope of Winnie's talent by citing her alleged similarity to vaudeville stars already famous for their comedy work, although they disagreed about which ones she resembled. One critic said she was "a comedienne of the Irene Farber type, but is decidedly prettier and can make her face decidedly more grotesque." Another called her "a second Frances White, even to the low-cut back of that green dress." A third labeled her "a comedienne of the Belle Baker type." A fourth thought her "a sort of combination of Eddie Foy and Elfie Fay, scoring many laughs." Finally, a fifth reviewer commented, "Resembling Florence Moore in some respects, Winnie always sings and grimaces herself into the hearts of the audiences and convulses them with laughter at the same time."

The *Variety* critic who said that Winnie displayed both "the Elfie Fay facial twist and the Eddie Foy grin" raised no objection to her using either one, but another writer for the same paper accused Winnie of borrowing too much from other performers. In her column "Among the Women," Patsy Smith faulted Winnie for "becoming a good chooser of other people's gags and business." Smith usually devoted her column to critiquing the clothing of female performers. In this particular piece she discussed fashions worn by several women starring in current films. But then at the end of the column, she suddenly switched to describing a recent appearance by the Lightner Sisters and Alexander at the Fifth

Avenue Theater. Smith said that Theo and Winnie made no change of costume during their act and that their outfits (one of them "blue pussy willow over lace" and the other "white and black silk over lace") were both "last season dresses." Then she added her gibe about Winnie swiping other people's jokes. If Smith's accusation was valid, one wonders why other critics did not say something similar. The *Clipper*'s review of the same show said that in spite of hot weather there was standing room only at the Fifth Avenue; that "the Misses Lightner and Newton Alexander" had "scored the big hit of the bill"; that Winnie was "a comedienne of marked ability and a remarkable personality"; and that "the audience demanded two encores of them and recalled them eight times more." In any event, Smith's comment on the Lightners' gowns was uncharitable. Smith herself mentioned that the Fifth Avenue was a small-time house, yet she made no allowance for the fact that a small-time booking was the logical time for a big-time act to send its latest outfits out for cleaning.

By the summer of 1917 the Trio was prosperous enough to lay off during the slack season. The three were at leisure from mid-June until late August, save for a single engagement the first week of July at Keith's Theater in Washington, DC. They spent their holiday at a rural property evidently owned by Theo or her relatives and located just outside the small town of Marysville, Pennsylvania. Theo's mother and brother had moved to Marysville from nearby Harrisburg sometime after 1910. In April 1914 Theo gave Marysville as her home address when she purchased three purebred Berkshire hogs, an unusual acquisition for a vaudeville professional. In May 1915 Newton and Theo visited Marysville, and soon afterward Russell Alexander instructed his music publisher to send his mail to "Lightner's farm, Marysville, Pa." Russell was by then too ill with tuberculosis to continue his career, so probably he was cared for at the farm until he was obliged to enter a sanitarium.

In June 1917 a Harrisburg newspaper reported on a party hosted by Newton, Theo, and Winnie at "the Alexander farm, about two miles from Marysville." Two dozen young adults hiked out from town for an evening "pleasantly spent in dancing and music." The hosts also entertained their guests by performing some skits. Also present were Newton's widowed mother and his ailing brother Woodruff. Probably both of them were being looked after in Marysville, just as Russell Alexander had been two years earlier. In August another newspaper report said that Winnie, Theo, and Newton attended a party held at a cottage located a few miles the other side of town. It appears likely that for some years thereafter the trio visited and vacationed at the Marysville property whenever their schedule permitted.

Following their summer holiday, the trio plunged back into vaudeville, booked for forty weeks on UBO time. In October 1917, two years after the Jolly Trio first played the Palace, the act again stepped out upon that most illustrious of all vaudeville stages. For Winnie, Theo, and Newton the thrill this time around was even greater, because they took the Palace by storm. All three of the nation's leading theatrical newspapers published enthusiastic reviews. "Opening intermission," reported the *Clipper*, "the Misses Lightner and Newton Alexander offered a routine of songs and comedy business which stopped the show. The girls are working great and did exceptionally well with their several songs, harmonizing, mugging and kidding all the way through for a decided hit." *Variety* declared the Jolly Trio "the applause hit of the show" thanks to Winnie's "mugging and business." *Billboard* said Winnie, "comedienne par excellence," had "walked off with the honors of a bill brilliant in the extreme. Miss Lightner tore around over a stage set in one and bellowed herself hoarse. She grimaced and made the world a brighter place to live in, tho she twisted her features into an awful mess. Together they are a real vaudeville trio. They haven't even scenery to help them out and yet they stopped the show because the audience never got enough of their songs and their fun." They performed for fifteen minutes, after which the audience held them for six bows and then demanded an encore.

Only six weeks after that triumphal appearance, the Palace brought the Jolly Trio back again. From then on the Trio played the Palace at least twice each year, nearly always receiving acclaim from both audience and critics. In May 1918 *Billboard* said the three "were accorded a reception by their many friends in front" and after delivering twenty minutes of "vaudeville at its best" received "many bows." At their appearance a year after that, however, *Variety* complained that Winnie's comedy had become routine. She evidently took that criticism to heart, for when the trio returned to the Palace just two months later, *Variety* praised the act as one of the best on the bill, in part because of "comedy references to timely topics culled from the *Literary Digest*." Describing this appearance *Billboard* said, "They were encored and took innumerable bows. They have long been great favorites of the Palaceites."

Usually the Trio's Palace engagements were accompanied by bookings at other houses like the Colonial, the Royal, the Alhambra, the Orpheum, the Bushwick, and the Riverside, thus allowing the players to spend a couple of months in New York City and its environs. Vaudevillians liked playing what they nicknamed the "subway circuit," as it provided a welcome break from the incessant travel that was their usual lot. Sometimes they could even make extra money by "doubling," that is, playing two theaters at the same time by being positioned early on one bill and late on another, thus giving them time to scramble from one house to the other. Once when Winnie and her partners played the Palace they were hastily called upon to double at the Colonial fifteen blocks down Broadway. Gus Van and Joe Schenck, a famous song and comedy duo, had walked out in a fit of pique over the way their names were displayed on the Colonial's outdoor electrical sign. Winnie and company pocketed extra cash while Van and Schenck were punished by the abrupt cancellation of their UBO contract.

Between their visits to New York City, the Jolly Trio played numerous Keith and other UBO houses in the East, and from August 1918 through February 1919 they made another swing around the Orpheum circuit that took them to St. Paul, Duluth, Calgary, Seattle, San Francisco, Memphis, New Orleans, and many other cities in the West and South. When they returned to New York and played the Palace in April 1919 they were given the coveted next-to-closing position. This honor did not mean the three were the headliners, for bills at the Palace included so many top-notch acts that performers did not squabble over their place on the program so much as who got the "star" dressing room. Still, being put on next to closing was a vote of confidence from the Palace management.

Winnie had emerged by then as the key figure in the trio, eclipsing her partners Theo and Newton. One reviewer of their Palace appearance commented that "Winnie Lightner, a clever comedienne, is now featured in the billing, and deservedly so, for no small portion of the act's success is due to her work." A few weeks later when they occupied the same slot at the Alhambra in Harlem a critic declared, "This is a clever trio, but Miss Winnie is the star of the act. She is a comedienne with a very striking personality." Another reviewer went even farther, saying, "When all scores are counted up and points placed to the individual credit of the participants in the current bill at the Alhambra, Winnie Lightner will undoubtedly be found to be the winner."

Her confidence bolstered, Winnie for the first and only time in her career overreached herself: She decided to forsake vaudeville for Broadway. Landing a role in a Broadway production was always an alluring prospect for vaudevillians, for if the show became a hit they could take up residence in a furnished apartment instead of living out of a trunk and moving on every week. Settling into a role on Broadway was even better than touring the subway circuit.

Winnie agreed to appear in a production called *While You Wait*, produced by Edward S. Keller, her vaudeville booking agent, in partnership with Elwood F. Bostwick, a promoter well known in Broadway circles. Keller and Bostwick planned to mount tryout weeks in New Haven and Washington, DC, and then open in New York. Winnie was the star, but the cast included Newton, Theo, and fifteen other principal performers, plus a bevy of chorus girls. The show was built around a theme that, while not original, was well executed. When the house lights dimmed and the curtain rose, the audience was surprised to see before it a stage that contained only some scattered fire buckets and jumbled scenery. Amid the disorder stood a stage manager and a property man. Their conversation revealed that the actors they were expecting had not shown up. Consequently they decided to prepare an entirely new play. First they selected some (supposedly) ordinary members of the audience to come up on stage and become actors. Then, having decided to expand the show into a musical revue, they invited the theater's female ushers to become chorus girls. The young women, led by Winnie Lightner posing as the head usher, readily obliged. Over the course of the evening the new show was developed, providing the pretext for a mélange of song, dance, and comedy. In one scene Winnie played the lead role in a burlesque of the opera *Carmen*.

Unfortunately, the tryout in New Haven did not go well. After opening night, a local reviewer said the show was "bright in spots," but lacked "the snap and consistency to make good at the two dollar price," as it provided no better entertainment than "practically any high-grade vaudeville house." The reviewer rubbed salt into the wound by adding, "It is difficult to see how, even with the work that will undoubtedly be done on the piece during the coming week, it can be whipped into shape so as to make a success."

Despite that setback, the producers gritted their teeth and pressed on with the tryout week in Washington. There they promoted the show with a barrage of advertising and press releases. The publicity included a report that the Lightner sisters worked in show business solely to finance their passion for agriculture. They were said to own a farm in the Berkshires, complete with orchard, cows, and pigs. Winnie, it was claimed, was "the practical farmer of the family," whereas Theo as "a student of botany" was busy trying to cross plums with walnuts. Perhaps the two women had embellished their memories of vacationing at the farm outside Marysville, Pennsylvania, in order to concoct this outlandish fable and pass it on to a gullible reporter.

In its second tryout, *While You Wait* received a much better reception from the local press. The *Washington Times* predicted a "prosperous run," pronouncing the show "a sure hit" and "the most unusual theatrical venture that has ever appeared on the legitimate stage in Washington." According to the *Times*, the talented cast "would do credit to the billing of half a dozen big-time vaudeville any week in the year." The *Washington Star* was similarly enthusiastic, describing the production as "a potpourri of entertainment—everything from soup to nuts, with a few unheard of extras thrown in for good measure." With its "snappy" songs, "lively" dancing, and the "bizarre" comedy of Winnie Lightner, it was "brimful of peppery action." The *Star* was confident the show would succeed, saying, "When a play is so far out of the ordinary that new adjectives are required to describe it and so entertaining that the encores become a habit with the audience, the box office problem appears to be solved."

It soon became clear, however, that the box office problem had not been solved. Word of mouth on the show evidently was less favorable than the reviews in the *Times* and the *Star*. A clue as to why may be found in a third review of opening night. The *Washington Herald* judged the theme of putting a new production together to be a "disquieting feature of this girl-song-joke show," even though "this thought germ and the kewpie eyes and Foyisms of Winnie Lightner are the pegs upon which hangs the production's hope of success." The *Herald* complained that although Winnie's "cherry lips, black eyes and Dixie deviltry" were "the very best reason for the show's existence," her *Carmen* spoof was "practically the only new stunt she does and there isn't enough of that." Also, said the *Herald*, the show suffered from "a handicap of jerkiness" and contained too many unimpressive "tinkly little tunes." Keller and Bostwick put on a brave face, declaring that they would revamp the show and bring it to Broadway in the fall. In reality though, they knew they were licked. The show closed after its week in Washington, never to be heard of again. If anybody in New York was waiting for *While You Wait* to arrive, they waited in vain.

Winnie and her partners did not to sit around licking their wounds. After a one-week hiatus they returned to vaudeville, although at first they had to make do with some low-grade bookings. Probably because it had been arranged hastily, their appearance at Henderson's Music Hall at Coney Island was promoted with the same description used at the start of Winnie's career: A publicity release said the Lightner girls would display "prettiness, cleverness and gracefulness, combined with the freshness of youth," and would demonstrate that "refined songs, cleverly and delicately sung, invariably appeal." In reality Winnie had of course long since traded gracefulness for mugging, and most of the trio's songs were neither refined nor delicately sung. Two months earlier a reviewer had pointed out that the act owed its success to "facial contortions," "frisky spirits," and songs "full of pep." The members of the Jolly Trio, said that writer, "are sort of rough house cut-ups, but nobody wanted to act as censor for all of their pranks were enjoyed."

In July the Trio returned to the big time by playing the Palace, where "as expected, Winnie Lightner clowned and mugged in her pleasing way." For the next three years the act toured the Keith and Orpheum circuits. The three partners' lives fell into a familiar pattern only occasionally interrupted by anything unusual. One such incident occurred in January 1920. Scheduled to play Sioux City, Iowa, on Orpheum time, they cancelled because for the first time in her career Winnie was felled by sickness so severe she could not go on. Possibly she was a late victim of the so-called "Spanish flu," the influenza pandemic that raged throughout most of the United States in 1918, lingering in some localities into 1920. Theo and Newton did not try to perform without Winnie. She had become indispensable, and her partners knew it. As a reviewer put it some months later, Winnie with her "wonderful personality and her cleverness as a 'nut' comedienne" was "the whole act." So it was, even though Theo was "a good piano player" and Alexander "a perfect foil" for Winnie's "pert and piquant repartee."

Despite their disastrous experience with *While You Wait*, Winnie and her partners still aspired to be something more than just a threesome with a piano, so in the fall of 1920 they tried again. This time, however, they did so in manner considerably less ambitious and much less risky. Instead of leaving vaudeville they merely developed a new act that was in effect a scaled-down version of a revue. There had always been some vaudeville turns that featured more performers and ran longer than the norm. These were known as flash acts, and they provided a welcome break from the usual solos, duos, trios, and quartets. Moreover, at this time the lavish Broadway revues put on by impresarios like Florenz Ziegfeld were doing spectacularly well, and their success inspired an imitative "revue craze" in vaudeville. The act mounted by Winnie and company was more successful and lasted longer than most other vaudeville revues.

The new act was called "Little Miss Vamp." Written by Newton Alexander, it featured Winnie in the role of a vamp, the contemporary term for a woman who charms and seduces men for her own advantage. The focus of Winnie's vamping was a dashing young fellow preparing to take part in an airplane race. Meanwhile Winnie was busy in a competition of her own, elbowing aside the several other women who were after the same guy. There was much more to the act than just the vamp-and-aviator business, however, for it featured songs, dances, and comedy bits, all of which were enhanced by an elaborate stage set and lavish costumes. Besides Winnie, Theo, and Newton, the cast included William Taylor, who played the aviator; a chorus of eight attractive young women; and the Dancing McDonalds, a male-female duo of whirlwind hoofers.

"Little Miss Vamp" opened with an elaborate full-stage set depicting a hotel lobby just off a seaside boardwalk, which could be seen bathed in bright sunshine through a rear doorway. The entire company swept into view through the doorway, the chorus girls all cooing over the handsome aviator as they pushed him along in a rolling chair. After a song by Winnie, Theo, and Newton, Winnie launched into the first of several comic exchanges with Newton acting as her straight man. Then Winnie and the chorus offered another number. A rapid change of costumes saw the whole company appear clad in white satin and playing drums while Winnie sang solo. The women of the chorus reappeared in colorful Spanish gowns, each one different. The Dancing McDonalds performed. The Jolly Trio sang again, as the chorus girls paraded in yet a fourth change of costume. Newton did a comedy bit with his cornet. Winnie surprised the audience by singing a serious ballad. Finally, the plot was resurrected with the news that the young aviator had injured his wrist, whereupon Winnie announced that she would enter the airplane race in his stead. Over the protests urging her not to do it, she exited the stage bravely declaring her determination to carry out her audacious plan. Moments later she returned, holding in her hand a toy airplane of the sort that buzzes around at the end of a wire, and asked if anybody knew how to fly the thing. That bit provided a good laugh as the curtain fell.

After an unadvertised three-day break-in at an anonymous small-time venue, "Little Miss Vamp" premiered at the Alhambra Theater in Harlem on 20 September 1920. Three weeks later it played the Palace. It was a smash. "And what a hit the new Lightner Sisters-Alexander act made!" proclaimed the *Dramatic Mirror*. "Wow, but they tumbled that Monday afternoon crowd over in a heap." Winnie was "the bright, shining star . . . a whole show in herself . . . peppery, vivacious, clowning one minute and singing a straight ballad the next." The reviewer praised every aspect of the new act: the scenery, the costumes, the chorus girls, the Dancing

McDonalds, and most especially the songs. There were, he said, "some corking numbers," including "Old Man Jazz" (sung by Winnie, Theo, and Newton), "Tric-Tric-Tricoline" ("a fast snappy number by Miss Winnie and the chorus"), and two solos by Winnie, "Wonderful Eyes" and "The Ragtime Drummer Boy." The reviewer concluded by saying, "All told the entire revue is just right for vaudeville and at the Palace Monday was the biggest kind of a hit."

For Winnie "Little Miss Vamp" was both a personal triumph and a career landmark. When she emerged as a movie star a decade later, it was in the role of an aggressive "gold digger" pursuing a wealthy gentleman amid a whirl of wisecracks, dancing, and songs. Clearly her experience playing Little Miss Vamp in vaudeville was a perfect rehearsal for the later breakthrough performance on film that made her the first great female comedy star of the talkies. As the *Clipper*'s reviewer observed of Winnie's vaudeville act, "She sings, dances, gets laughs and shines as the star all the way through. . . . In fact, the remainder of the company is almost passive in comparison to her, for she is all through the act, here, there and everywhere with a laugh, gag or smile." Winnie also sang a serious ballad, and she did it with an emotional force that literally stopped the show. The audience demanded and received two encores before they would let her move on. "In this," said the reviewer, "she sprang a real surprise, for she displayed a richness of voice and depth of feeling we did not believe her capable of."

With a year's worth of Keith and Orpheum bookings in hand, Winnie and company set off on another tour of the West. This time around they usually were the headliners. Western travel remained arduous, but there was much to see and do and ample opportunity to see and do it. Usually they performed just twice a day, with each performance lasting only twenty minutes. Even allowing for the many hours required to arrange such things as orchestral accompaniment, scenery changes, and lighting cues at every theater, and to don makeup and costumes for each performance, there was still time to enjoy life. Newton Alexander, an avid golfer, was out on the links almost every morning while the act toured California, joining in a foursome with three other vaudevillians whose acts were playing the same Orpheum houses. On one of those same mornings Winnie visited an indoor swimming pool at the Los Angeles Athletic Club. The sight of Winnie in a bathing suit generated so much male interest that Bull Montana, a famous professional wrestler, had to block the pool entrance in order to keep back the crowd. Winnie was accompanied by some of the chorus girls from the act, and she amused onlookers by trapping them in a revolving door from which they could not escape until she stopped pushing it around in a circle.

While headlining at the Los Angeles Orpheum in February 1921, Winnie was interviewed by Edwin Schallert, theater critic of the *Los Angeles Times*. Not yet hidden behind a phalanx of publicity agents, as she would be during her film career, Winnie spoke jokingly but candidly about her current circumstances and future plans. Schallert was much taken with Winnie because, he said, "She has a temperament like a saxophone, and everything she says is funny." When he arrived at her dressing room, she was arranging her hair. On stage she wore it pressed tight against her head and shining like patent leather, but now she was smoothing it over her ears into a more conventional style. She was, Schallert thought, "about three times as good-looking as you'd suppose seeing her in vaudeville." Unable to keep still even for a moment, Winnie fiddled with little ivory animals and other gewgaws. If she ever went into the movie business, Schallert mused, "I would hate to think of her waiting around between scenes in the films." Winnie told Schallert that she had no intention to get into the movies immediately, but did expect to some day. "I don't go in for the slapstick, though," said Winnie. "No pies in my face. I'd rather stay on the stage." (That was a vow Winnie would not keep, for in one of her films she would indeed receive a cream pie in the kisser.) It is interesting that Winnie contemplated a movie career even before the arrival of the talkies. Evidently she calculated that her gift for comic facial contortions and body language would serve her well in silent pictures, even though her prodigious singing talent could not be displayed there.

For now Winnie was happy in vaudeville, although she did remark that some people in the business were envious of her success. "I never was that way myself when I wasn't a headliner," she said, "but now I'm in a headline spot, I'm going to stay there just for meanness." Winnie was just kidding about being mean, but she no doubt expressed real frustration at the pettiness and jealousy she encountered among her peers. Although well aware that she could easily headline as a single, Winnie told Schallert she had no intention of leaving Theo and Newton. "I don't think I'd like it," she said. "I'd be too lonesome out on the stage. I've got to have somebody to punch when I get excited." She thought, in fact, that she and her partners might eventually leave the two-a-day in order to put on their own full-scale musical comedy or revue. Despite having crashed and burned in *While You Wait*, Winnie still dreamed of starring on Broadway.

Despite her openness, Winnie was not entirely straightforward when she spoke of her past and present circumstances. She said she was born in the theater district in New York City, which while not true was close enough to be forgivable. But she also gave no hint that she had not been born with the surname Lightner, and in fact spoke explicitly of Theo as her older sister. When Schallert asked if she was married or engaged, she replied that she was neither. "I had a sweetheart once," she added wistfully, "but I don't know whether I've even got him now." Only a little over a month after Winnie made that statement, the news suddenly broke that vaudeville star Winnie Lightner had begun divorce proceedings against her husband, Richard L. Pyle. That Winnie was married came as a surprise, but that she was both married and getting divorced was a bombshell. The news created a particular stir in Los Angeles, both because Winnie had so recently headlined at the local Orpheum, and because her soon-to-be-ex husband was starring in a touring show that was about to open at another theater in the city.

Just a few years older than Winnie, five feet eleven inches in height, weighing in at a well-proportioned 167 pounds, and sporting bright blue eyes and light brown hair, Richard Pyle was a strikingly handsome young man. A native of Muskegon, Michigan, he was an actor, dancer, and singer in musical comedies, including three Broadway productions and many road companies. When and where Winnie and Richard met and married is uncertain, but it may have been in the summer of 1920 when they both were in New York City. Winnie played the subway circuit of UBO houses, while Pyle appeared at the Knickerbocker Theater in the Victor Herbert musical *The Girl in the Spotlight*. After that, though, their paths divided. By the start of 1921 Winnie was touring California on Orpheum time, while Pyle was in Atlanta and later New Orleans as the leading man in a road company of George M. Cohan's hit musical comedy *Mary*. In late March, Pyle's road company came to Los Angeles, but by then Winnie had decamped for Chicago, where she filed her divorce suit. The divorce was granted on grounds of desertion on 13 April 1921.

One wonders how Winnie and Richard ever imagined they could make their marriage work. Because both of them could sing, dance, and do comedy, they possibly could have formed a vaudeville twosome. Or alternatively Richard might have joined with Winnie and her existing partners to turn the Jolly Trio into a jolly quartet. But there is no indication that the couple ever contemplated any such thing. It appears they married on impulse and separated soon after. Following the divorce they continued along their separate ways. A year later Richard was in Los Angeles again where he replaced Edward Everett Horton in a show called *Buddies*. Pyle then left the stage for the movies and played supporting roles in more than thirty features filmed between 1923 and 1928. Early on he had a small part in the classic Buster Keaton comedy *Sherlock Junior*. There Pyle played a posh villain in two brief scenes of the film-within-a-film that the Keaton character steps into after dozing off while working as a theater projectionist. For reasons unknown Pyle elected to go by the name John Patrick when appearing in films. His movie career petered out just as Winnie's took off.

Winnie's second marriage was even more curious than her first. Just twelve days after divorcing Pyle, Winnie married again. Her new spouse was William J. Harold. While it is clear who Pyle was, next to nothing is known for certain about Harold. When Winnie eventually divorced him, a newspaper reported that he had conducted the orchestra when Winnie's act played New Orleans. The report gains credence from the fact that Winnie had indeed played the Orpheum in New Orleans the week of 25 April 1921. Moreover, on that occasion a local reviewer said the act did not go over well because "Winnie Lightner's mugging and tricks somehow missed." Perhaps Winnie was paying more attention to the orchestra conductor than to her own performance.

If Harold really was the orchestra conductor in a vaudeville theater, then Winnie's second foray into marriage was just as impulsive as her first one, and even more impractical. When Winnie married Pyle, a man with theatrical abilities somewhat similar to her own, it is at least conceivable that they could have combined their careers. But when Winnie married Harold, it is difficult to imagine how either party thought such a union could work. An orchestra conductor was attached to a single theater in a single city like a mollusk to a rock, whereas a vaudeville star like Winnie blew around the country like a tumbleweed. Small wonder then that Winnie and Harold separated within days of being wed, according to the divorce petition that she filed when she officially dumped him after two years of matrimony. The 1930 federal census reported that a man named William Harold, age thirty-two, was living in Chicago and was a musician employed by an orchestra. If that was the same William Harold Winnie had married in New Orleans, and if he subsequently moved to Chicago, then his residence in the latter city may explain why Winnie filed her divorce suit there.

Now unburdened by domestic attachments—not that they had ever slowed her down—Winnie continued her career with her usual vigor.

By the autumn of 1921 she and her partners had been doing "Little Miss Vamp" for nearly a year, and had been booked at least once into virtually every big-time vaudeville house in the country. Not surprisingly, there had been changes to the supporting cast. Two of the chorus girls, Louise Robinson and Betty Martin, had dropped out in order to marry Edward Tierney and James Donnelly, respectively. Their new husbands were fellow vaudevillians, both of them partners in a dance act starring Frances Pritchard. William Taylor had left his role as the aviator in order to train as an opera singer. Tessie Darling, formerly of the Marion Morgan Dancers, had joined "Little Miss Vamp." Other newcomers included Marion Davis, Jack Good, and Bobby Devant. Despite all of these comings and goings, the content of the act itself had not changed, so a revamp was in order. Whereas Newton Alexander had written "Little Miss Vamp," he and his partners could now afford to pay for outside help. Accordingly, they turned to two of the best song and sketch writers in the business, Neville Fleeson and Albert Von Tilzer, to help them develop a new mini-revue. Unlike "Little Miss Vamp," the new act did not have a specific title, being billed simply as a "one-act musical comedy featuring Winnie Lightner & Co." It carried over some of the more successful songs and gags from the earlier turn, but of the former personnel only Winnie, Theo, and Newton remained. New secondary performers were hired, the most important named in the billing as "The Gosman Sisters, Jack Haley, Vada Russell, and Ramona." In retrospect, the most notable of the new faces was Haley, who would go on to a long career in show business capped by his unforgettable film role as the Tin Man in *The Wizard of Oz*.

The new act found its legs at places like Poli's in Bridgeport and the B. F. Moss in Flatbush, and then debuted at the Palace on 26 September. It was a success, although nothing like the blockbuster hit "Little Miss Vamp" had proven to be at its debut the previous year. One critic said the new act "would be more pleasing if there were less of Winnie and if her performances were subdued to a certain extent." (That was a hopeless suggestion, for Winnie could do many things, but being subdued was not among them.) The *Dramatic Mirror* griped that the new act was too similar to the old one, but acknowledged that "Winnie's clowning was good for laughs" and that overall "the trio did well." *Variety* noticed that there now were only four chorus girls but thought the change had "rather aided the offering, with Winnie Lightner easily the star of the interlude." The same paper offered the prescient comment that Winnie's clever handling of a ballad number was "an indicator of musical comedy possibilities."

Over the next few months, as the new act toured the East, it received a warmer reception. In late October it was the headliner at Keith's Eighty-First Street Theater, although it had to share honors with the sensational German horror film *The Golem*. A reviewer praised Winnie as "a snappy miss with a keen sense of comedy," adding that "her scene with Alexander and his cornet was funny and well handled." When Winnie delivered Alexander's ballad "It's a Wonderful World After All" the applause was so prolonged that she had to sing it again. In November when Winnie and company played Keith's, Philadelphia, their turn was shifted from its original mediocre place on the bill to the headline slot, and a local reviewer hailed it as "one of the most decided and spontaneous hits seen here this season." The following month there was a minor but amusing hiccup when they played Keith's, Boston. A barelegged solo dance by Ramona, although well received everywhere else, proved too much for the Puritans of Beantown. At the opening matinee Ramona's naked limbs were visible for just a few seconds before the spotlight man hurriedly put on a colored filter that made them appear clothed. For subsequent shows she wore leggings. After Boston there was smooth sailing until March, when Winnie fell ill and had to have her tonsils removed. Winnie and company were booked to open on 13 March at the Palace, which would have been their fourth engagement there within a period of only eight months. But they were forced to cancel both that booking and the one for the following week. They resumed their usual punishing schedule with an appearance at the Alhambra on 27 March and continued to tour throughout the spring and on into the summer of 1922.

It might have been expected that the troupe, now settled comfortably into their new act, would then have visited the farther reaches of the Keith circuit, followed by another western odyssey on Orpheum time. But it was not to be. Although Winnie did not know it yet, the vaudeville phase of her career was drawing to a close. She would not forsake vaudeville entirely, and indeed her greatest triumph there was still to come, but her focus would shift elsewhere. It was just as well, because vaudeville had passed its peak. Throughout the nation many small-time theaters were giving up live acts altogether and switching to all-movie programs. Even big-time vaudeville was in decline. Many of the theaters affiliated with the Keith-Albee booking agency (formerly the UBO, but now calling itself the Keith Vaudeville Exchange) and even some of the Keith-Albee houses themselves, were shifting from big-time, two-a-day shows to small-time programs that copied the old Loew's formula of coupling a modest number of live acts with a feature film. Even the greatest stars now had to include small-time bookings on their routes. Those engagements often required them to perform several times rather than only twice daily, sometimes in split-week arrangements that doubled their unpaid travel time and costs. For thousands of minor acts the situation was far worse. Bookings were dwindling, and life was becoming a grim struggle for survival. Many thousands of vaudevillians had to leave the business entirely and find some other line of work.

As a well-known standard act, the Lightner Sisters and Newton Alexander were high enough up in the pecking order not to have to worry about becoming unemployed. But they did have to supplement their appearances at the flagship Keith houses with more and more engagements at small-time venues like the Prospect in Brooklyn, where they played a Monday through Wednesday split-week in May 1922. They were the headliners, but many people in the audience had come not so much to see them or any of the other acts as to catch the new Buster Keaton film that was on the program, or to compete for prizes in the flapper and cake-eater dance contest that was a special added feature on Monday night. The Jolly Trio was described by a reviewer as "one of the few survivors of the revue craze" that had swept vaudeville in happier days. It was time to move on. Fortunately for Winnie a new opportunity beckoned. One of the regular attendees at the Palace on Monday afternoons was George White, producer of an annual revue on Broadway. White had seen Winnie and her partners on many occasions, and he liked what he saw. In July 1922 he announced that he had signed the Lightner Sisters and Newton Alexander to appear in the upcoming fourth edition of *George White's Scandals*. Winnie had long aspired to star on Broadway. Her dream was about to come true.

Scandals and Revels

IN THE EARLY 1920S BIG-TIME VAUDEVILLE FALTERED, BUT BROADWAY revues flourished. At first glance that disparity seems odd, for they were similar forms of entertainment. They both presented an unconnected series of songs, dances, and sketches. The big difference was simply that a revue was far more elaborate than a vaudeville show. A revue had a vastly larger cast and contained two, three, or even four times as many separate scenes, many of them decked out with spectacular costumes and scenery. Because revues were expensive to produce they necessarily commanded ticket prices higher than those at even the most prestigious vaudeville houses, and they were marketed to a narrower demographic. The revue audience was urban, sophisticated, and affluent. Consequently, while the burgeoning motion picture industry was eating away at vaudeville, it was not undermining the revues. In fact, a staggering total of more than 150 revue productions were mounted on Broadway in the 1920s.

The granddaddy of them all was Florenz Ziegfeld's *Follies*, a fresh version of which had arrived every year since 1907. Ziegfeld's revue remained the biggest and best known. Second only to the *Follies* was George White's *Scandals*, the first edition of which appeared in 1919. *Scandals* was somewhat less elaborate than *Follies*—but only somewhat. Every year from 1922 onwards George White made a pilgrimage to France where Erté, the legendary master of art deco, supplied him with designs for magnificent settings and costumes. *Scandals* moved along more briskly than *Follies* and had more of a Jazz Age zing. The zing was especially evident in the editions of 1920 through 1924, for which George Gershwin composed most of the music. Also, the comic sketches in *Scandals* tended to be more topical and biting. Finally, *Scandals* put more emphasis on dancing because White himself had won fame as one of the best hoofers in show business. For each of his annual productions he now trained a corps of pretty young women to perform with remarkable skill and precision his own steps and routines.

Winnie Lightner made her Broadway debut in *Scandals* of 1922. George White had to scramble to put together this, the fourth edition of his show. The previous three had all made good money, but White's fondness for racetrack betting had left him unable to finance the fourth on his own. He managed eventually to dredge up the necessary backing, including a $25,000 loan from Al Jolson. White then quickly recruited the obligatory chorus of young beauties and began whipping them into shape with a speed and rigor that only a dance master like himself could sustain. He also hired some big name talent to top the cast list. He managed to lure the great comedian W. C. Fields away from his usual home in *Follies*. An even bigger catch was Paul Whiteman, whose jazz orchestra had rocketed to nationwide acclaim as a result of its immensely popular recordings on the Victor label. Several other stars of the show, while less famous than Fields and Whiteman, were still quite well known in show business. Among them, of course, was Winnie. This galaxy of talent did not come cheap. A newspaper columnist joked that the salary checks "bore curious resemblance to the statement of the Corn Exchange Bank."

Along with Winnie came her partners Theo Lightner and Newton Alexander. On opening night the three of them had a scene to themselves in which they performed their familiar piano-and-song act. They had no inkling that they were appearing together as a trio for the last time. Because the opening-night show ran far longer than intended, substantial cuts were made before the next performance. One of the dropped items was George Gershwin's jazz opera *Blue Monday*, now recognized as a work of genius foreshadowing his masterwork, *Porgy and Bess* (1935). Another jettisoned scene was the one that had featured the Lightner Sisters and Alexander. At the time the loss of their personal spot seemed unimportant to the trio. They still had plenty to do because all three of them made numerous individual appearances scattered among the scenes that remained. Seven years had passed since Newton and Theo had given Winnie her start. All of them knew that she was now the one with star power. Winnie, Newton, and Theo would remain close friends all of their lives, but in her show-business career Winnie was now on her own.

Winnie appeared in eight of the show's twenty scenes. In a sketch called "The Flapper," she had the title role. In "Three Different Homes with the Same Quarrel" she played the wife of the Poor Man (Lester

Allen), whose domestic difficulties were paralleled by those of the Well-To-Do Man (Newton Alexander) and his wife (Olive Vaughn), as well as by those of the Rich Man (Arthur Brooks) and his wife (Theo Lightner). The scene took place within a sort of triptych displaying the interiors of three apartments. Within them the three husbands spoke simultaneously to their spouses, with pictures of George Washington falling from the walls when the men lied. The skit climaxed with the three declaring their absolute faith in the fidelity of their wives, at which point within each apartment another man emerged from behind the furniture and fled for the door.

Three skits paired Winnie with W. C. Fields. In "Ten Years Backward" they were the Husband and the Wife, while in "The Radio Bug" he was Papa Shugg and she was his daughter. It must have been one of those scenes that included a celebrated incident in which Fields and Winnie carried on a verbal altercation while what appeared to be a live canary chirped in the background. A tirade from Fields came to a sudden halt when Winnie grabbed the canary and swallowed it. Their third sketch together was "Terrific Traffic," in which Mr. Bimbo (Fields) struggled with a disintegrating motorcar as well as with Mrs. Bimbo (Winnie), Baby Bimbo (Olive Vaughn), and a traffic cop (Newton Alexander).

While the skits gave Winnie ample opportunity to display her gift for making wisecracks and rubber faces, her more important contribution to the show was her singing. The first act included a whole scene in which she stood alone before the footlights and put over several numbers, two of them salvaged from the deleted scene with Newton and Theo. "Where the Bamboo Babies Grow" described a sailor's fondness for a South Sea island where the king's daughter could be had for a quarter. "True Blue Sam" was the lament of a traveling man who always carried with him a picture of his girlfriend, until he showed it to a bunch of other traveling men, all of which had her picture, too. Both songs required Winnie to assume a male persona, but that was something she could always accomplish with great comic effect.

Elsewhere, Winnie introduced two of George Gershwin's best compositions. In the second act she warbled the plaintive melody "Where Is the Man of My Dreams?" while surrounded by the principal males of the show, all dressed as tramps. But her best number—by far the biggest hit of the entire production—came when she closed the first act by premiering the Gershwin masterpiece "I'll Build a Stairway to Paradise" within a spectacular setting called "The Patent Leather Forest." Winnie stood front and center. Behind her Paul Whiteman's orchestra sat nestled amid a grove of shiny black palm trees. On either side, dozens of chorus girls clad in shimmering black climbed heavenward on curving white staircases, while Winnie belted out Gershwin's rousing anthem urging her listeners to ascend toward utopia "with a new step every day." Afterwards Winnie danced, joined by other cast members including George White himself.

A reviewer of the opening night described the scene as "one of those big, smashing stairway things in black and white" and added, "if we applaud enough, as, of course, we do, the shapely ladies involved divest themselves of their sable garments and are enjoyably exposed in their underclothing." In subsequent performances the disrobing was handled more cleverly. At the conclusion of the scene, the main curtain descended. Then it immediately rose again, revealing the chorus girls stripping off their patent leather and standing about in skimpy lingerie. The audience gasped at what seemed a startling miscue—until the realization dawned that it was just a naughty joke. As that alteration to the proceedings exemplifies, revues were always more or less in a constant state of revision. Scenes were added, reordered, or dropped. A gag that fell flat was scratched and a new one substituted. Any song that became popular in vaudeville or anywhere else might be interpolated. Sometimes even the star performers might come and go, although that rarely happened in George White's productions until long after they had left Broadway and gone on tour.

Because of the time it had taken White to secure his financing, the 1922 *Scandals* opened many weeks later than usual. It had its Broadway premiere on 28 August. It closed on 11 November after eighty-nine performances. It was then staged in Philadelphia, Chicago, and other cities throughout the winter and into the spring of the following year. Winnie took advantage of the sojourn in Chicago to obtain, on 28 March 1923, a quick and uncontested divorce from her second husband, William Harold, on grounds of desertion. The *Chicago Tribune* described Winnie as an "ebullient young person" whose antics had "stopped the show" at the Illinois Theater. Elsewhere there was surprisingly little comment about her. One reviewer complained, "Mr. Fields might have been given longer opportunity to mess around with his family Ford," but failed to mention Winnie's role in that or any other scene. Many critics commented on the superb musicianship of the Paul Whiteman orchestra but said nothing at all about Winnie's vocals, ignoring even her stirring rendition of "I'll Build a Stairway to Paradise." Winnie evidently was far outshone by the brighter stars.

But if Winnie had not dazzled the critics, she had satisfied George White, for he assigned her a much bigger role in his next edition, *Scandals* of 1923. Her role became even more prominent following tryout performances in Atlantic City and New Haven. De Lyle Alda, an operatic soprano who had appeared often in vaudeville and stage musicals, quit the show just after its New York opening, complaining that her part had been reduced "to one scene and two songs," and that everything taken from her "was given to Winnie Lightner, who now appeared in practically every scene of the show and who also has several specialties in one for her individual appearance."

The 1923 *Scandals* ran on Broadway from 18 June through 4 November for a total of 168 performances, a new record for White's revue. Thanks to the success of his offering the previous year—plus a modicum of restraint, or perhaps just better luck, betting on the ponies—White had the means to stage the 1923 edition on his own. This time around he did not hire any superstars of the magnitude of W. C. Fields or Paul Whiteman, but he did spend lavishly on sets and costumes that were more spectacular than ever. The show was studded with extravagant production numbers, including one in which women dressed exquisitely to represent various jewels pirouetted against a velvet background. There also were some clever surprises. When the house lights dimmed following the overture, what should appear but a filmed newsreel. That would have been unremarkable at a cinema or maybe even a vaudeville house, but it certainly was not expected at a revue. It soon became apparent, however, that the film was a parody featuring members of White's company in burlesque versions of notorious recent events, such as the marriage of a seventeen-year-old Chicago heiress to a riding instructor twice her age. The film ended with some dancing girls, and then faded out as those same girls appeared live on stage. Another surprise, and the biggest sensation of the entire show, was a special curtain that descended at intermission. Upon it were arranged an assortment of beautiful women, naked but for some strategically placed golden leaves and branches. Observers wondered whether the young ladies had been suspended up in the flies throughout the first act. But "regardless of this inconvenience," remarked a critic, "the effect was striking."

Winnie was not quite so ubiquitous in the 1923 production as De Lyle Alda claimed, but she did star in several skits. In "Moscow Players" she was the Wayward Wife, wearing a brilliantly colored Russian peasant dress that a *Variety* columnist said "suited her unusually." Her funniest skit was a burlesque of *Romeo and Juliet* that paired a boisterous Winnie with an equally ridiculous Tom Patricola. Although a newcomer to the *Scandals*, Patricola was well known in vaudeville as a superb dancer and mandolin player. In this and other scenes he and Winnie both scored big with the critics. The reviewer for the *New York Herald* said, "The best assets of the revue in the way of principals are two vaudevillians, Tom Patricola, who danced like a Red Indian . . . , and the bouncing Winnie Lightner, who is a combination of Blanche Ring, Nora Bayes and Eva Tanguay, who delivers comic songs with remarkable speed and finish, and who has developed an unsuspected lot of good looks." Later on, a writer in the *New York Times* concurred: "Tom Patricola and Winnie Lightner, so long among the pets and prides of Keith vaudeville, always hitting the high spots on any bill, were drafted for this year's 'Scandals' by George White, himself a veteran of the two-a-day, and both have justified his faith in them as production people. 'That hoofing Patricola can act and Winnie Lightner can play a part as well as "sell" a ditty,' said White, after looking them over at the Palace, and he was right. They ran away with the 'Scandals.'"

Another big scene for Winnie was the one that closed the first act (and was followed by the infamous "living curtain"). It consisted of a spirited attack on Prohibition. In it Winnie belted out the Gershwin song "Throw 'Er in High." The scene embodied an attitude of "anything goes" permissiveness that would raise eyebrows even today. It not only celebrated the unrestricted consumption of alcohol, it also featured showgirls costumed to represent cocaine, opium, and morphine. Critic S. Jay Kaufman, while conceding that this "anti-blue law scene" was "magnificently done," declared its portrayal of drugs "something which the balcony and gallery of a theatre should not be allowed to see." Kaufman did not explain why he saw no harm in having the dancing drugs paraded before the elite people down in the orchestra.

Just as important as Winnie's appearance in the various scenes was her delivery of songs during the intervals. While the stage was reset, she would step out in front of the main curtain and keep the audience entertained. The critic for the *Brooklyn Eagle* reported that on opening night, "Winnie Lightner, singing between scenes, delayed the proceedings several times by pleasing the audience better than the scenes she followed and preceded. She has an abundance of vitality and that trick of putting songs over, the absence of which in many performers possessed otherwise of better equipment makes them uninteresting." The reviewer for the *New York Times* wrote, "At the art of singing a comic song there are few who are her equals." Many other critics also praised

Winnie's singing, although they sometimes objected to one or another of the songs themselves, pronouncing their lyrics vulgar or even obscene. Robert Benchley wrote that Winnie "by dint of very hard work, succeeds in putting over several songs which are hardly worth the trouble." S. Jay Kaufman described Winnie as the female equivalent of Eddie Cantor, except that "Eddie's songs are invariably good. Miss Lightner's charm makes one forget—almost forget—the cheapness of some of her songs."

Winnie's selections varied from one performance to another, both while the show ran on Broadway and after it went on tour. She included at one time or another: "More, a Modern Maiden's Prayer," "Take a Look at This (Take a Look at That)," "Somebody Nobody Loves," "Stingo Stungo," "Hula Lou," "Cannibola," "The Gold Digger," and "Last Night on the Back Porch." All of them became popular enough to be published as sheet music featuring Winnie on the covers, but none of them was the work of George Gershwin. In fact, Gershwin was off his form in this edition of Scandals. None of the songs written for this season became hits, and all of them are now forgotten. "Last Night on the Back Porch," the only tune in the whole show that became a truly notable success, was written originally by a college boy named Carl Schraubstader and then tweaked by Lew Brown of Tin Pan Alley. Al Jolson sang a version of it in a Broadway musical in 1920, but it received little notice. Now Winnie's rendition turned the song into a nationwide hit, one of the biggest of 1923.

Less than two months after the 1923 Scandals ended its Broadway run, George White announced that Winnie would star in the next edition of his revue. The press release said she had "only recently passed her teens" and "made her stage debut a few seasons ago in vaudeville." Actually, Winnie was twenty-four, and the "few" years since her stage debut totaled eight. More accurately, the press release added that Theo Lightner and Newton Alexander, too, would have roles in the new show. According to a report in Variety, White "tried to engage Winnie alone, as others have done, but found he had to take all three or none." Furthermore, "because another revue producer tried to wean Winnie away he has to pay $400 more weekly to the trio starting next season."

Knowing she would be spending another lucrative season on Broadway, Winnie made an important personal decision. On 8 February 1924 she embarked upon her third foray into matrimony. Her new spouse was George Holtrey. Born in Ohio in 1896, Holtrey worked on the technical side of the theater business, serving at various times as a carpenter, electrician, stagehand, and assistant stage manager. His romance with

Winnie probably began during the Broadway run of the 1923 *Scandals*, when he likely worked at the theater where she performed. Marrying Holtrey was at least a bit more practical than Winnie's earlier matrimonial decisions, as she and he both were based in New York City. They moved into a suite in the elegant Osborne Apartments on West Fifty-Seventh Street and remained together for the next five years, a record for Winnie.

The 1924 *Scandals* tried out in Atlantic City and then opened on Broadway on the last day of June. Hailed by reviewers as the best one yet, it ran through 13 December, racking up an impressive 196 performances. The show began cleverly with a song, "Just Missed the Opening Chorus," which taunted the tardy folk who were still finding their seats. There had been no opening chorus, but the mortified latecomers had no way of knowing that. Just to rub it in, the song was followed by four skits, all of them dealing in various comic ways with the consequences of being late.

The most elaborate production number in the show was "Year After Year We're Together," which celebrated the joys of enduring matrimony. It began with a wedding scene peopled with pretty showgirls gowned in white lace and backed by a "living curtain" containing more girls similarly outfitted. That was followed by representations of silver, gold, and diamond anniversaries, each featuring girls costumed as anniversary gifts and backed by curtains displaying still more girls clad in (or, more accurately, dotted with tiny bits of) the relevant precious metal or jewels. A less elaborate scene, but one that left the audience even more wide-eyed, was entitled "Lover of Art." It, too, displayed the beautiful young women of the chorus, now dressed in colorful bathing suits and cavorting on a beach. Suddenly the women stood still, there was a flash of light, and the bathing suits vanished. The women now stood there, recalled a reviewer, "chaste and white as marble pieces at the Luxembourg. Or as naked as the day they were born, if you wish to take that view of them. Considerably more naked, as a matter of truth, because there is so much more of them." This miracle was achieved via the "Samoiloff Effect," whereby lights shining through colored filters produce startling changes in the way fabric dyes appear—or in this case, disappear. Other notable segments of the show included a burlesque of "mammy songs" and other Old South nostalgia; a celebration of the current fad for the Chinese game of Mahjong; a spoof of Greenwich Village intellectuals; and an exhibition of Spanish dancing by girls festooned with roses, shawls, and combs.

Those scenes were just some of the more interesting ones that did *not* feature an appearance by Winnie Lightner. There were plenty that did, however, and it was her name that headed the lengthy cast list. In her most notable scene she introduced to the world the Gershwin composition "Somebody Loves Me." It was the hit of the show and went on to become an enduring classic. Winnie's solo rendition was followed by spoken lines in which she contemplated an array of male paragons who might fulfill her hopes for a perfect lover: Ancient Rome's Mark Antony, Shakespeare's Romeo, and current film stars Harold Lloyd, William S. Hart, and Jackie Coogan. (It was made clear that Winnie intended to woo Coogan only after he had grown up. That was a good thing, as he was nine years old at the time.)

Another high point for Winnie was a comedy skit in which she partnered with Lester Allen in a parody of *Abie's Irish Rose*, a play that had been running on Broadway for two years, despite the critics having panned its schmaltzy story about an Irish Catholic girl and a Jewish boy who marry over their parents' vehement opposition, are disowned for a time, but then win over the old folks by having twins. It was a story deliciously ripe for satire, and Winnie and Lester were perfectly suited to their roles because she really was an Irish Catholic girl and he a Jewish boy. The *Scandals* audience enjoyed seeing *Abie's Irish Rose* skewered, but the send-up made no difference to the play's popularity among the less sophisticated folk who had made it such a hit. *Abie's Irish Rose* continued to pack them in on Broadway until October 1927, when it at last closed after a record-breaking run of 2,327 performances.

"Leave It to the Audience," another big scene for Winnie, contrasted censored with uncensored versions of the same dialogue and dances. Needless to say, the unexpurgated versions were more fun. Winnie sang "Tune in to J.O.Y." (the call letters of a mythical radio station), and the scene climaxed with Winnie and other members of the cast, including George White himself, doing the Charleston. Additional appearances by Winnie included her role as the Heroine in "Ups and Downs in Pogotown," a melodrama performed on pogo sticks, and as the Girl (paired with Newton Alexander as the Man) in a skit with the one-word title "Suicide." In another scene Winnie recited what the program called "colorature poetry" (which the critics did not much like), and in yet another she put across a jazzy Gershwin number, "Congo Kate," within an African setting. Finally, there was a segment in which Winnie simply stepped out in front of the main curtain and sang. The songs varied from performance to performance. One of the most popular was "Nothin's

Gonna Stop Me Now," a non-Gershwin composition that was interpolated into the show.

The 1924 *Scandals* was so successful that after leaving Broadway it remained on tour with the original cast until late April 1925, when it was time for George White to start putting together the next edition of his revue. Even then, though, the 1924 show was still doing such good business that a new cast was hired for it, and it continued to tour even throughout the 1925 edition's entire Broadway run. By December 1925, both the 1924 and the 1925 *Scandals* were on tour at the same time. They did not conflict, because the newer show played major cities like Chicago, Boston, Philadelphia, and Detroit, while the older one visited a long string of lesser places like Utica, New York, and Orlando, Florida. In the summer of 1926 a renewed road show version of the 1924 *Scandals* was assembled with a mostly new cast. The remounted show toured throughout the remainder of 1926 and into the early months of 1927. Toward the end it was playing communities as small as Escanaba, Michigan, and Murphysboro, Illinois. Oftentimes the production would visit a town for just one day, putting on a matinee and an evening performance, only to repeat the same routine elsewhere the next day. That was a remarkable logistical feat, considering that an entourage of about one hundred people, along with three baggage cars full of props and scenery, had to be hauled from one community to the next, installed in a theater, and launched into a performance—all within the span of about fifteen hours.

Although Winnie had departed in April 1925 along with the rest of the original cast, she retained a personal connection to the 1924 road show. While her own part was taken over by an actress named Nyra Brown, one of the other prominent roles was assumed by Winnie's brother Fred. When baby Winnie had gone to live with her foster parents in Manhattan, brother Freddie had remained with his father in Greenport, Long Island. Freddie grew up there, served in the army during the First World War, and then embarked upon what he hoped would be a career as a professional baseball player. That hope was shattered, however, when he suffered a severe ankle fracture in June 1919 while playing on the Marysville, Pennsylvania, team of the Dauphin and Perry Counties Baseball League. With baseball no longer an option, Fred turned to show business. Not surprisingly, it took him a few years to make the transition. The 1920 federal census reported him as boarding with a family in Marysville and working as a railroad track laborer. But by 1922 he was touring in small-time vaudeville as an actor in a comedy playlet, and after that he appeared on the Proctor circuit and elsewhere as a comedian, paired with a succession of female partners.

It was a big break for Fred when he joined the touring company of the 1924 *Scandals*. That Winnie had a hand in Fred landing the job seems likely. In any case, she clearly helped kick-start his career by letting him use Lightner as his stage name and advertise the fact that he was her brother. In the *Scandals* road show Fred took over the key position that had been occupied by comedian Will Mahoney in the original production. Fred played no less than nine different characters in various skits, and he also sang songs. He appeared in close to half of the show's scenes. It was the first major highlight of his forty-year career on stage, radio, and screen. It also was a turning point in his personal life. While touring with *Scandals* he became acquainted with Roscella McQueen, one of the pretty chorus girls in the production. In June 1926 while the show was working its way east from the Pacific coast, Fred accompanied Roscella on a visit to her parents' home in Mingo Junction, Ohio. When the *Scandals* tour ended in 1927, Fred went off on his own for a bit, appearing both in vaudeville and in some musical comedies on Broadway and elsewhere, but by 1929 he and Roscella had married and she was assisting him in his vaudeville comedy routine. Their marriage was a lasting one, in marked contrast to Winnie's earlier misadventures in that department. Although two years older than Winnie, Fred remained active in show business three decades after she bowed out.

While Fred toured in *Scandals*, Winnie starred on Broadway in a revue called *Gay Paree*. The new show was the brainchild of promoter Rufus Le Maire, who originally planned to call it the "Greenwich Village Scandals." That title angered George White, who felt that the scandals label was his personal property. Equally indignant were A. L. Jones and Morris Green, who since 1919 had been staging their own revue called the *Greenwich Village Follies*. They objected to Le Maire's use of the name Greenwich Village (which was rather cheeky of them, given that they themselves had snitched the follies label from Flo Ziegfeld). When Le Maire ran short of money, his project was taken over by the Shubert brothers, who wisely decided to drop Le Maire's controversial title and instead call the show *Gay Paree*. George White remained miffed, however, and let loose a rumor that he was planning a revue called "Parisian Artists and Models," a title that would thumb its nose at both the Shuberts' new production *Gay Paree* and also their long-established revue *Artists and Models*. But White did not really intend to mount any such show. Instead, he took more direct action.

On Saturday, 1 August 1925, Rufus Le Maire took his newly signed star Winnie Lightner to dinner at Reuben's, a Park Avenue restaurant popular among show folk. Soon after they were seated, George White approached their table and politely congratulated Winnie on her new engagement. Then, turning to Le Maire, White said, "As for you, I call my shots"—and let fly a punch. The two men exchanged words. White socked Le Maire a second time and dared him to come outside. White walked out the door and waited on the sidewalk. When Le Maire failed to join him, White came back in and slugged Le Maire a third time.

Despite those nasty preliminaries, *Gay Paree* opened as scheduled at the Shubert Theater on 18 August 1925. It ran until 30 January 1926, for a total of 181 performances. The content of *Gay Paree* had almost nothing to do with its title, but nobody seemed to mind. It offered the usual mélange of songs, skits, an occasional big production number, and much dancing and posing by scantily clad showgirls. Winnie's name topped the cast list. Her co-stars were comedians Chic Sale and Eddie Conrad. Also included in the cast was Newton Alexander, but not his spouse. Theo had given up performing in order to manage Winnie and Newton's business affairs, which, according to a newspaper report, now included ownership of a couple of tea shops in Manhattan.

Gay Paree's thirty-four scenes included three especially colorful ones. "Vision of Hassan" featured women costumed to represent a sequence of four perfumes: Mimosa, Narcisse Noire, Tabac Blond, and Infini. (All four scents were from the House of Caron, which looks suspiciously like what nowadays is called product placement.) "Glory of the Morning Sunshine" concluded the first act, with the entire company cavorting in a profusion of red, yellow, and orange. "Venetian Nights: The Wedding of Venus to the Adriatic" centered on Frances Blythe, wearing a fig leaf and surrounded by the show's forty dancers. Comedy skits spoofed such current fads as Florida land speculation, plastic surgery, and bootlegging. A skit about memory training featured an instructor who had forgotten to put on his trousers. The scenery and props were so voluminous that the Shubert Theater could not accommodate them all. Consequently some were at first kept at the Broadhurst Theater next door, and later the alley between the two theaters was roofed over so that scenery could be stashed there. Even then vans had to carry still more stuff back and forth from a warehouse for each performance. The Shuberts also had to build additional dressing rooms both on the roof and in the basement of the Shubert.

As the headliner of *Gay Paree*, Winnie performed in a variety of settings. She was Mrs. Low Brow in the domestic comedy "What Every Man Suffers." She was Tillie of Longacre Square in "Seeing New York." She was Miss Brodie in "Riverside Drive at Any Time." In the last one she played a young woman arguing with a young man (Jack Haley) whose behavior had forced her to get out of his car and walk. They were interrupted by the young man's father (Newton Alexander), who, it developed, had once compelled the young woman to do the same thing. The punch line, delivered by Winnie, was "So's your old man!" In what may have been the most memorable scene of the whole show, Winnie teamed with Eddie Conrad in "A Piano and Song Recital," which ended with Winnie delivering in high register the passionate musical plea "Give Me the Rain" and Eddie drenching her with a bucket of water. Elsewhere in the show Winnie sang the tunes "Hocus Pocus," "Toddle Trot," "Sugar Plum," "Wide Pants Willie," and "Oh! Boy, What a Girl." The last named became the biggest hit of the whole production. Its composers later claimed that the sheet music sold a hundred thousand copies, and recorded versions by Eddie Cantor and others sold well, too. *Gay Paree* also included an entire scene called simply "Winnie Lightner in Some Songs," in which Winnie put across a selection that changed with each performance.

The closing scene of the show, "Night Club in the Roaring Forties," featured Winnie belting out yet more songs in a setting that evoked a glorious, post-Prohibition future. That scene likely triggered Jack Haley's memory four decades later when he described how Winnie would put over pop tunes and ballads; act in sketches with comedians and straight men; "dance in front of a line of chorus girls and make them look like they were standing still"; and finally "at the end, at eleven thirty at night, after two shows that day, when everyone else in the company was spent, deliver three songs all by herself and tie the whole show up in a knot!"

Critical reaction to *Gay Paree* was varied but generally favorable. The revue did receive one resoundingly negative assessment from a rather prudish critic writing in, of all places, *Variety*. That critic was appalled by the chorus girls' attire, or rather lack thereof: "The minimum loinclothes are rhinestone studded. Brassieres are discarded, tummies are bare. This isn't nudity; it is nakedness." Furthermore, said the reviewer, the show's comedy skits were "a succession of stale-beer barroom dirty stories acted out, each cracker delivered with a sledge hammer." There was the scene "Puritan Hotel" in which a man met a pretty and willing girl in a hotel lobby, registered himself "and wife" with the desk clerk, and was then handed over a big bill with the explanation that his wife had been staying there for weeks. In the skit titled "Beds" a salesman said to an old maid, "You can't go wrong in a mahogany bed." She replied, "I'll take a walnut one." In "The Yogi" a seer told a couple expecting a baby that if the child were a girl the mother would die, and if the child was a boy the father would die. It was a boy. The iceman dropped dead. That the reviewer regarded such jokes as stale is understandable, but that he found them offensive makes one wonder if he had seen any other Broadway revues. At least he did not castigate Winnie for her part in the proceedings. "Miss Lightner," he said, "has perhaps the poorest stuff to do that she has ever fallen heiress to in her whole stage life, but she survives on the gifts God gave her, which cannot be inundated completely." He also acknowledged, however grudgingly, that in her "Wide Pants Willie" number "she knocks in a hit that will sizzle up and down Broadway."

The *New York Times* said *Gay Paree* was "filled to satiety with the regal wealth that we now expect of so pretentious a form of entertainment." It crackled with "breathless hurry and high spirits. All this was best epitomized in the number entitled 'Wide Pants Willie,' danced furiously by Margie Finley and the entire chorus dressed in sweaters, soft hats and wide-bottomed flannel trousers after the ultra-mode of university chaps across the sea." The *Brooklyn Eagle* described *Gay Paree* as "a gorgeous, if not a particularly humorous or brilliant, revue," in which the best song was "Wide Pants Willie," which the reviewer thought "not so well sung by Winnie Lightner, but cleverly danced by Margie Finley." The most favorable review of all came from critic Brett Page, who declared *Gay Paree* "the most hoarsely mirthful" revue of the season. He praised especially Winnie's contributions, declaring, "Miss Lightner, lured away heaven knows how from George White's annual Scandals, is in positively grand form. The loudest of our warbling clowns, she emits noises which have both melody and boiler factor magnetism. When, attired in garments that suggested nothing so much as cycloramas from the Hippodrome, she sang 'Wide Pants Willie,' my joy was stintless, and her 'Give Me the Rain,' the climax of which found her immersed by Eddie Conrad (with bucket) was as absurd a bit of foolery as has ever been devised."

While one might think Winnie's exertions on stage would have exhausted even her formidable energy reserves, she had enough left over to devise an excellent publicity stunt. Two weeks after *Gay Paree* opened, a theatrical columnist announced that Winnie had persuaded the Shuberts

to let her organize a block party in Shubert Alley, the little passage between the Shubert Theater and the Astor Hotel. The party began immediately after the evening performance on 10 September and was a
raucous, roaring success. The audience was invited to stay for the party,
and thousands of other people, invited or not, jammed into the area.
They were entertained by a dance orchestra, a potato race, a pie-eating
contest, a needle-threading competition, and impromptu performances
by cast members from *Gay Paree* and other current Shubert attractions. A
nearly nude gentleman posed as Venus in a parody of the big production
number in *Gay Paree*. Al Jolson, currently starring in *Big Boy*, served as
master of ceremonies. He and Winnie jointly presided over a Charleston
contest, judging the dancing and handing out prizes. The party raged on
into the wee hours, when it finally broke up because of mounting com-
plaints from guests at the Astor who wanted to get some sleep.

After *Gay Paree* ended its Broadway run it toured other cities, beginning with Boston. There Winnie created another barrage of publicity, this
time unintentionally. Late one evening a police officer named Crowley
was on his way to the Hotel Charlesgate responding to a call, when at
the intersection of Beacon Street and Massachusetts Avenue he chanced
upon a band of noisy revelers. Crowley told them to go home. Later, on
his way back from dealing with the incident at the hotel, Crowley discovered that the party animals were still there and carrying on as before.
An argument ensued, and then a young woman in the group socked the
officer. The young lady and her friends were hauled off to the station
house. Local newspapers trumpeted the fact that the lady pugilist was
none other than Winnie Lightner, star of *Gay Paree*. Fortunately, Officer
Crowley did not take Winnie's assault too seriously and filed no charges.
The incident probably did not hurt the show's box office receipts; neither
did it detract from Winnie's reputation for high spirits.

The show continued touring as late as October 1926, although by
then its principal players had long since departed. The two biggest stars,
Winnie Lightner and Chic Sale, were hard at work rehearsing for a second Broadway edition of *Gay Paree*. Newton Alexander came along, too.
After playing to near-capacity houses for six weeks in Philadelphia, followed by a week in Brooklyn, the new production opened at the Winter
Garden Theater on 9 November 1926 and ran five months for a total
of 192 performances. One of its biggest production numbers was titled
"Beautiful Fan." It began modestly with a woman seen purchasing a fan,
but soon led to a stage filled with fan-wielding Spanish dancers, followed
by a Japanese equivalent. Finally, the rear curtains parted to reveal a

gigantic fan adorned with curling feathers and curvaceous women. Other elaborate scenes were "Kandahar Isle" (with a South Seas setting), "Morocco Drill," "Bachanol," "Vintner's Dream," "Oriental Nights," and "The River of Gold." The grand finale, "There Never Was a Town Like Paris," featured both a new song of that same name and an old one with the cringe-making title "Paris is a Paradise for Coons." The latter had raised Al Jolson to Broadway stardom when he introduced it in 1911. It celebrated the fact that African Americans were better off living in Paris than in the United States because, among other things, they did not have to fear being lynched. In *Gay Paree* the number was sung by whites wearing blackface, as was the norm in Broadway revues—further evidence that black people really were better off in Paris.

The most memorable song of the show, "I Can't Believe That You're in Love With Me," was not included at first but interpolated later on. Sung by Winnie and then published as sheet music, it was the only song in the show that became a popular hit. Comedy skits in the new *Gay Paree* included a parody of the movie *Beau Geste*; a monologue entitled "Eagle-Eyed Elmer" (by Chic Sale); "The Zither Club" (Sale again); "Lulu Belle and the Censors"; "Mrs. Craig Picks His Stenographer"; "Now and Then"; "Three Old Men"; and "The Doctor's Waiting Room." Another sketch, "For Her Husband's Benefit," teamed Winnie with Frank Gaby and required the latter to deliver a swift kick to the former. The stunt gave the audience a good laugh but became painful for Winnie, who endured it every performance, day after day, week after week.

A happier role for Winnie was her spoof of Maurice Chevalier. Outfitted in the famed French entertainer's customary suit and boater, she danced and sang, imitating his mannerisms and accent. Winnie's successful male impersonation was an early manifestation of an image that would become pervasive during her film career, when she was heralded as "the tomboy of the talkies." The germ of that later persona was already evident in Winnie's boisterous behavior in vaudeville and revues, as she herself readily acknowledged. "I am called 'America's Tomboy' on the stage," she said, "because my work is just about the sort of thing a real tomboy would do. Yet it is clean and decent—and rough in its breezy style. . . . It gets across because every single man in the audience remembers involuntarily some similar tomboy who used to be his pal in sneaking hitches on wagons, running to fires, or engaging in countless other boyhood sports years ago. There is something responsive in every man to the appeal of good fellowship from women."

By the spring of 1927 the second edition of *Gay Paree* was flagging, its box office receipts falling below $25,000 a week. The Shuberts decided to refresh its appeal by introducing new songs, skits, and cast members. Sophie Tucker joined the cast, bringing with her three new sketches, as well as Ben Bernie and his jazz orchestra. Two other newcomers, George Raft and Oscar Levant, were not important enough to receive any mention in the press. Raft was a dancer, while Levant was a pianist in Bernie's orchestra. The revised, so-called "spring 1927 edition" of *Gay Paree* premiered on 21 March.

By coincidence, on that very day Winnie launched a lawsuit against the manufacturers of a bathing preparation called Sparkling Burgundy for using a photograph of her in such a way that she appeared to be posing inside a bottle of their product. It is understandable that Winnie objected to the unauthorized commercial use of her portrait, but there was more to it than that. The story began a year earlier at the theater where a revue called *Earl Carroll's Vanities* was playing. *Vanities* was the raunchiest of the leading annual productions. If *Follies*, *Scandals*, and *Gay Paree* were extravagant versions of vaudeville, then *Vanities* was an equally souped up version of burlesque. On 22 February 1926 Earl Carroll hosted a backstage party, the highlight of which was a perfect embodiment of the freewheeling spirit of the Roaring Twenties: A seventeen-year-old showgirl named Joyce Hawley climbed naked into a bathtub filled with champagne. The gentlemen in attendance gathered around to dip their glasses in the tub. Toasts were made, glassfuls were gulped, and a jolly time was had by all. Unfortunately for Carroll, the incident became the talk of the town. Newspapers recounted the details, and local authorities felt compelled to act. Testifying before a grand jury called to investigate the alleged violation of the Volstead Act (the national prohibition law), Carroll said that the bathtub had contained only ginger ale, and that nobody, nude or otherwise, had entered it. Subsequently convicted of perjury, he spent several months in a federal prison.

In her lawsuit Winnie contended that the use of her photograph implied that she "bathed in and recommends liquid which would apparently be, and perhaps is, of alcoholic content." That tended "to connect the plaintiff in the mind of the public with orgies and occurrences of the notorious Earl Carroll wine bath incident." Winnie asked for $100,000 in damages and an injunction forbidding any further use of her image. The suit must have been settled out of court for there were no more reports about it in the press.

Besides her lawsuit Winnie had a more personal preoccupation: her relationship with George Raft, the dancer who had just joined the show. Decades later Raft recollected that he had performed a fast Charleston while Oscar Levant played "Sweet Georgia Brown." Raft said that while dancing he had cast a wary eye upward at the hundred-pound sand-bag counterweights that hung above the stage. He feared that Winnie's husband, who was the assistant stage manager, had discovered Winnie and Raft were having an affair and therefore might "accidentally" clob-ber Raft with a sandbag. While Raft's story is uncorroborated, it seems unlikely that he made it up. Raft had affairs with so many female screen legends that he scarcely needed to pad a résumé that already included such names as Carole Lombard, Norma Shearer, Betty Grable, and Mar-lene Dietrich. Evidently Winnie had overcome her Catholic upbringing enough to realize she did not have to marry a man just because she wanted to consummate a mutual sexual attraction, a scruple that seems to have applied to at least the first two of her marriages. Winnie's fling with Raft lasted only a few weeks. Although the rejuvenated version of *Gay Paree* delighted the packed house that attended its opening on 21 March, ticket sales soon dwindled. The Shuberts decided to throw in the towel, and the show closed on 9 April. George Holtrey either did not learn about Winnie's brief extramarital excursion or else forgave her for it, as their marriage survived the episode.

Winnie returned to vaudeville, starting with an engagement the last week of April at the Palace, still the pinnacle of the vaudeville world. The big time had shrunk to the point that there remained only about sixteen top-notch, two-a-day houses, about one-third the number that existed when Winnie left for Broadway in 1922. But there was still good money to be made in those big-time venues that endured, especially in New York and Chicago. Winnie now performed solo in an act called "A Song a Minute." The name was apt, for she simply strode out in front of the main curtain and reeled off one number after another in quick succession.

When Winnie played Chicago in May she stayed in an elegant hotel suite, accompanied by both her little dog and a personal maid. But even a life of luxury can have its annoyances. When Winnie checked in she was informed that the maid must use the service elevator to take the dog out for its walks. Unfortunately, the maid promptly fell ill, so Winnie had to attend personally to the needs of her pet. Not wanting to create a fuss, she donned the maid's uniform and set off for the service eleva-tor, confident that nobody would realize who she was. Nobody did, but complications arose nevertheless. In the elevator she was joined by an older woman employed as a bath maid. A conversation ensued:

BATH MAID. Huh, manicurin' the dog are you? Who you work for? That actress? Well, actresses ain't much, nor their maids, either. And you don't look like any exception to the rule.

WINNIE. Oh, judge us not too harshly.

BATH MAID. Now don't talk stagey. After all, you're not the actress herself, you know. Don't put on airs with me.

When Winnie reached the staff exit, she encountered a doorkeeper who required everyone passing in or out to punch a time clock and sign a register. When he learned the nature of her errand, he made her a business proposition: For the modest sum of twenty-five cents, he would, whenever she liked, record her as having been out of the hotel for an appropriate period of time. That way whenever she felt like it she could take a nap instead of walking the mutt. Winnie politely declined the offer as too expensive. She had a harder time dealing with another hotel employee, a room service waiter named Clarence who took a shine to the pretty new maid. Clarence presented her with treats that he filched from the meals he delivered. Not wanting to blow her cover, Winnie graciously accepted the olives, fancy little pastries, and pickled watermelon. She drew the line, however, when Clarence proposed matrimony. It was a relief when her Chicago engagements drew to a close.

In June Winnie worked the subway circuit in New York. When she topped the bill at the E. F. Albee Theater in Brooklyn, a reviewer declared, "Miss Lightner, who is extremely pretty, is suggestive of Eva Tanguay, in that she does not spare herself nor her audience in the nervous energy of her abandonment to her songs. Every muscle, facial and otherwise, is brought into play." The reviewer added, however, "Despite her charm, pleasing voice and infectious humor one wishes she did not grimace quite so often." The following week, Winnie played the Palace. Even though she shared the bill with George L. "Doc" Rockwell, the most famous comic monologist in vaudeville, it was Winnie who was assigned the "star" dressing room. As all show-business insiders knew, that meant she had attained the highest pinnacle of vaudeville. Not only was she playing the Palace, she was the headliner.

Her opening performance on the afternoon of Monday the thirteenth drew only a meager crowd. That was no reflection on Winnie, however, for while the sparse audience at the Palace watched her sing and dance, everybody else in New York thronged Fifth Avenue to see a tickertape parade saluting Charles Lindbergh, recently returned from his epic solo flight across the Atlantic. The Palace devoted part of its program to pictures of Lindbergh being received both at home and abroad, but neither that feature nor Winnie could compete with the opportunity to participate in the rapturous salute to Lucky Lindy. Still, Winnie gave it her all, working "in one" in front of the red velvet curtain and backed by the house orchestra as she blasted through one song after another. Sid Silverman in *Variety* reported that although she had "turned loose some lyrics that may have had a couple of blushes in them for the unwary . . . they were very much in the Lightner style and what this girl can do with such a number is well known." She was, Silverman added, "fast, furious and always to the point. This girl can stay in vaudeville for so long as she wills." During her next booking, at the seaside New Brighton Theater, Winnie scored a similar success, especially with her hit song "It All Depends on You." The *Brooklyn Eagle* reported that the audience demanded and received three encores "probably under the impression that Miss Lightner could continue ad infinitum with her songs a minute."

In July Winnie returned to Chicago where Rufus Le Maire was putting together the second edition of a revue called *Le Maire's Affairs*. He hoped to present it first in Chicago and then take it to Broadway. That is what he did the previous year, when his production featuring Sophie Tucker scored a big hit in the Windy City, racking up 127 performances. Unfortunately for Le Maire, Tucker quit the show before it opened in New York, causing *Le Maire's Affairs* to fail miserably there. This time around Le Maire chose Winnie as his female star. She was joined by male lead James Hussey and a dozen other veterans of vaudeville. The show was a typical full-scale revue with the obligatory chorus girls, songs, sketches, and production numbers. The productions included an elaborate showboat scene at the close of the first act. Perhaps not surprisingly in a town where Al Capone was in his heyday, one of the skits ended in gunfire. The setting was a deluxe movie house, where the ushers were trained to shower the customers with exceptional service. A female patron received so much attention that she couldn't stand it anymore and said she wished she were dead, whereupon one of the ever-helpful ushers pulled out a gun and shot her. In another skit a distraught mother rushed into a doctor's waiting room exclaiming that her baby had swallowed a bullet. She was told to take the infant home, keep him quiet, and "don't point him at anyone."

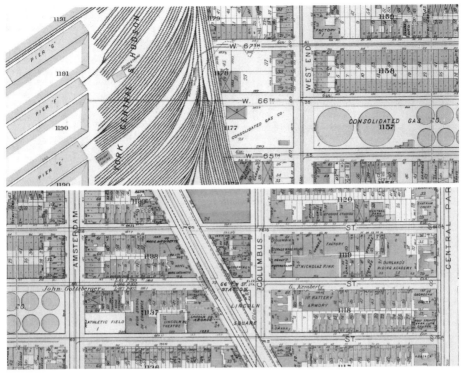

Winnie's childhood world: From the docks and rail yards along the Hudson River (top left), Manhattan's West Sixty-Sixth Street extended eastward, crossing Broadway and terminating at Central Park (bottom right). Winnie lived with her foster parents in a tenement on the south side of Sixty-Sixth Street just west of Broadway and just north of the Lincoln Square Theater. (G. W. Bromley & Co., *Atlas of the City of New York, Borough of Manhattan*, 1911, New York Public Library Digital Collections.)

At age nine Winnie would sneak into the empty Lincoln Square Theater and pretend to entertain an audience, until one day a janitor caught her in the act and smacked her with a mop. (New York Public Library Digital Collections.)

Prior to becoming Winnie's partner in vaudeville, Newton Alexander (far left, hands on knees) performed for many years in an act called the Exposition Four. (C. L. Barnhouse Company archives, courtesy Andrew Glover.)

Winnie's other future partner, Theo Lightner, teamed with Dolly Jordan in a song and piano act.

THE SAN FRANCISCO CALL, MONDAY, JULY 21, 1913.

POPULAR BILL AT EMPRESS THEATER

Race Track Skit Is Feature of the Program

Instrumental and vocal music furnished by the "Exposition Four" at the Empress heads the program for popularity. The "Trainer," a racetrack skit, is pathetic and pleasing. An educated mule adds to the merryment of the entertainment in White's comedy circus. Many encores were accorded Theo Lightner and Dolly Jordan, who sang many popular songs. There was more singing by Raymond Teal in blackface. Marco cast unusual animal pictures by means of his hands and Jones and Sylvester sang and chatted their way to favor.

Newton and Theo become acquainted while touring the same small-time vaudeville circuit. In July 1913 both of their acts were on the bill at the Empress Theater in San Francisco. (California Digital Newspaper Collection, University of California, Riverside.)

THEA **LIGHTNER** WINNIE
AND
NEWTON ALEXANDER

In 1915 Newton and Theo hired fifteen-year-old Winnie to join them in their new vaudeville act. She adopted Lightner as her stage name in order to pose as Theo's sister.

The new act was an immediate success, and Winnie accomplished the remarkable feat of playing the Palace Theater in New York only three months after beginning her career.

In 1920 the trio expanded their act into a mini-revue called "Little Miss Vamp," with Winnie in the title role.

Shifting from vaudeville to Broadway, Winnie starred in three annual editions of *George White's Scandals*. There she introduced many hit songs including "I'll Build a Stairway to Paradise" (1922), "Last Night on the Back Porch" (1923), and "Nuthin's Gonna Stop Me Now" (1924).

While heading the cast in *Scandals* of 1924, Winnie posed for photographer Alfred Cheney Johnston, renowned for his erotic portraits of actresses and chorus girls. (Courtesy Gary Flannery.)

Winnie topped the cast in two annual editions of the Shubert brothers' *Gay Paree*. Her hit songs included "Oh! Boy, What a Girl" (1925) and "I Can't Believe That You're in Love with Me" (1926).

While starring in her final Broadway revue, *Harry Delmar's Revels* (1927), Winnie posed for celebrity photographer Herbert Mitchell.

B. F. KEITH'S
PALACE

Broadway and 47th St. Bryant 4300.
SUNDAY CONCERTS 2 AND 8 P. M.
WEEK BEGINNING JUNE 13TH

2:27	**VANLANE & VERONICA**	8:27
2:32	**PAUL KIRKLAND & CO.** In "The High Stepper."	8:32
2:44	**THE INGENUES** 20—Musical Maids—20 With PEGGY O'NEIL.	8:44
2:56	**ROBINS** Walking Music Store	8:56
3:06	NEVILLE BOBBY **FLEESON & FOLSOM** In "THE SONG PAINTER."	9:06
3:21	Their Hit Compels a 4th Week America's Aristocrats of the Dance HARRY BILLIE **ROYE & MAYE** With Charles Embler & Boyd Davis.	9:31
4:04	**GEO. & JACK DORMONDE** In "Scientific Nonsense."	10:04
4:14	Return to Vaudeville **WINNIE LIGHTNER** Late Feature of George White's "Scandals" and "Gay Paree" in "A SONG A MINUTE."	10.14
4.26	**DR. ROCKWELL** "QUACK. QUACK. QUACK."	10:26
4:46	Madelyn-**THE MEREDITHS**-Hoyt Little Aristocrats of Danceland.	10:46

Returning to vaudeville, Winnie headlined at the Palace in June 1927.

Le Maire's Affairs premiered on 15 August. According to a reviewer in the *Chicago Tribune*, the opening night crowd gave a tumultuous welcome to all of the show's principals and subsequently "registered immense delight" at their performances. The reviewer himself had reservations. He complained that some of the show's skits contained dirty jokes so hoary they probably had been told "to entertain General Winfield Scott in the campaign against Mexico." As for Winnie, the reviewer said that her "lung-power and her self-confidence are undiminished" but "she has learned nothing in the five years since she first clicked in the Scandals," and her songs sounded too much alike. The reviewer particularly disliked a number called "Nagasaki Butterfly." As he described it, "They have her in this dressing up as a sailor and putting all she has into one of those 'I-hate-to-leave-my-Butterfly' ballads wherein the poet implies that 'Europeany guys' and 'Puccini guys' make a dandy little rime." Still, the reviewer praised many other elements of the show, including "the most violent variant of the Apache dance I have so far encountered" and the song "Since Henry Ford Apologized to Me," in which James Hussey, using a heavy Yiddish accent, made fun of the automobile tycoon's recent renunciation of his notorious anti-Semitism.

Considering the show's strong points and its warm reception by the opening-night audience, *Le Maire's Affairs* might have thrived had it not faced a formidable competitor. The eighth (1926) edition of *George White's Scandals* had been an extraordinary hit on Broadway, where it ran for a solid year before closing on 18 June 1927. George White then brought it to Chicago, where it opened on 10 July. By the time Rufus Le Maire launched his own show five weeks later, *Scandals* was so well established that *Affairs* could not gain traction. *Le Maire's Affairs* ran for less than a month in Chicago and never made it to New York. It appears likely that White deliberately hurried his show to Chicago in order to sabotage Le Maire's. Certainly neither impresario had forgotten their violent confrontation two years earlier, which Winnie had witnessed. In June the *Tribune*'s theatrical columnist observed "that Mr. Lemaire's dislike of Mr. White is acute, and that Mr. White's regard for Mr. Lemaire is poisonous," and therefore it would be "sort of comical-like" if both of their shows were to play Chicago at the same time.

No doubt happy to escape the not-so-comical situation in Chicago, Winnie returned to New York. There she played the 5,400-seat Capitol Theater, then the flagship of the mighty Loew's chain. The Loew's formula of pairing a feature film with a live show was still going strong;

indeed, it had been copied by most of the diminishing (although still substantial) number of theaters that still staged vaudeville. The Capitol had recently beefed up its programs to an unprecedented level of opulence. The week Winnie appeared, the screen entertainment included two newsreels and a feature-length comedy, *The Fair Co-ed*, starring Marion Davies. The stage show included four vaudeville turns: Bert Darrell doing fancy tap dancing; Harry Jans and Harold Whalen in a comedy routine; Gus Van and Joe Schenck, with their vocal harmonizing and dialect humor; and Winnie Lightner, putting across a medley of popular songs. All but Darrell were well-known, top-notch acts that had headlined in vaudeville (and were now being paid more than they ever had been there).

Supporting the acts were a seventy-piece orchestra, an onstage band, a choir, and thirty Chester Hale dancing girls. Two production numbers bookended the stage show. The first was a display of ballet and precision dancing with elaborate scenery and costuming built around the theme of roses. The scene climaxed when the choir in full voice rose on an elevator platform behind the dancers. Later on in her solo act, Winnie echoed the roses theme by appearing in a simple black dress adorned solely with a single red rose on her shoulder. "Miss Lightner," said *Variety*, "did nine minutes and left them begging." After all four acts had performed, the stage show concluded with its second production number. This time the Chester Hale girls danced in French doll costumes. Then the choir flowed in from both wings, dressed in white robes. Finally, the rear drop lifted to reveal several tiers of still more women wearing filmy silver gowns and star headdresses. In the middle was "a witch-like figure of a girl suspended in a rising full moon" amid a spectacular lighting effect, a sort of simulated fireworks display of whirling and shooting stars. All in all, said *Variety*, the show at the Capitol was "a rather staggering layout of entertainment." The admission price was ninety-nine cents.

Meanwhile, four blocks down Broadway at the Palace, the people in the orchestra seats paid over three dollars to watch vaudeville acts that were greater in quantity but no better quality, and were not accompanied by a feature film, an onstage band, a choir, a chorus, or a production number. The Palace still made a profit, but a diminishing one. As *Variety* remarked, "You don't have to figure hard to understand why vaudeville of the old school is tottering."

Winnie next performed for a week in a similar but less grandiose program at the Fox Theater in Philadelphia. Then she suddenly found herself immersed in a frantic effort to prepare for what turned out to be her final engagement on Broadway. This was in a show called *Harry Delmar's Revels*. *Revels* was the brainchild of Harry Delmar, a vaudeville dancer who decided to follow the example of George White and stage his own revue. Delmar had to surmount many obstacles, including the loss of costumes worth $20,000 in a fire, and then the cancellation of a scheduled tryout week in Hartford owing to flooding. He persevered, however, and engaged vaudeville stars Blossom Seeley and Frank Fay as his leads. He also hired Bert Lahr, an up-and-coming comedian. Then, just days before the show began its rescheduled tryout, in Brooklyn this time, disaster struck when Blossom Seeley abruptly quit the cast in order to pursue a more lucrative opportunity elsewhere. Winnie took Seeley's place and saved the day. Winnie brought her old partner Newton Alexander along with her as usual, although his participation was so minor that he was not even named in the program. The preview in Brooklyn was a solid success, and *Harry Delmar's Revels* opened on Broadway on 28 November 1927.

Revels featured three elaborate production numbers. One was "My Rainbow," in which Frank Fay sang the title song, while a succession of lovely young choristers paraded in gowns of chartreuse, blue, green, violet, orchid, magenta, and white, followed by one more beauty whose ensemble employed the full spectrum of a rainbow. Another big scene, "Milady's Boudoir," featured chorus girls costumed to represent a dozen different perfumes. But the most remarkable production number was "Undersea Ballet." Within a set that looked for all the world like the bottom of the ocean, thanks to greenish lighting behind a scrim curtain, a pair of adagio dancers flung themselves about amid an assortment of Chester Hale girls costumed as jellyfish and other creatures of the briny deep. Suddenly an enormous octopus descended from the flies, grabbed the female adagio dancer, and hoisted her upward. She fought free and fell backwards ten feet into her partner's arms. Critics unanimously praised the scene. In the *New York Times* Brooks Atkinson commented tongue-in-cheek that the Chester Hale girls had given "one of the best collective impersonations of jelly fish that have been seen on the New York stage this season."

Comedy skits in *Revels* spoofed such things as the formal manners of an English teatime and the snooty pretensions of theatrical groups like the Provincetown Players. Winnie participated in the comedy, appearing along with Frank Fay in a sketch called "The Peacemaker." In another skit she played a young wife with theatrical ambitions who ends up murdering her husband when he threatens to get in the way. As might be expected, however, her main contribution was singing numerous songs, including two that became hits: "I Love a Man in Uniform" and "Naga-saki Butterfly," the latter a carryover from the ill-fated *Le Maire's Affairs*. *Revels* included two other numbers, apparently not sung by Winnie or any other prominent performer, that attracted no notice at the time and were not among the half dozen published as sheet music. They were "Me and My Shadow" and "I Can't Give You Anything But Love." Both later became wildly popular when featured in other shows.

Reviewers noted that *Revels* even more than other revues followed the template of vaudeville. Its principal players were all vaudevillians. It even included a "pony ballet," presumably either an animal act or an imitation of one. This was not, however, the first item on the program, though it probably would have come first on a vaudeville bill. The *Brooklyn Eagle* said *Revels* was "nothing more or less than glorified vaudeville" but "ripping good fun" and "a mighty good evening's entertainment" nonetheless. "From beginning to end," added the *Eagle*, "'Harry Delmar's Revels' has snap, pep, and go. What more can one want in such an entertainment?" Atkinson in the *Times* called the show only "pretty good" rather than mighty good, but he agreed that it was a success. Robert Benchley in *Life* magazine said that the twenty-three scenes of the *Revels* hit "a pretty high average of amusement," and praised "Miss Winnie Lightner, whose songs are gradually getting more sanitary, much to her advantage." The *New Yorker* magazine did not describe Winnie's songs or anything else in the show as sanitary, instead characterizing *Revels* as "a good, rowdy show bordering on old-fashioned burlesque with even a suggestion of that institution in the hips and chests of its choruses."

Although it pleased the critics, *Revels* did not become a hit. Entertaining as it was, it proved unable to compete with the several other revues and the dozens of musical comedies and other attractions playing on Broadway. *Revels* would have closed in less than a month had not some of its performers accepted pay cuts and even chipped in their own money to keep it going. Bert Lahr, who was making his Broadway debut, invested the entire $5,000 that he had saved up from earlier work as a comic in vaudeville. Lahr gambled that the exposure he was getting would justify his investment, and he was right. *Revels* launched him on his way to stardom on stage and screen. Winnie, though, already was a star and thus had no such incentive to join in the rescue effort. She left the cast in early January 1928. Lillian Roth replaced her, and the advertising that previously featured Winnie Lightner and Frank Fay as leads now named Frank Fay and Bert Lahr. *Harry Delmar's Revels* managed to survive until

3 March 1928, but by then Winnie had long since moved on to greener pastures.

As it happened, these pastures were in England. Sailing from New York on the steamer *Columbus*, Winnie and her husband landed at Plymouth on 17 January and set off for London, where they were ensconced in the swank Savoy Hotel. In London Winnie made her first and only appearances outside North America. In the week beginning 23 January she headlined at the Alhambra on Leicester Square, the most prestigious variety house in Great Britain.

Many American vaudeville stars tried their luck abroad. Some scored, others bombed, and nobody ever could figure out exactly what made the difference. The same was true of British artists who crossed the pond in the other direction. Winnie fared somewhere in between the two extremes. She was not one of the abject failures who had to catch the next boat home, but she was not a spectacular success either. *Variety* reported that she "opened indifferently on her first show, due to improper routining" but "fared better" after that. A rumor drifted back to America that the Brits just "didn't get her." No doubt there was some truth to the report. In class-conscious Great Britain, the relatively high social stratum that patronized the Alhambra tended to be reserved and self-conscious in such a public setting. They felt uncomfortable when confronted with performers, especially female performers, who were boisterous and uninhibited—like Winnie.

Winnie had to cancel her second week's engagements because of a throat inflammation brought on by the notorious London smog. She got her voice back by 6 February in time to play the enormous Coliseum at Charing Cross, where a diverse audience filled the theater's thousands of seats. There she was not the headliner, but she was good enough to be held over for a second week and promoted to a more prominent place on the bill. A reviewer commented favorably, although with typical English restraint, "Miss Winnie Lightner, from America, claims to 'sing a song a minute,' a feat which she achieves without spoiling her material or surfeiting her audience."

Surprisingly, the prestigious Alhambra offered three shows a day, one in the afternoon and two in the evening, whereas the more plebeian Coliseum, like the top vaudeville houses back home, gave only two. Even more surprisingly, during both of the weeks Winnie played one or the other of the two theaters, she also gave two performances nightly at the Kit-Cat, a famous nightclub located on Haymarket in the West End. That was possible because all three venues—the Alhambra, the Coliseum, and the Kit-Cat—were within walking distance of one another. Even when she appeared twice nightly at the Alhambra, Winnie could nip out to the Kit-Cat in between her two turns and again after the second one. At the Kit-Cat she performed up close and personal to a well-heeled clientele that could afford to pay fifteen shillings six pence for an evening of dinner, dancing, and entertainment.

On the evening of 24 January a writer for the *Daily Mail* witnessed Winnie's debut at the Kit-Cat. He said that at her first performance "the applause was rather grudging" because "the audience was still sipping its brandy and coffee and reluctant to have its attention diverted from the comfortable laziness induced by a good dinner." It was a different story at the midnight show, where a happy, boisterous crowd "applauded her with all the enthusiasm that she deserved." The writer praised Winnie's strong voice, energetic gestures, and "a rhythm in her singing that no English actress of the variety or musical stage can emulate." Like two other Americans, Aileen Stanley and Sophie Tucker, she could "make an idiotically worded song popular by sheer drive and rhythm of singing." Whereas British singers tended to pause at the end of a line, "these Americans, if only because they have greater lung power and a longer breath, go straight on."

There was a final surprise to Winnie's London sojourn: She was pregnant. She must have known she was before embarking for Great Britain, yet she went ahead with the trip. Moreover, after she had completed her engagements in London, she and her husband visited Paris for a week before sailing for home from Cherbourg at the end of February. Even more remarkably, when she returned to the United States she plunged right back into vaudeville. The Keith and Orpheum circuits had now merged into a single organization. Winnie first played theaters in the East and Midwest. In Pittsburgh, where she had been scheduled to headline for a week and give as many as four shows a day, she fell ill after opening night and had to cancel the rest of the booking. Otherwise, she treated her pregnancy as a mere inconvenience, no reason not to perform with her accustomed vigor. Soon she headed for the West Coast to headline at the Orpheum houses in California. In Oakland, she was described as "singing, capering, laughing, clowning in her aptly termed 'Song a Minute.'" In Los Angeles, the return of "the radiant Winnie Lightner" was said to "lend effervescence to vaudeville." She was, said a reviewer, "a full-fledged star, singing song after song with hardly a moment in between to catch her breath, and entertaining generously, wholeheartedly and humorously." She also was seven months pregnant, a fact that would have astounded the reviewer had he known her secret.

After Winnie performed the last week of June in Youngstown, Ohio, it was announced that she had fallen ill and would be resting for three weeks. The nature of her illness was not specified, nor was there any public announcement when on 27 July 1928 George and Winifred Holtrey became the parents of a baby boy. They named him Richard. Precisely two weeks and three days later, Winnie headlined at the New Brighton Theater in Brooklyn. She was, according to the *Brooklyn Eagle*, "supplied with sparkling material, which, coupled with her refreshing personality and talents," made her "a distinct hit." In September she played the Palace. There, according to the *New York Times*, she delivered "several of Tin Pan Alley's newer masterpieces with her usual abundance of gusto." The following week, she doubled at two Brooklyn theaters, headlining simultaneously at the E. F. Albee and the newly opened Kenmore. Then she played the Eighty-First Street Theater in Manhattan. Amidst all that activity, she somehow found time to join with several other actresses in forming a "Smith-for-President Club" aimed at "going out to line up the stage vote for Al Smith" by staging a big party at the Ritz-Carleton Hotel. And what of her two-month-old baby? Perhaps George Holtrey was playing househusband back in the apartment on Fifty-Seventh Street. If not, Winnie could easily afford to hire a nurse.

Following six weeks on the subway circuit, Winnie again ranged farther afield. Even a star of her caliber now had to accept bookings that would have been beneath her back in the glory days of vaudeville. The first week of November found her playing a split-week shared between Fort Wayne, Indiana, and Akron, Ohio. In Fort Wayne the feature film was accompanied by a measly two vaudeville acts. Although such signs of decay were increasingly evident, neither Winnie nor anybody else knew that this would be her final tour under the auspices of the Keith Vaudeville Exchange. Still less did she or anyone else suspect that within a few short years there would exist not a single theater anywhere in North America, not even the fabled Palace, devoted solely to big-time, two-a-day vaudeville. Of course everybody was aware that vaudeville had been declining for many years in the face of the expanding motion picture industry. But what had been a gradual retreat was about to become a rout. The most conspicuous advantage of live over filmed performance was disappearing; the movies were starting to talk.

Winnie was part of that sound revolution. Before leaving for England she had stood before a grinding camera and concealed microphone to belt out two songs for a one-reel short subject. After returning to the United States she made two more film shorts at around the time of her vaudeville appearances in Los Angeles. When she played the Palace in September, *Variety*'s reviewer hailed her as a showstopper, but criticized her for including in her repertoire two songs from one of her films. On the same 10 September 1928 newspaper page that hailed Winnie's final appearance at the Palace, an adjoining advertisement for a motion picture house announced that its feature film would be accompanied by one of her talking shorts. The movie theater was at Broadway and Forty-Sixth Street, just one block from the Palace. Winnie in person was competing head-to-head with Winnie on film. It was an uneven contest. Soon big-time vaudeville would be no more. But Winnie would not disappear along with it. Instead, audiences all over America and around the world soon would be flocking to cinemas to see the first great female comedian of the sound era: Winnie Lightner, the tomboy of the talkies.

CHAPTER 6

Movies That Talk and Sing

IN LATE DECEMBER 1927 THE FOX FILM CORPORATION ANNOUNCED TO exhibitors that it had available for booking a dozen short subjects equipped with sound tracks. Some of them were recycled newsreels of events like Charles Lindbergh being welcomed home after his heroic flight. Others were pure entertainments such as vaudeville turns. One of the latter was titled *Winnie Lightner Singing Two Songs: Nagasaki Butterfly and Everybody Loves My Girl*. It was Winnie's first appearance on film. She had sung "Nagasaki Butterfly" in Chicago in *Le Maire's Affairs* and then on Broadway in *Harry Delmar's Revels*. The other song, "Everybody Loves My Girl," had been featured in the *Ziegfeld Follies*, but Winnie had not offered it in any of her own Broadway revues. She likely had included both numbers in her recent vaudeville repertoire. As early as March 1928 Winnie's one-reeler was shown in a few locations. By September it became sufficiently well known to draw comment from *Film Daily*, which said that Winnie delivered her two songs "in her characteristic manner and does it as if she really enjoys it. Her voice is clear and strong, and she shapes up as one of the best femme vocalists putting over the pop stuff who has yet appeared in the sound shorts. They should feature her in a series, for she is the kind of thing the crowds seem to like."

When Winnie made her film debut, talking pictures were just beginning to be recognized as an important innovation rather than a passing fad. When in 1926 the brothers Warner inaugurated what we now recognize as the talkies era, nobody else had an inkling of what was to come. Even the Warners did not at first make feature-length all-talking films. Instead, they merely incorporated an orchestral background into features that otherwise remained silent. From the beginning, though, the Warners did produce short subjects that talked. Their immediate aim was to improve the quality of entertainment at those lesser cinemas that could not afford to maintain a house orchestra or present live vaudeville acts. Now, when watching a feature film the patrons of even the tiniest theater would be able to hear a recorded orchestra of fine musicians instead of just listening to a person of dubious talent flail away at a piano. Those same patrons might also be treated to a selection of filmed short subjects in lieu of live vaudeville turns. Scarcely anyone imagined that movies with sound might someday drive silent films, house orchestras, and live vaudeville to virtual extinction. That only happened after years of gradual improvement had brought the talkies into full flower.

Warner Bros. called its sound technology Vitaphone. It was a system in which the camera that captured visual images on a film reel was mechanically connected to a machine that simultaneously recorded sound on a disk. Such systems had existed experimentally since the turn of the century, but it had taken decades to develop a practical version that could reliably synchronize sound and image, especially one that could amplify the sound enough to be heard throughout a theater without distorting it so much as to render it unintelligible. Vitaphone almost immediately had a competitor when the Fox Film Corporation pioneered a rival technology it called Movietone. By converting sound waves into patterns of light, the latter system created a sound track alongside the visual images on the film itself. While sound-on-film was destined to become the industry norm, it was not clear at the outset which system would prevail. Early on many theater owners hedged their bets by installing both.

From the beginning Movietone had advantages over Vitaphone. It was less expensive to equip a theater for Movietone, partly because the Fox corporation deliberately held the cost down in order to encourage early adoption of its system. Movietone required less labor in the projection booth, as operators were obliged to handle only film reels rather than both reels and disks. Movietone reels could be of varying lengths, whereas every Vitaphone reel had to last no more than ten minutes in order to jibe with the capacity of its accompanying disk. Most importantly, with Movietone it was easy to edit or repair a film by snipping out any frames that were unwanted or damaged and then splicing the portions that were left. On the rejoined film, picture and sound would still be synchronized. With sound-on-disk, on the other hand, cutting out frames would ruin the coordination of images on the truncated film with the sound on the unaltered disk.

But despite its drawbacks, Vitaphone did at first possess one key advantage over Movietone: Its sound quality was better. Whereas wear and tear, or even fingerprints or specks of dust, could cause annoying pops and squeals when a Movietone film was projected, Vitaphone disks were far less prone to such problems. True, the sound quality of a disk became noticeably impaired after it had been played about twenty times, but at that point it was easy to substitute a cheap new disk for the worn one. Not so with Movietone, where only a costly new film print could make the sound good as new.

Neither Warners nor Fox knew which system would win out. Furthermore, both companies realized that their main challenge was not to battle for their particular technology, but rather to persuade theater owners to install a sound system of any kind. After all, the way Warners and Fox were going to make serious money was not by selling sound systems, but by making movies and then renting them out to as many theaters as possible. Therefore, the two companies entered into an agreement whereby each was allowed to use the other's system. When the quality of sound-on-film improved to the point that it matched that of sound-on-disk, the latter system became obsolete. Warner Bros. stopped recording directly to disk in 1930, although until 1934 the company continued to supply disks to those theaters that still wanted them.

The top Hollywood studios—MGM, Paramount, and United Artists—did not commit themselves to sound until May 1928. Talkies were still in their infancy. Of the estimated twenty thousand movie venues in the United States, only around three hundred had been wired for sound. One of the earliest showings of Winnie's short subject was at a theater in Uniontown, Pennsylvania, which in early March exhibited a feature entitled *Flying Romeos*. The feature itself, a comedy about an airplane race, was entirely silent, but the theater boasted that its customers would also "Hear That Sight Sound Marvel Movietone" featuring "Winnie Lightner, Vodvil's Favorite Star." A few weeks later a cinema in Aiken, South Carolina, announced that it, too, was being equipped for Movietone, "the first time this newly perfected invention has been exhibited in this part of the South," and that William Fox himself would be present for a special inaugural program of newsreels and short subjects, including Winnie's short. In April the Globe Theater in New York City premiered a Fox feature called *Street Angel*. It had an orchestral background via Movietone, and it was shown along with Winnie's short, as well as others.

The future of sound remained uncertain. In July a theater owner in Waterloo, Iowa, announced that he was installing both Vitaphone and Movietone equipment and that the Warner Bros. Vitaphone picture *State Street Sadie*, a crime melodrama starring Conrad Nagel and Myrna Loy, would be shown during his theater's inaugural "talker week" along with the Fox Movietone short subjects "Lindbergh and Coolidge" and "Winnie Lightner in a musical number." Although the installation of both Vitaphone and Movietone might appear to demonstrate a firm commitment to sound, the theater owner was still hedging his bets, for he added, "The new policy contemplates no present change in the personnel of the theatre aside from an increase in the number of projection operators required. 'Casey' Jones and the stage band, the visiting vaudeville entertainers and Ralph Jones at the organ, will be continued as now." The owner's caution was understandable, for it was still early days. The opening night feature at Waterloo, *State Street Sadie*, included some talkie sequences with fairly realistic spoken dialogue, but most of the film was silent, the flow of images interrupted only by occasional flashes of stilted prose on conventional title cards, such as the one that read, "I, too, have lost some one I loved. The man who killed your father drove my brother to suicide."

In late August, Winnie's short accompanied *Lights of New York*, the first true feature-length all-talkie ever made. Released on 8 July by Warner Bros., *Lights of New York* was another crime melodrama and entirely unremarkable except that it contained dialogue in its virtually every scene. That was no mean feat, considering that the boom microphone had not yet been invented. On sets that contained just one or two concealed stationary microphones, the actors had to stop talking whenever they shifted position. Some of them also spoke slowly, evidently thinking that was the best way to be sure of being heard. Messy as it was, the picture was a huge hit with audiences intrigued by the novelty of a movie that talked with almost no interruption for fifty-seven minutes. *Lights of New York* played simultaneously at all of the Fox theaters in New York City. At the foremost Fox house, the Academy of Music in Manhattan, a *Variety* reporter who attended one showing said that there were standees nine deep at the back of the auditorium. The reporter also said that the film was accompanied by a vaudeville show that was, in his words, "half real—half reel," in that it consisted of four live acts and four Movietone shorts. Remarkably, the audience liked the filmed turns better than the live ones. As the reporter put it, in vintage *Variety* prose, "The talker vaude portion eclipsed the others from a palm slamming angle, which may give the straight vaude moguls something to worry about." As indeed it did.

By then Winnie's Movietone reel was not her only screen appearance. In May, Warner Bros. announced that it had signed her for two

Vitaphone shorts. She must have made them during or soon after her vaudeville bookings in Los Angeles that same month, which means she was seven months pregnant at the time. That appears to have made no difference to Winnie, who, a reviewer said, belted out her songs "in her characteristic nut manner, bouncing from one into the next without stalling." Warners paid her $6,000 for each short. One was titled *Winnie Lightner, the Song a Minute Girl*, a reference to her current vaudeville act. The other was *Winnie Lightner, Broadway's Favorite*, harking back to her years with *George White's Scandals* and other revues. Each short contained three songs. The first one included "Heaven Help a Sailor on a Night Like This," "Raise Myself a Papa," and "We Love It." The second had "That Brand New Model of Mine," "You've Got a Lot to Learn," and "Lala Pa Looza."

The first of Winnie's Vitaphone releases hit the theaters in July, and the second followed in August. *Variety* said Winnie was "a hot number for a talking short" and her first effort was a "mob pleaser." *Variety* liked the second one even more, saying, "There has hardly been time as yet for the development of favorites on the talking shorts, but when the votes are counted it seems probable Winnie Lightner may be one of the chosen." Winnie's second short was "better in every way" and "apt to come very close to being as near a show stopper as canned entertainment ever can be." At a showing in Clinton, New York, at a theater that *Variety* regarded as "typical of all or most wired houses," the audience was "strong for Winnie, applauding her name when announced and giving audible expression of their regret when she was through. They yielded reluctantly to the encoreless finality of that argument-denying caption, 'Finis.'"

While Winnie's Movietone numbers were pleasantly innocuous, her Vitaphone offerings were just as enjoyable, but not so innocent. Her first song on Vitaphone, "Heaven Help a Sailor on a Night Like This," was the lament of a seaman overwhelmed by the abundant and accommodating women of Honolulu. "Now what can I do?" he cried. "I'm only a gob. They need a Sultan here on the job." Winnie's second number, "Raise Myself a Papa," was even more provocative. She declared that because the men in her life had all proven unsatisfactory, she decided to latch on to a twelve-year-old boy and bring him up to be the partner of her dreams. Nowadays it is shocking to encounter a song that makes fun of child abuse, but in 1928 sex between an adult woman and an underage boy was not taken seriously. The boy was not physically injured and could not become pregnant, so he had merely "got lucky" earlier than usual—or so it was assumed. There was no public awareness of the psychological damage that precocious sexual experience can inflict upon a young male. "Now twelve is pretty young they say," the lyrics went, "but when they're older than that they're too blasé." The song went on to say that the singer intended to avoid the mistake of her sister, who had taken up with a boy of five when she was forty-three. That experiment failed because by the time she "taught him to be just what he should," she was "too darn old for him to do her any good." Winnie's final song on her first short, "We Love It," was less controversial. It was a joyful celebration of connubial bliss by a woman who was happy, even though she and her husband lived in a dilapidated bungalow and drove a rubbish car stuck in first gear. "We don't go to the moving pictures for our thrills," she explained. "Our love scenes would make the movies look like stills."

Of the tunes in Winnie's first short, *Variety* said, "All three have double entendre lyrics that seem to be sure fire before a pop audience." As to the songs on Winnie's second short, according to *Variety* the middle number was "pretty blue" and the final one "snappier, even bluer." Much as *Variety* liked Winnie's performances, the paper suggested that "the talking short people had best decide how they are to handle that sort of stuff for the screen. It's not for matinees or for family time."

Actually, the talking short people already were worrying about how to handle that sort of stuff. In 1927 the moviemakers trade organization, the Motion Picture Producers and Distributors Association of America (MPPDA), fearful that the coming of sound had heightened the threat of government censorship, drew up a list of "Don'ts and Be Carefuls" to be observed by its members. One of the items on the long list was an instruction to avoid profanity. In June 1928 the president of the MPPDA, Will H. Hays, wrote to Jack Warner expressing concern about the presence of the words "hell" and "damn" in some Vitaphones. Warner replied that the films in question had been made long before and recorded vaudeville acts exactly as they were presented on stage. "However," he went on, "in the last few months we have watched very carefully and in all the sketches and acts we have eliminated every censorable line." It appears, though, that Warner Bros. had not been watching carefully enough, for Winnie now achieved a permanent place in motion picture history as the first performer ever to be censored for spoken words.

Censorship itself was nothing new. Chicago enacted a film censorship ordinance in 1907, and Pennsylvania created the nation's first state board of review in 1911. Half a dozen other states and more than thirty cities followed suit. When the talkies appeared, censors quickly claimed jurisdiction over sounds as well as images. Winnie's run-in with the censors took place in Pennsylvania. Unfortunately, the relevant records of the Pennsylvania Board of Motion Picture Censors are no longer extant, so it is impossible to determine exactly which of Winnie's words were expunged, and whether they were excised from just one or both of her Vitaphone shorts. It is certain, however, that the censorship did occur.

In June 1928 *Variety* reported that Winnie's Vitaphones were being "held up in Pennsylvania through censorship of dialogue." The two films contained a combined total of six songs. The *Variety* report named five of them, but did not explicitly state that they were the ones that had provoked the censors. The one song title the report did not mention was "Raise Myself a Papa," the number that spoke of grooming a twelve-year-old boy to become a perfect partner. From today's perspective, it is hard to imagine any song could have invited censorship more than that one. It must be borne in mind, however, that public attitudes about what is objectionable have changed a great deal since the 1920s. In October, *Variety* provided some additional detail in a brief item that read,

> There are 600 Vitaphone acts now on hand and available to wired houses. It is explained at Warners it is possible, although troublesome and difficult, to resynchronize shorts that have been censored. It was necessary to do this in Pennsylvania, where some lyrics in Winnie Lightner's songs were ordered out. The resynchronized record was made from the master record by an intricate and highly technical cut-out and pick-up system. The average filmcutter and assembler is worthless for this task, which requires an expert technician.

The Pennsylvania censors definitely did demand the removal of particular spoken words, and Winnie Lightner was indeed the first person in motion picture history to have her voice censored.

Both Fox and Warners tried to prevent the bowdlerizing of their films by arguing that the 1911 Pennsylvania law applied only to visual images. That was a plausible assertion given that there had been nothing else to censor at the time the law was enacted. The argument was strengthened in the case of Vitaphone by the fact that the sound was on a disk that was physically separate from the film itself. The censors were unmoved, however, and their right to censor film dialogue no matter what the sound system was upheld in two 1929 decisions handed down by the Pennsylvania Supreme Court.

For a period of about two years, from mid-1928 through mid-1930, Winnie's shorts were widely distributed. She was seen and heard by more people than ever before. Winnie's vaudeville tours had carried her to the far corners of the nation, yet even when the Keith-Albee and Orpheum circuits were at their peak, only a minority of Americans had the opportunity or the resources to patronize their big-time theaters. Most people, if they attended vaudeville at all, did so at the far more numerous small-time houses of the sort that Winnie's partners Newton and Theo had toiled in for many years, but in which she herself had seldom appeared. Winnie's stardom on Broadway did even less to spread her fame to the hinterlands across the Hudson. Advertisements for her second Vitaphone often described her erroneously as a star of *Ziegfeld's Follies* or *Earl Carroll's Vanities*, rather than of *George White's Scandals* or any of the other revues in which she actually appeared. Most folks far from New York City did not know one Broadway revue from another.

Even people who enjoyed watching and listening to Winnie belt out songs in a talkie short would not necessarily remember her name. She was well known to show-business insiders, but much less familiar to the public at large. That would change, though, because of developments that occurred during the latter half of 1928. In July, the extraordinary success of *Lights of New York* made it evident to the Hollywood bigwigs that an all-talking feature-length picture was a viable proposition. Then in September, Warner Bros. released *The Singing Fool*, starring Al Jolson. The result was an earthquake that rocked the industry. In popular legend, it was Jolson's earlier film, *The Jazz Singer*, released in October 1927, that created the talkie revolution, but that was not really the case. *The Jazz Singer* was a hit all right, but it was a predominantly silent film with just a couple of short talkie sequences. Furthermore, and contrary to legend, the audience on opening night was not thunderstruck to hear Jolson say "You ain't heard nothin' yet," and then break into song, because audiences had been hearing Jolson and other performers do similar things in Vitaphone shorts for more than a year. *The Singing Fool* was a far more significant breakthrough. Even it was not a total talkie, but two-thirds of it was, and the talkie portion included seven splendid songs that Jolson put over with panache. More to the point, *The Singing Fool* raked in money at a breathtaking rate. Its total domestic gross reached $3,821,000, a record that would remain unmatched by any other movie until *Gone with the Wind* came along more than a decade later.

In 1929 the talkies reached the tipping point in their transformation of the motion picture industry. By mid-year more than five thousand theaters had been wired for sound. That was still only about a quarter of the movie houses, but it was the most important quarter. All of the nation's largest cities now had wired houses, some two thousand in all. New York City had 500, Philadelphia 125, Chicago 120, and Los Angeles 87. But there also were more than three thousand theaters wired for sound in places with populations under a hundred thousand, which means that many minor cities and even some small towns had at least one cinema that had invested in the new technology. A vast new market had opened.

With dollar signs dancing before their eyes, Hollywood's moguls now raced to turn out movies that talked, and especially movies that sang. To do that, they needed actors with vocal ability, and it seemed obvious that the best place to find them was within the ranks of those men and women who were trained for the stage. After all, it was thought, seasoned performers who knew how to enunciate clearly and loudly enough to make themselves heard throughout a theater must surely be able to do as well before cameras and microphones in film studios. That assumption turned out to be a costly mistake, for the talkies in fact required an entirely new style of acting and speaking as different from stage performance as it was from the pantomime of silent film. Some former silent film actors succeeded in adapting to the demands of sound, and some did not. The same was true of those performers who came from the stage. But for now, the studios all joined in a headlong scramble to raid vaudeville and Broadway for vocal talent. It was only natural that Winnie Lightner was among the recruits. In March 1929 she arrived in Hollywood, signed by Warner Bros. for an important role in a feature-length all-talking musical comedy called *Gold Diggers of Broadway*.

Winnie's move to Hollywood marked not only the biggest turning point in her professional career, but also an important transition in her personal life. She brought along her infant son, but not her husband. Although it would be another three years before Winnie Lightner and George Holtrey were legally divorced, their relationship was at an end. Winnie was going to have more than her baby Richard for company, however, because her old friends Newton Alexander and Theo Lightner accompanied her to California. Winnie took them with her when she shifted from vaudeville to Broadway, and she saw no reason to abandon them now. Winnie, Richard, Newton, and Theo took up residence together in an unusual but harmonious Hollywood household.

CHAPTER 7

Gold Diggers of Broadway

THE FIRST OF THE GREAT HOLLYWOOD MUSICALS SHOULD HAVE BEEN *The Desert Song*, which Warner Bros. completed by January 1929. It was a filmed version of an operetta that had been a big hit on Broadway for over a year, and was still packing them in at road show performances all over the country. Unfortunately, the movie was not released until May. The delay resulted in part from a legal challenge by a road show producer who claimed that the film rights that Warners had acquired did not include the right to make a talking film. Only in February did the courts decide in favor of Warner Bros. Even then, though, Warners foolishly clung to its predetermined schedule and did not release *The Desert Song* for another three months. Consequently, it was not the breakthrough that would have made it a sensation. Instead, that role was usurped by MGM's *The Broadway Melody*, which premiered in early February.

The Broadway Melody was a backstage story, that is, a depiction of the goings-on among a group of actors who were putting on a show. The film mixed scenes of real life among the actors with scenes from their show. That setup was already a cliché. In 1923, for example, Warner Bros. had distributed a silent feature titled *The Gold Diggers*, a backstage story derived from an earlier Broadway play. What made *The Broadway Melody* an exciting new experience for moviegoers was not its plot, but its music. Audiences were enthralled by this, the first feature-length all-talking, all-singing musical comedy. Although most of the songs were mundane and their lyrics sometimes difficult to grasp, one of them, "You Were Meant for Me," became a popular hit. A minor element of the film's backstage story that passed largely unnoticed by the viewing public, but not by Warner Bros., was that one character, a nasty cad and philanderer, was given the name Jacques Warriner. Jack Warner, head of production at Warners, was not amused.

Warner Bros. scurried to catch up, releasing *The Desert Song* at the beginning of May and following it up at the end of the month with *On with the Show*, a backstage story about actors putting on a stage musical with a plantation setting. The songs in *On with the Show* were highly forgettable—"Lift the Juleps to Your Two Lips," for example—except for two numbers superbly sung by Ethel Waters. The big thing *On with the Show* had going for it was its color. While both *The Desert Song* and *The Broadway Melody* included brief color inserts, *On with the Show* was the first feature-length all-talkie to be filmed entirely in color. Experiments with color date back almost to the dawn of motion pictures, but as with sound technology, it took decades to devise a process that was commercially viable. After years of experimentation, the Technicolor company succeeded in producing several feature-length movies in color, the first released in 1923. The method used was far from ideal, however, as it involved cementing one layer of celluloid on top of another. The resulting film scratched easily and was prone to cupping that made the screen image pop in and out of focus. Another deficiency was that the process did not display the full color spectrum.

By 1929 Technicolor had devised a better method that produced normal, single-layer film. The other major limitation of the earlier process had not been overcome, however, for Technicolor still could not reproduce the entire spectrum. Color was achieved by using a camera in which a prism created two duplicate images, one of which passed through a red filter and the other through a green filter. The image that passed through the red filter was then dyed green, while the image that passed through the green filter was dyed red. Finally, in a series of unbelievably complicated chemical manipulations, the green and red images were processed separately and then combined in a final print. The colors of the final print were mostly shades of red, green, pink, and brown. There was also a touch of blue, but no yellow. While the Technicolor company would eventually add a third filter and thereby reproduce the full spectrum, that technique was not yet available. It was horrendously difficult to process and then combine two images—never mind three—without the final print becoming hopelessly blurred by colors that overlapped and bled into each other.

In June MGM regained the upper hand when it released *The Hollywood Revue of 1929*, a pastiche of production numbers, songs, and skits not connected by any storyline. Modeled on Broadway revues like *Follies* and *Scandals*, this film was the first to employ the second most common format for the early Hollywood musical. Backstage stories were the

most prevalent, revues a distant second, and operettas a still more distant third. All three basic formats had now been introduced, as had the
key technologies of sound and color. The time was ripe for a movie that
would raise the standard of production to a new level by incorporating
and improving upon the best aspects of the musicals that had already appeared. This time Warner Bros. took the prize.

Gold Diggers of Broadway, a backstage musical filmed entirely in Technicolor, premiered at the Winter Garden Theater in New York City on
30 August 1929. Reviewers unanimously lauded the picture for its unprecedented technical quality. Mordaunt Hall of the *New York Times* said
it was "an extraordinarily pleasing entertainment" that "caused one to
meditate in the end on the remarkable progress of the screen, for not
only are the voices reproduced with rare precision, but every opportunity is taken of the Technicolor process in producing the hues and glitter
of a musical comedy." While not quite the "all natural color" that Warner
Bros. advertised, the color in *Gold Diggers of Broadway* surpassed all previous efforts and looked stunningly beautiful. Flesh tones came through
remarkably well, and scenery and costumes displayed all sorts of lovely
tints because the moviemakers had learned to select paints and fabrics
not on the basis of how they looked to the naked eye, but rather how
they would appear on the final print.

The improved sound and color greatly enhanced the picture's elaborate musical production numbers, which were filmed on an enormous
soundstage, the largest in the world at the time. While the productions
were nothing like the jaw-dropping extravaganzas devised in later years
by Busby Berkeley, they were nonetheless remarkable achievements at
a time when filming in color was so difficult and expensive that retakes
were all but unknown. To prevent the whirr of the camera from being
picked up on the separate sound recording system, the camera and its
operator had to be enclosed within an airtight box with a sealed glass
window in front. Although the box was mounted on wheels, it was cumbersome to move, dragging its attached cables along the floor. It was
barely possible for the poor cameraman to complete a ten-minute reel
before he passed out from heat and lack of oxygen. At the first possible
moment he burst out of the box, gasping for air. Everybody else on the
set panted, too, for Technicolor necessitated lighting of such intensity
that the heat from a multitude of 10,000-watt lamps at times singed hair
and clothing.

Although *Gold Diggers of Broadway*, like the earlier musicals, included
long stretches in which the full set was photographed straight-on by an

almost stationary camera, choreographer Larry Ceballos managed to keep scores of chorus girls in view by using the old stage trick of having them traipse up and down stepped platforms that ran horizontally across the set. Meanwhile, director Roy Del Ruth devised camera work that critic Mordaunt Hall characterized as brilliant. Hall particularly praised a scene in which a succession of dissolves and angles conveyed the way that Ann Pennington, dancing on a tabletop, was perceived by her inebriated companions. At the start of the film's grand finale, Del Ruth even managed to pull off the miracle of a nearly overhead shot of the chorus girls moving into position.

Del Ruth also hit upon a novel method of improving sound quality. When making silent pictures, he and other directors routinely used a megaphone to call out instructions to the actors, both at rehearsals and when their movements and gestures were being filmed. A megaphone obviously could not be employed that way during the filming of a talkie. Nevertheless, throughout the making of *Gold Diggers of Broadway* Del Ruth kept his megaphone handy not only at rehearsals, but also during filming. At rehearsal he used it in the conventional manner, voicing instructions to the cast. During filming he adapted it to an entirely different purpose by placing its small end next to his ear and aiming its larger opening at an actor. That way he could hear the actor's voice distinctly and make an educated guess as to how well it would be picked up by the microphone.

Although it looked and sounded better than any of its predecessors, *Gold Diggers of Broadway* borrowed its plot from the similarly named silent film Warner Bros. had produced in 1923. It was a conventional backstage story. The plot revolved around a cluster of showgirls, played by Helen Foster, Winnie Lightner, Ann Pennington, Gertrude Short, Lilyan Tashman, and Nancy Welford. One of the girls was in love with a young man who came from a rich family. The young man's uncle (Conway Tearle), having leapt to the conclusion that the girl must be an opportunist out to raid the family fortune, roared into town determined to prevent the couple from marrying. Tearle brought along his lawyer (Albert Gran), a portly old gent equally certain that the girl must be a gold digger. The misunderstanding was eventually cleared up, and the story ended happily with Tearle giving his blessing to the young couple's engagement and himself falling for one of the other girls (Nancy Welford).

What was intrinsically a routine backstage tale was enlivened by spirited acting and a terrific script. Whereas the earlier musicals had sometimes been stalled by turgid conversations, *Gold Diggers of Broadway* had only short, snappy dialogue that drove the story along briskly. Better yet, the dialogue was peppered with funny lines, the vast majority of them either delivered by or directed at Winnie Lightner. Winnie is at the center of a subplot that is far more entertaining than the main storyline. She plays a buxom, uninhibited, rambunctious young woman who is determined to land herself a man. As she puts it near the start of the film, "I'm gettin' to the point where I don't care what kind of man he is, as long as he has pants and an income." To which Lilyan Tashman replies, "And you're not so particular about the pants, are you, Darling?"

Winnie's character is a sheer delight because although she is indeed a gold digger, she proclaims her intentions with such candor and good humor it is impossible not to like her. When introduced to Albert Gran she declares, "Oh, I adore lawyers. They get you alimony." In no time at all, she is addressing him as "Sweetie" and entreating him to buy her a "nice little bitty automobile. . . . Not one of those great big foreign cars. Just a simple little Lincoln. . . . Maybe purple with ducky green wheels." When Gran tries to fend her off by saying he could not possibly buy her a car without harming her reputation, Winnie is momentarily nonplussed. "Oh, that's right," she says hesitantly. "People would talk, wouldn't they, Sweetie?" Relieved that Winnie has seen his point, Gran eagerly responds, "Why of course. You see, a man doesn't buy a girl a car unless he's engaged or married or something." Whereupon Winnie exclaims, "Oh, Sweetie, you're proposing!" Aghast, Gran cries, "No, I'm not! Oh no, no, no! You have nothing in handwriting! You have no witnesses!" But it is too late, for Winnie is already exulting, "Sweetie proposed! Sweetie proposed!"

Despite his continued protests, Gran begins to relish Winnie's vivacious company as she drags him out shopping and partying. In fact, he is having the time of his life. In the end he really does propose. On the way to that denouement Winnie adds to the fun by singing three comic songs. Of the picture's many tunes, the biggest hits were "Painting the Clouds with Sunshine" and "Tip-Toe through the Tulips with Me," both sung by Nick Lucas. But Lucas also was saddled with some decidedly mediocre selections, whereas all three of Winnie's were first rate. Winnie's first number, "And Still They Fall in Love," is less risqué than her other two, but just as funny. It describes how a woman's romantic dreams are shattered once she gets married. The man who was so polite and attentive when wooing her now goes out drinking and gambling, leaving her at home to toil over the kitchen sink. He is more interested in a good cigar than in her, and, worst of all, he eats peanuts in bed. In her second song, Winnie declares that despite living in an age of technological wonders like airplanes, radio, and talking pictures, what she really wants is what we now call a robot. That word had not yet been coined, however, so Winnie sings instead of her longing for a "Mechanical Man" who will cook and clean and otherwise satisfy her every need. "Say, if he doesn't love me in a great big way," trills Winnie, "I'll have his batteries charged and then he'll be okay." Or if a recharge doesn't do the trick, she will trade him in for "a man who can, a brand new mechanical man." Winnie's final song is "Keeping the Wolf from the Door," in which she observes, "a girl without finances often must accept advances" and celebrates the gold digger ethic with such lyrics as, "I've got a conscience, let me park it somewhere, somewhere in the care of a nice millionaire." Winnie belts out that last number from a tabletop shared with Ann Pennington and surrounded by boisterous, tipsy companions. At Winnie's insistence, Gran chimes in with "Woof! Woof! Woof!" at the end of each stanza. The song ends with Winnie losing her balance and plopping her ample body onto Gran's lap. (She later claimed in interviews that her tumble had been an unplanned accident, but that seems unlikely. In any case, critics singled it out as one of the most hilarious moments in the movie.)

A running joke throughout the film is Winnie's inability to master the tiny speaking part that she has been given in the stage show. While striking a pose resembling the Statue of Liberty she is supposed to say, "I am the Spirit of the Ages and the Progress of Civilization." At intervals she is seen rehearsing her part, sometimes holding aloft either a bunch of flowers or an absurdly oversized Liberty torch. She invariably misspeaks, coming up with such bizarre iterations as: "Into the Valley of Death rode the six . . . . No, that's the wrong one"; "I am the spirit of the Shuberts. No that's wrong"; and "I am a fai-, a fai- . . . No, I'm not a fairy." The movie concludes with a giant production number depicting the grand finale of the stage show. Before an enormous backdrop displaying landmarks of Paris in distorted perspective, a vast array of performers puts on a spectacular display of frenzied dancing and acrobatics, while an unseen orchestra reprises the songs heard earlier. Finally, the stage show reaches its climax. In front of the assembled company, male dancers lift Winnie into the air. She strikes her Statue of Liberty pose and declares, "I am . . . I am . . . Oh, darn it, I've forgotten that second line." The music swells, and *Gold Diggers of Broadway* comes to its glorious end.

Winnie's performance was so magnificent that even before the picture had been completed, and months before it received its first public showing, Warner Bros. signed her to another contract. That proved to be an astute move, for when the rave reviews of *Gold Diggers of Broadway* poured in, nearly every critic singled out Winnie as central to the film's success. Sime Silverman of *Variety* wrote, "Somebody tossed the picture right into Winnie Lightner's lap, or else she stole it. . . . Mugging, talking, singing or slapsticking, she can do them all and does in this picture." Other trade papers agreed that she "runs away with the honors" (*Movie Age*) and is "far and away the high spot" (*Film Daily*). Walter Winchell in *New Movie Magazine* said, "Her quickly-tempoed melodies not only leave you limp with laughter, but her scenes, in which she enlivens the proceedings, are masterpieces." Norbert Lusk in *Picture Play* said that in addition to "the sheer gusto of her clowning, Miss Lightner adds to it a warmly human friendliness that makes you feel it wouldn't be right to utter a word of reproach if she spilled the soup down your back. She saved the show."

Reviewers in the popular press were similarly effusive, both during the movie's initial engagement at the Winter Garden and after the picture went into general release. *Life* magazine singled out Winnie as "the bright particular star" of the film. The *Brooklyn Standard Union* said she was "as humorous as it is possible to be." The *Albany Evening News* called her "the solid gold" in *Gold Diggers*. The *Chicago Tribune* said the film's "outstanding features are the work of the irrepressible Miss Winnie Lightner . . . a distinct and original screen personality." When the picture was used as the opening attraction at the new Warners Downtown Theater in Los Angeles, the *Los Angeles Times* said Winnie "scored a hit well nigh sensational." In Canada the *Montreal Gazette* reported that Winnie, the "main reason" for the film's success, "was greeted at every turn of the story with, literally, roars of laughter." When the picture reached the United Kingdom, one report from London described it as "a marvellously glittering affair" in which Winnie, "whose appeal was only moderate when she appeared in the London music halls, makes the great laughing hit." Another report said she was "probably the greatest comedienne find in years. . . . Nothing funnier has been seen on the screen." The *Daily Mail* review of the film said,

> The fact that one will remember it, and even see it twice willingly is entirely due to the extremely clever performance of Miss Winnie Lightner, a tall, gawky young woman with a rare and perfect talent for comedy. She sings one song, "Keeping the Wolf from the Door," simply inimitably. Here is a first-class talent, and indeed she

saves the picture. . . . One cannot call her manner that of a vamp; it would be to mistake the operation of a lawn-mower for that of a hearty steam-roller.

In Australia, where the movie was banned by censors but then released after an appeal, the *Adelaide Advertiser* said nobody should miss seeing *Gold Diggers* at least once, for "Winnie Lightner's deft hand on the reins of high comedy turns its splendor into spectacular channels."

Winnie had so successfully transitioned from stage to screen one Hollywood journalist later credited her with having singlehandedly convinced the studio bosses that the moviegoing public would accept the substitution of new stars for old. "When the talkie cyclone first loomed up," wrote Florabel Muir, "the old-time stars felt secure behind their bulwarks." They were confident their loyal fans would not warm to interlopers from the stage. "They may be big shots on Broadway," thought the veterans of the silent screen, "but who knows them out in the sticks?" Jack Warner decided to test the issue:

He put on a picture called Gold Diggers of Broadway, and cast it without one prominent player from the movie ranks. The star was Winnie Lightner, a comedienne from the variety stage. The sticks gave Warner his answer by turning out in droves to guffaw at Winnie's tricks, and Gold Diggers earned a most gratifying profit for Warner Brothers. This encouraged other producers and the axes began to fall right and left. The expensive contracts that producers had been glad enough to sign in order to hold their stars were cut away as rapidly as they expired. Hollywood had learned that pictures could be made profitably without the lure of long-established favorites.

Gold Diggers of Broadway did indeed make a gratifying profit. Exhibitors from coast to coast reported it was doing far more than normal business, sometimes half again or even twice as much. In Tacoma, Washington, a theater owner declared, "The appeal has been so general that it is a shame to have the run cut, even in its third week." In Salt Lake City the picture was the first one ever to play for a solid month. In North Adams, Massachusetts, where *Gold Diggers* was already running continuously from 1:00 p.m. to 11:00 p.m., the local theater added an 11:00 a.m. showing "to relieve the congestion." In Altoona, Pennsylvania, the manager urged potential customers to "attend matinees and avoid standing."

In Syracuse, New York, *Gold Diggers* was held over for six weeks and broke local records previously set by the Al Jolson films and by a stage production of *Abie's Irish Rose*. In Rochester *Gold Diggers* was seen by two hundred thousand customers at 360 showings over ten continuous weeks. Even in tiny Weedsport, New York, when the film was brought back for a third time the local manager reported that its first two engagements had already set a new house record by playing to eight times as many people as had seen *Ben Hur* or *The Big Parade*. The manager added, "We have had requests to show this picture again from people who have seen it five and six times."

Gold Diggers of Broadway was in wide release throughout 1930 and 1931 and continued to be shown in some locations in 1932. It was exhibited at more than six thousand theaters and seen by millions of moviegoers. Warner Bros. had spent $532,000 to make it and an additional $74,000 on advertising. The film's domestic revenue, after the exhibitors had claimed their usual one-third or so of the box-office takings, reached $2,540,000. Foreign earnings brought the total Warner Bros. receipts to $3,967,000. The picture was so successful that Warners would make five more movies on the same pattern: *Gold Diggers of 1933*, *Gold Diggers of 1935*, *Gold Diggers of 1937*, *Gold Diggers in Paris* (1938), and *Painting the Clouds with Sunshine* (1951). This steady stream of remakes may explain why, after its initial spectacular run, *Gold Diggers of Broadway* was never released again. It may also be the principal reason that it is now a lost film. The sound disks survive virtually intact, but only a fraction of the visual element is extant, and the surviving frames provide only a few fleeting glimpses of Winnie giving the greatest performance of her life.

Although *Gold Diggers of Broadway* was a great earner for Warner Bros., its success should not be exaggerated. Contrary to some reports, it did not make more money than any previous talkie, much less set a record that endured until 1939. In fact its worldwide total was significantly less than the $4,366,000 that MGM received from *The Broadway Melody*, and even the latter figure was dwarfed by the $5,916,000 that Warners earned from the Al Jolson vehicle *The Singing Fool*. The reality was that novelty trumped quality in attracting audiences to the early talkies. *Gold Diggers of Broadway* was easily the best of those three high-grossing films, but unlike *The Singing Fool* it was not the first talkie to feature a slew of songs by a great performer, and unlike *The Broadway Melody* it was not the first full-blown Hollywood musical.

But if it was neither a great innovation in terms of content and technology, nor a record setter as measured by its revenues, *Gold Diggers of*

Broadway was unquestionably a consummate evocation of the legendary Roaring Twenties. With its pretty flappers cavorting in feathery pastel gowns, its gleeful banter about fancy cars and diamond necklaces, and its glamorous nightclub and party scenes in which men in evening dress downed bootleg whisky and watched women dance on a tabletop, it captured the intoxicating spirit of the Jazz Age. While Winnie and her compeers were frolicking in front of the cameras, none of them could have imagined how quickly the movie they were making would become a relic of a vanished era. Just two months after the film's premiere, the New York stock market crashed spectacularly to earth. During the next two years, while millions of people flocked to see *Gold Diggers of Broadway*, millions of others joined the unemployment lines. Only slowly did the realization dawn that this was no ordinary downturn like the one that had prevailed before the stimulus provided by the First World War kicked in, or the one that occurred after that stimulus ended. The steepest economic decline in American history had begun. By 1933 when the Great Depression reached its nadir, all of the spectacular economic growth of the 1920s, and most of the growth since the turn of the century, had vanished into thin air.

In the popular imagination the Roaring Twenties are still pictured as a time of burgeoning prosperity and happy times for all. In fact reality fell short of that golden image. While national income soared in the twenties, it was unequally distributed. A wealthy elite prospered as never before, but half the population remained mired in poverty. Winnie knew full well that the character she played on film was good for laughs, but had little counterpart in the real world. "If there are any girls hypnotic enough to have men transfer to them important cars, jewelry, clothes and certified checks, why then all I can say is more power to them," she told an interviewer. But she had worked with a lot of chorus girls, and none of the ones she knew had snared herself a millionaire. "The show girls I have known," she said, "have been putting up a pretty stiff fight, and a stiff upper lip, making things go. Part of the year they've got a job, and the other half they're 'at liberty,' as we put it—at liberty to make up excuses to your landlady for not having the rent money handy."

But as the already straitened circumstances of many Americans worsened to the point of actual hunger and starvation in the most extreme cases, Winnie herself was entering the most prosperous period of her life. She once testified in a legal proceeding that between 1929 and 1932 she earned a total of $249,462. That means that her yearly income (at a time when income tax rates were low) had a purchasing power equivalent to

more than a million dollars today. She could afford to live the extravagant style of a movie star, and for a while she did. Her sensational success
in *Gold Diggers of Broadway* made her the toast of Hollywood. Everybody
invited her to parties, and she reciprocated by throwing shindigs of her
own around the swimming pool of her rented mansion in Beverly Hills.
Such hedonistic behavior came easily to her, for it was merely a more
lavish version of her pre-California lifestyle. Throughout her Broadway
career she enjoyed life to the hilt. "I was a playgirl for years," she acknowledged. "In London and Paris and New York I was fairly wild—ask
the nightclub proprietors if you don't believe me. I partied lots and I never took time off to think. I was like that when I first came to Hollywood.
And then a lot of things happened. The most important was that I found
it required more energy to make pictures than it ever did to play on the
stage." She realized that her social life was getting out of hand. "The
crowd started Sunday-dropping-in on me," she recalled. "Sometimes the
weekend went on for days. I wasn't getting any rest. The place was like
a hotel. So I called the parties off and really began to enjoy Hollywood."

There was another reason for Winnie's withdrawal from the whirlwind party scene. She had begun a relationship with Roy Del Ruth, the
director of *Gold Diggers of Broadway*. Six years older than Winnie, Roy had
been a journalist before becoming involved in motion pictures. In 1915,
the year Winnie started out in vaudeville, Roy became a script and gag
writer at Mack Sennett's Keystone Studios. Soon Roy was directing comedy shorts starring Harry Langdon and others. In 1925 he began turning out feature films at Warner Bros. He was a prolific and remarkably
versatile director, working throughout his long career in virtually every
movie category from musical comedy to film noir. The coming of sound
did not faze him. In 1928 he directed *The Terror*, which was the second
all-talking feature ever made, and the first in the horror genre. The film
produced scary effects by the creative use of sounds such as creepy organ music and the increasingly audible thud of footsteps as a murderer
approached unseen. Later that year Roy directed an utterly different all-
talkie, *The Desert Song*, the operetta that would have become famous as
the first great Hollywood musical if only its release had not been delayed.

Roy and Winnie kept quiet about their relationship because they both
were married to others. Winnie was still the legal spouse of George Holtrey, although she had left him behind when she moved to Hollywood.
Roy had married a young actress named Olive Simon in 1921. Their
son Richard was born the following year. At some point thereafter they
began living separate lives while residing under the same roof. Jimmy

Starr, a screenwriter and gossip columnist, got to know Roy while working with him on the silent comedy *Ham and Eggs at the Front* (1927). In his published memoir *Barefoot on Barbed Wire*, Starr wrote that he became fond of Roy despite finding him "a strange, talented man who seemed to like his own company best." Starr also became acquainted with Roy's wife, whom he described in decidedly unflattering terms: "Of all the spoiled-brat wives of Hollywood, Olive Del Ruth, probably, was the worst of the lot." According to Starr, Olive had no interest in motherhood or anything else of value. Instead she devoted herself to throwing around Roy's money, showing off her designer gowns and full-length mink coat, and tooling through Hollywood in her spiffy new Duesenberg roadster with chrome side pipes. Despite Starr's antipathy toward Olive, he began spending time with her because, he explained, "We didn't like each other, but we could be useful to each other." Olive liked to get her name in the newspapers by hanging out at the smartest restaurants and clubs. Starr needed to frequent the same places in order to pick up material for his gossip column. When Starr asked Roy how he felt about Starr and Olive's relationship, Roy's reaction was, "Why not? Have a good time. I don't care what she spends as long as she leaves me alone. The kid is stashed away in a boarding school. It's a hell of a life."

It may seem strange that a noisy, outgoing woman like Winnie should find happiness with a quiet, introverted man like Roy. In fact, though, Winnie's public persona reflected only one side of her personality. Certainly she had reveled in being loud and aggressive when she was on stage in vaudeville or on Broadway, or even when just out partying at Paris nightclubs or New York speakeasies. But she needed an audience in order to behave that way. That held true even when she was making movies. She told an interviewer, "I've heard of movie actresses who chase everybody off the set when they act. Not little Winnie. When I do a scene all the electricians and carpenters and everybody else around the place can step right up and have a look. In fact, I want them to. They usually do. That's my audience. I play to them instead of to the camera. I forget all about lenses and mikes. I just try to be my old fat self."

When not playing to an audience, Winnie was a different person. Soon after arriving in Hollywood, she startled the eminent screenwriter Herman J. Mankiewicz by saying, "You know, people frequently get a girl wrong. I like a good time as well as anybody, I guess, and yet where I'd really like to be often is out in the open spaces alone, in a tent, with the blue sky stretching to an infinity above me, with the millions of stars twinkling their eternal message, and with just enough moonlight to read

Variety by." It was typical of Winnie to end her soliloquy with a wise-crack, but there was more than a grain of truth in what she said. She did not like crowds. Once she got over her initial euphoria at having become a movie star, she much preferred to relax in the company of people she liked, rather than hobnob with celebrities or frequent places where she was sure to be recognized by hordes of adoring fans. Hollywood columnists often mentioned that Winnie rarely attended the premieres of new movies, especially her own. She preferred to slip in unrecognized at a later showing in order to see for herself how an ordinary audience reacted to her performance.

Along with her little boy Richard and her old friends Newton and Theo, Winnie lived comfortably and contentedly in her Beverly Hills mansion. Roy Del Ruth visited often but did not actually move in with Winnie until many years later. Winnie was delighted to have settled down in a place she could call home. "Watch me spread all over this big house, after living in hotel rooms," she said. "I've got things in the closets in every room just to show I can if I like." She also indulged her fondness for dogs by acquiring several, including a new favorite named Bim. "I've got a police dog and a bull terrier," she explained, "but I thought I wanted a big dog. So I bought one of Harold Lloyd's Saint Bernards. They're the breed that trots around the Alps with a flask of gin tied onto them. He's only nine months old now, but he eats six pounds of meat at a sitting and drinks a gallon of water." Winnie was frequently seen buzzing around Hollywood in her little green American Austin coupe, accompanied by Bim. Or perhaps it would be more accurate to say that she was frequently not seen, because Bim pretty much took up the whole car.

Winnie confessed that she missed New York, but she loved Hollywood. She hoped to stay in movies and definitely did not want to go back to vaudeville. "It isn't like it used to be," she groused. "I've played on bills with the Duncan Sisters, Valeska Surratt, T. Roy Barnes, and wonderful dance acts. But now vaudeville is just the same. It opens with acrobats. The second spot is a couple of hoofers. Third is a guy with a violin. Fourth, a skit. And so on. The scenery is fierce. An old rag hung up with a few rhinestones on it, and they think it's swell. And a few trick lamps that the girls in the act made in a Cincinnati hotel." Here Winnie voiced a complaint that would be repeated for decades by former performers who blamed the demise of vaudeville on its having become formulaic and boring. The real problem was not, however, the vaudeville formula, but simply that vaudeville could not compete with Hollywood in paying for talent. Like Winnie herself, all of the performers that she named had left vaudeville for films. If vaudeville scenery and props were less elaborate than they had been, that, too, reflected the financial squeeze that was slowly strangling the life out of vaudeville.

Winnie was paying $650 a month rent for her house in Beverly Hills. She also was still shelling out $350 a month for an apartment in Manhattan because, she told an interviewer, "My husband is there all alone—he directs plays in New York." In fact, George Holtrey worked as a stagehand and never directed anything. Perhaps Winnie had her new partner Roy in mind when she made up that little fib. The only thing detracting from Winnie and Roy's happiness was their inability to escape their respective marital entanglements. Neither of them wanted to go through the ugliness of a bitterly contested divorce, but neither of their spouses would let go without one. George Holtrey was happy residing at Winnie's expense in a much nicer apartment than he could afford on his own modest earnings. Olive Del Ruth was even happier living lavishly off Roy instead of having to support herself. The problem would have to be tackled if Winnie and Roy were ever to formalize their relationship with a wedding. For now, though, they could console themselves with the realization that although they were unable to shed their respective spouses, they were at least well equipped to bear the resultant financial drain. Roy was one of the most successful and highest paid directors in all Hollywood. Winnie had the prestige and the income of a major star. Best of all, they had each other.

CHAPTER 8

She Couldn't Say No

CONFIDENT THAT WINNIE'S BRAVURA PERFORMANCE IN *GOLD DIGGERS* *of Broadway* would make her popular, Warner Bros. hurriedly thrust her into other projects. Her first assignment was a relatively modest role in *The Show of Shows*, which was Warners's response to MGM's *The Hollywood Revue of 1929*. The MGM film, which pioneered the revue format and showcased the company's brightest stars, many of them being heard for the first time in a talkie, had been a hit. It cost $426,000 to make and earned a domestic gross of $1,527,000, plus a further $894,000 abroad.

Jack Warner figured that to achieve an even greater success all Warners had to do was copy MGM, but make everything bigger and better. *The Hollywood Revue of 1929* had twenty-five stars. Warners topped that in *The Show of Shows* by featuring more than three times as many of its own players, ranging from John Barrymore to Rin Tin Tin. Winnie Lightner was one of the first five cast members to be named, with others added as the project took shape. MGM had employed two hundred showgirls in its production numbers. Warners would advertise that *The Show of Shows* had "by actual count 1,000 Hollywood beauties. All of them tinted by Technicolor—and none of them tainted by time." Finally, Jack Warner threw caution to the winds, blowing a grand total of $795,000 on costumes, sets, and every other aspect of production. With all of those vast resources plowed into *The Show of Shows*, what could possibly go wrong?

Well for starters, although Warners wanted to film *The Show of Shows* entirely in color, doing so became impossible. All of the studios were piling into color, and the Technicolor company could not build its complicated cameras anywhere near fast enough to keep up with the demand. Warners still bested MGM in this respect, however, for while *The Hollywood Revue of 1929* had been a black and white film with a few color segments, *The Show of Shows* was a color film with a few black and white segments. The main problem with *The Show of Shows* is that it frequently lapses into bloated overkill. As it rolls along reel after reel for two hours, great throngs of dancers perform again and again with impressive precision, but at sometimes tedious length, amid sets that are busy to the point of distraction. Curtains open and close, drops rise and fall, and enormous pieces of scenery roll in and out of view, as though everybody had forgotten they were making a movie rather than a stage show. One sequence presents songs and dances by eight pairs of sisters, one after the other. Even the most gormless of vaudeville managers could have told Jack Warner that it was fine to have a sister act on a bill, but to have two was unwise, and to have eight in succession was tiresome beyond belief. Another problem with *The Show of Shows* is that it bunches its overabundance of stars together in scenes that give them little opportunity to display their individual abilities. Viewing the film now, it is painful to watch a brilliant talent like Beatrice Lillie straining against the confines of a lackluster skit.

Fortunately, most of these deficiencies do not apply to Winnie's participation in the film. She appears in two sequences, both of which center squarely on her. While her second sequence does contain one of the film's many elephantine production numbers, in that instance the over-the-top staging adds to the effectiveness of the scene, because the whole thing is an elaborate joke rather than an attempted work of art. The impact of the scene is all the greater because it contrasts so markedly with Winnie's first appearance in the picture. The setting of her earlier sequence could not be simpler: a bare stage backed by a shimmery curtain. As master of ceremonies Frank Fay and his little dog walk off to one side, Winnie races into view from the other and immediately begins belting out "Pingo Pongo," a comic song about a tropical island where the native king enjoys the favors of his forty-seven wives, and where any bothersome missionary who shows up is eaten. The song, which thumbs its nose at the conventional moral values of chastity and monogamy, is perfect for Winnie, and she puts it over with the same matchless verve she displayed all those thousands of times she stepped out "in one" to sing solo in vaudeville or on Broadway. Critics today might complain that the song embodies a racist and imperialist attitude toward so-called primitive peoples—which is true enough—but sensitivity to such matters was not to be expected in 1929. Besides, the song does, after all, enthusiastically side with the uninhibited Pingo Pongo folks, rather than the western missionaries and their repressive moralism.

The second sequence in which Winnie appears begins in a similar fashion, with Winnie launching into another humorous song, but it quickly becomes something else entirely. This time the song is "Singin' in the Bathtub," which extolls the pleasure of warbling through the soap-suds while taking a Saturday night bath. In 1929 the idea of bathing only once a week was not in itself funny, because that was still a common practice, but the song's gloriously silly lyrics and Winnie's exuberant de-livery make it a treat. One highlight is a spoken portion in which Win-nie, in the tones of a preacher, exhorts "Saturday's children" to accept their "Judgment Day," saying, "Now the ordeal begins, so lift up your chins and wash all your sins away." The wonderfully zany song becomes even zanier when Winnie is joined by a bevy of dancing chorines dressed in 1890s bathing costumes. The chorines are tall and peculiar looking, because as soon becomes apparent, they are in fact men sporting truly awful wigs as well as female attire.

Winnie and her gender-bending companions cavort about, and then the curtain behind them opens to reveal an array of steaming bathtubs, each occupied by a fleshy gentleman clad from neck to knees in a hori-zontally striped bathing suit and holding a cigar in one hand while wav-ing a fan with the other. The burly bathers spring from their tubs and join in the singing and dancing. Finally, Winnie ascends to the top of what appears to be a colossal bathtub covering the entire rear of the set, and the "Singin' in the Bathtub" number comes to an end. Yet there is one more surprise. Winnie is joined from stage left by a huge man decked out in top hat and tails. The two of them sing "You Were Meant for Me," their duet ending in an embrace. Moviegoers were sure to be startled when they recognized the man as Bull Montana, a famous professional wrestler who also appeared in movies playing a thuggish gangster. To see him suddenly appear in this weird setting and in his incongruous formal attire is jarring, and to hear him sing even more so. His vocalizing is ex-ecrable compared to Winnie's, but that he sings at all adds one final fillip to this, the wackiest and most entertaining sequence in the whole movie.

Funny as it was, the sequence also delivered a poke in the eye to MGM. It was Jack Warner's revenge against MGM boss Louis B. Mayer for having given the name Jacques Warriner to an unpleasant character in *The Broadway Melody*. "Singin' in the Bathtub" is a take-off on "Singin' in the Rain," which had been the big hit song of *The Hollywood Revue of 1929*. The satirical thrust of "Singin' in the Bathtub" becomes particularly biting when Winnie cries out the lyrics "Never take a shower. It's an awful pain. Singin' in the shower's like singin' in the rain!" Moreover, when Winnie and Bull Montana warble "You Were Meant for Me," they are not spoofing another MGM song, they are stealing it outright. "You Were Meant for Me" had been featured in both *The Broadway Melody* and *The Hollywood Revue of 1929*. To have one of his hit songs mocked and another stolen enraged Louis B. Mayer. He considered suing for damages but abandoned the idea after he calmed down.

In *The Show of Shows* Winnie appears to enjoy herself immensely. Her ebullience is, however, more a display of her talent and professionalism than of her true state of mind. She later told an interviewer that she didn't want to do any more "odd jobs like the bathtub gag in 'Show of Shows.'" In Winnie's view, "That was one of those things they started making on the spur of the moment, when they shove you onto the set in an idle half-hour and request you to be comical." Well, she most certainly had been comical, spectacularly so. If she really had not been afforded ample direction and preparation time, then her accomplishment was all the more remarkable. Unlike most of Winnie's other early appearances on film, both of her scenes in *The Show of Shows* still exist (although sadly, only in black and white), and they are now the best surviving evidence of those rare qualities that raised her to stardom on the stage prior to her movie career. Anyone who watches her put over "Pingo Pongo" can readily see why the "Song a Minute Girl" headlined in vaudeville, and anyone who views the "Singin' in the Bathtub" production number will understand why Winnie shone in *George White's Scandals* and other Broadway revues.

While *The Show of Shows* was still in production, but with Winnie's scenes in the can, Warner Bros. set her to work on another feature called *She Couldn't Say No*. By making Winnie the unequivocal star of the latter, Warners made a high stakes bet that once *Gold Diggers of Broadway* was released, there would be such a groundswell of enthusiasm for Winnie that moviegoers would flock to any picture in which her name topped the marquee. Warners was in such haste to meet that expected demand they slotted Winnie into a role that was not a good fit for her. While everything about Winnie's sensational performances in *Gold Diggers of Broadway* and *The Show of Shows*—and for that matter everything about her previous stage career—screamed out for her to star in a musical comedy, *She Couldn't Say No* was no such thing. Instead, it was a melodrama in which Winnie plays a woman besieged by heartache and tragedy.

She is a nightclub singer used to rough surroundings and harboring no illusions. Although deeply in love with her manager (Chester Morris), she knows he does not feel quite the same way about her. Morris is a petty gangster, but he promises Winnie that he will give up his criminal activity. The mob boss (Tully Marshall) allows Morris to try going straight but predicts he will not last long. "You'd come back," Tully says. "It's in the blood. I know. I've seen kids like you strain at the bit and break the traces and run away, but they always come back." Tully also cannot understand why Morris cares for Winnie, who, he observes, is packing "twenty pounds of beef she don't need." Morris's good intentions soon go by the board when he falls for another woman (Sally Eilers), a wealthy socialite, and begins working for the mob again in order to get the money to keep up with her affluent lifestyle. When Morris tells Winnie he is in love with Eilers, Winnie responds that she is willing to give him up. "Oh, what's the use of crying over spilled milk and melted hearts or apple sauce or nothing; it's life, ain't it?" she says. She adds, however, that she thinks he is making a terrible mistake. She says he is infatuated with Eilers because he always has been "a guy who wanted to climb out of his class," but for Eilers he is just a new pet, a novelty that will soon fade. "She'll commence to look you over for fleas," Winnie predicts. "She'll notice that you don't speak her lingo. . . . Then she'll realize that her Russian Wolf Hound is nothing more than just an ordinary Pollack mug."

Disconsolate after losing Morris, Winnie struggles to keep her emotional turmoil from ruining her performances as a singer. Her piano accompanist and devoted friend (Johnny Arthur) does his best to comfort her. Eventually she gets back on track, scoring big with one of Arthur's new songs and landing a role in a Broadway show that becomes a runaway success. As the story nears its climax, Arthur has just persuaded Winnie to marry him when a policeman arrives to report that Morris, grievously wounded in a shoot-out, is asking for her. Winnie races to his bedside. He tells her he realizes now that he would "have been the luckiest fellow on earth to have had you." His dying words are, "I'm going, Winnie, and I'd like to fade out calling you my pal." In the film's final scene, back at the theater Winnie is about to be called to the stage when she learns that months earlier Morris secretly provided the backing for her Broadway show. Reassured that he really had loved her, she finds the strength to go on.

Never before had Winnie attempted a serious role, so everyone involved—and especially Winnie herself—probably wondered if she could pull it off. The only reassuring thing was that being cast as a nightclub singer afforded her considerable opportunity to make use of her vocal talent. Over the course of the movie she sings five songs. Three of them are humorous, which means she is a sort of female Pagliacci, masking her personal unhappiness while striving to entertain. By far the best of the three is "Pingo Pongo," the same number she had put across with great success in *The Show of Shows*. Another one, "The Poison Kiss of that Spaniard," is a brief and rather labored piece about a "Spanish hill billy" who "kissed me and that made me silly." The third is "Bouncing the Baby Around," which advises mothers to amuse themselves by doing just that. The lyrics are funny, although nowadays child welfare advocates would likely protest if mothers were urged to "spank his little bottom" and "use the kid as a medicine ball."

Besides the three comedy tunes there are two serious ones, and it was those two that became popular hits, selling widely as sheet music. "Watching My Dreams Go By" and "A Darn Fool Woman Like Me" are wistful laments, but that posed no problem for Winnie, who had proved long ago that she could put over a serious ballad when called upon to do so. Unfortunately, *She Couldn't Say No* is a lost film, so we cannot now see or hear Winnie's evidently impressive rendition of those songs.

She Couldn't Say No was completed just as *Gold Diggers of Broadway* premiered. The positive response to the latter, and especially the over-whelming praise for Winnie's part in it, showed that the Warner Bros. decision to make Winnie a star had been a wise one. Now they put her to work on another feature, this time a more appropriate vehicle. *Hold Everything* is a musical comedy that revolves around the world of box-ing. A stage version starring Bert Lahr had been a big hit on Broadway. Now Roy Del Ruth directed the film adaptation. Winnie was partnered with Joe E. Brown, an actor whose career paralleled Winnie's in moving from vaudeville to Broadway and then to motion pictures. A spirited co-median with a remarkably large mouth, Brown had been praised for his supporting role in *On with the Show*, although he had not scored anything like Winnie's sensational hit in *Gold Diggers of Broadway*. Consequently, Winnie was given star billing and a much higher salary when she and Brown were assigned the leads in *Hold Everything*.

Another role went to an actor and singer named Georges Carpentier. He plays a boxer preparing to fight for the light heavyweight champion-ship of the world. Carpentier was eminently suited for the part, because he actually was a former prizefighter who had been light heavyweight champion (and would have become heavyweight champion in 1921, had he not been knocked out by Jack Dempsey). In marked contrast to Carpentier, Joe E. Brown plays a second-rate boxer and sissified braggart who is to be a contestant in a preliminary bout preceding Carpentier's

big match. Bert Lahr later complained that Brown copied the effete mannerisms Lahr had displayed in the stage show (and would use again in
his unforgettable role as the Cowardly Lion in *The Wizard of Oz*), but of
course Lahr was hardly the first performer to adopt such a persona. Winnie plays Brown's girlfriend. Most of the film's comedy revolves around
Winnie and Brown's tempestuous relationship. Winnie amorously pursues him, yet also vigorously lambastes him for showing an interest in
other women and for guzzling beer instead of concentrating on reaching
qualifying weight for his upcoming fight. Once she nearly fries him in a
sizzling contraption said to be an electric reducing machine.

Winnie and Brown trade insults, and they both are so adept at physical comedy they make even lame gags work. For example, Brown says to
Winnie, "With that face of yours, you'd be safe in a lumber camp. When
you die, I'll be the homeliest." That remark made no sense, as Winnie
had a pretty face except when deliberately contorting it for comic effect.
The writers did a better job giving Winnie a good comeback: "Every time
you open that mouth of yours," she tells Brown, "it looks like the hanger
for the Graf Zeppelin."

Another well-scripted moment comes along when Brown boasts that
he is "in training for a terrific fight"—which Winnie interprets as a decla-
ration that he is going to marry her! Near the end of the movie, after both
Carpentier and (more surprisingly) Brown have both won their bouts,
Brown drunkenly but sincerely tells Winnie that he truly loves her and
does want to marry her. "But what I wanna know," he slurs, "has there
ever been any other man in your life? Has any other man crossed your
threshold? I demand to know that." A long silence follows. "I ask you
and you answereth not," protests Brown. "What are you thinking of?"
There is another silence. Then Winnie says, "I'm countin'." Still, all ends
happily, with Brown not only reaffirming his proposal of marriage, but
also promising to give up boxing and become a mattress stuffer.

The unfolding of this inconsequential but amusing story is interrupted
at intervals by a song from either Winnie or Carpentier. Two of Winnie's
numbers are in her usual light-hearted vein. In "Take It on the Chin,"
she urges other women to follow her example and treat any love affair
as a fight to the finish, in which "stupid Mr. Cupid" is the referee and female sex appeal the key to victory over any man. In her second number,
"Physically Fit," Winnie declares with a good deal of sexual innuendo
that the man of her dreams need not be intelligent or educated, so long
as he has "muscles of steel" that are "a pleasure to feel." Provided he
knows what Winnie wants and finishes what he starts, then despite not

having an Ivy League degree he can "succeed where college men fail." Winnie's final number, "Isn't This a Cock-eyed World?" is a change of pace. It is a thoughtful and serious song about the painful paradox that we often fall for someone who does not care for us, while we spurn someone we do not care for who loves us. Listening to this song today (which we can do, because the sound disks for *Hold Everything* survive even though its visuals are lost) is a revelation. It makes one understand why Winnie stopped the show at the Palace in 1920 when she put across a serious ballad with "a richness of voice and a depth of feeling" that surprised the critics. That same unexpected richness and depth is present in her rendition of "Isn't This a Cock-eyed World?"

Joe E. Brown recalled decades later that Winnie had been a great partner who never tried to upstage him. Some actors, Brown said, "have their minds more on how they look to the cameras than on their parts, and the results are contrived and artificial. Winnie Lightner was never like that. For that reason she was wonderful to work with." Brown also spoke positively of Roy Del Ruth, describing him as a fine director but also a practical joker. Brown said he once foiled what must have been one of Roy's tricks when he caught him practicing Brown's handwriting. On another occasion Roy succeeded in forging Jack Warner's signature on a memo ordering a prop man to decorate a set with all of the furnishings from the office of another director who was out of town. When the absent director returned and opened the door to his office, he was astonished to find it completely bare except for a telephone sitting on the floor. According to Brown, Roy eventually left Warner Bros., complaining, "no one on the lot had a sense of humor."

After the completion but prior to the release of *Hold Everything*, Warner Bros. offered Brown a contract to make additional pictures with himself as the star. For Brown, *Hold Everything* represented the same kind of personal breakthrough that *Gold Diggers of Broadway* had for Winnie. Brown jumped at the offer, but asked that his elevation to stardom be made retroactive to include the just completed film. Waiving her right to be the sole star, Winnie readily agreed to share equal billing with Brown. Many an actor would have breathed fire at the idea, but here again Winnie was never like that.

With *Hold Everything* wrapped up and Warner Bros. beginning its annual shutdown between filming seasons, Winnie left for an extended sojourn back east. She arrived in New York City in early November. She first visited with relatives, most particularly her foster father, Andrew Hansen, whose wife Margaret had died while *Gold Diggers of Broadway* was in production. It was a great sadness to Winnie that Margaret had not lived to see that great breakthrough film, for up to the time of her death Margaret had read everything written about Winnie and seen every new vaudeville act, Broadway revue, and film short that she had ever done.

But Winnie soon had other preoccupations. It was widely reported that she would make a vaudeville tour, but she did not. According to columnist Walter Winchell, when Winnie saw the rushes of her forthcoming films, she realized that she had "gone the way of Aunt Jemima" and resolved not to make any public appearances until she lost weight. Being curvaceous and a bit on the hefty side had never been a problem in vaudeville or on Broadway, but her body naturally seemed far larger on a movie screen than it did on a stage, where she was viewed from a distance. In the 1920s the slender and rather androgynous figure of the flapper had come to be regarded as the ideal feminine form. There was no way that Winnie could become flat chested and boyish, but she could try to lessen the girth of her waist and thighs. Walter Winchell said the Palace offered Winnie $10,000 for a two-week engagement. She said no even though the offer was five times the highest pay she and her two partners had ever received collectively when they played the Palace. Winchell thought her refusal was amazing. "Now with Winnie rated as a $5,000 per week single act, she won't take it. Golly!" he exclaimed. "Sophie Tucker, who is twice Winnie's size, never got that much coin! And Paul Whiteman, who gets $9,000 a week, has to pay 32 musicians!"

Instead of playing the Palace, Winnie patronized a gymnasium run by Jack O'Brien, a former boxer. Conveniently located in the Manhattan theater district, O'Brien's gym was popular among actors who wanted to acquire trimmer figures. O'Brien's methods were not for the fainthearted. After a newcomer had been weighed and measured, O'Brien and the client would negotiate what was to come off and where. The client was then expected to show up daily for a workout lasting four hours. At each session, heavy rubber bands were fitted over the client's unwanted bulges. The client then donned a bathing suit, padded trousers, and a sweatshirt. Then the client went up to the roof to alternately run and walk ten laps around a track. Back down in the gym, that warm-up was followed by fifteen minutes of vigorous calisthenics, such as swinging each arm alternately to touch one foot and then the other. Then came still more exercises, this time performed while lying on a table. That was followed by a spell of either jumping rope or pulling on a rowing machine. Finally, after a quick steam and shower, the client pressed various body parts against a machine with rapidly spinning bumpy rollers. It is doubtful that certain aspects of O'Brien's regimen, such as the rubber bands and the bumpy rollers, did much good, but the hours of intense exercise burned a lot of calories. It worked for Winnie. She shed seventeen pounds in just three weeks.

Months later some of the reviews of *She Couldn't Say No* must have reassured Winnie that her weight-loss effort had been worthwhile. One critic, although sympathetic, remarked upon how bulky Winnie looked in the movie, adding, "Anybody with the substantial proportions of a good old Pennsylvania barn who can compete with the lovely ladies of the screen and put it over as well as Winnie does, once again deserves a hand and a big one." Another reviewer said, "A word for the future. If you think Winnie is too fat to be cute, watch her next film. They say she has gymed off about twenty pounds."

Although Winnie refused to be seen before losing weight, she had no objection to being heard. Consequently, anybody who tuned in to New York City radio station WPAP at noon on 20 November 1929 got to hear her sing. It was part of the Warner Bros. publicity campaign for the premiere that evening of *The Show of Shows* at the Winter Garden. Winnie did not attend the premiere, but plenty of other people did. The next morning's *New York Times* carried a story headlined, "Police Hold Throng at 'Show of Shows' / Drive Horses on Sidewalk to Check Rush of People Eager to See New Talkie." The story went on to assess the film favorably, and presently Warner Bros. published an advertisement quoting ten other New York City newspapers describing *The Show of Shows* in such glowing terms as "an extraordinary production" (*Morning World*), "spectacular and colorful" (*Telegram*), "a photoplay extravaganza that is lively, entertaining and well staged" (*Herald Tribune*), "the most elaborate, highly technicolored spectacle that has come in since the first talkie began" (*Sun*), and "the Revue to End All Revues, for surely none can top it in presenting to the public a miraculous melange of entertainment" (*American*).

Winnie's fame had been growing since the release of *Gold Diggers of Broadway* three months earlier, and *The Show of Shows* only added to her luster as the first great female comedian of the talkies. Such was her drawing power that when *The Show of Shows* went into national release, some local theater managers named only Winnie in their advertisements for the film, ignoring all seventy-six of the show's other stars. Although the picture was popular, it fell short of Jack Warner's grandiose expectations. With a domestic gross of $1,259,000 and foreign receipts of $336,000, it earned considerably less for Warner Bros. than the *Holly-wood Revue of 1929* had for MGM, which was particularly disappointing in view of the vastly greater cost of producing *The Show of Shows*. Winnie's "Singin' in the Bathtub" sequence was an inspired act of revenge on Jack Warner's part, but Louis B. Mayer got the last laugh at the box office.

"Singin' in the Bathtub" had a long afterlife. The sheet music was published by the long established firm of M. Witmark and Sons. That meant more revenue for Warners, which had recently purchased the Witmark company. Several artists made phonograph records featuring the song. The first Looney Tunes cartoon, released by Warner Bros. in 1930, was called "Sinkin' in the Bathtub" and was a parody of Winnie's parody. It is remarkable that Winnie herself never made a commercial recording of this, or indeed any of the many other songs she turned into popular hits over the course of her career on stage and screen. She never explained why not, but the answer may simply be that she had insufficient financial incentive. Warner Bros. owned Brunswick Records from April 1930 through December 1931 yet never released for popular sale any recordings featuring Winnie. Had Warners done so, it would be a lot easier now to hear Winnie's hit tunes sung in her own splendid voice.

While not persuading Winnie to make phonograph records, Warner Bros. did succeed in keeping her in their stable of film stars by signing her to a lucrative new contract. In an agreement dated 22 November 1929, she agreed to make three movies during the fiscal year beginning 2 April 1930. She was to be paid $25,000 for each picture. The contract specified that in screen credits and advertising her name would appear before that of any other female member of the cast. The contract gave Warners the option to retain Winnie's services for one or two subsequent years in exchange for even greater remuneration. Should the company elect to keep her on for the year beginning 2 April 1931, she would be paid $35,000 for each of three pictures. If thereafter the company decided to exercise its option for the year beginning 2 April 1932 she would make a further three movies at $50,000 each.

The Warner Bros. publicity department worked feverishly to boost Winnie's fame. Photos of her modelling the latest fashions appeared in the women's pages of newspapers, and she was pictured along with other female stars in advertisements for Lux soap. Newspapers from coast to coast printed accounts of her background. Those accounts were, however, so varied that one wonders why Warners could not at least have been a bit more consistent with its myth-making. Often Winnie was said to be from Greenpoint, Brooklyn, a very different place from her actual birthplace of Greenport, Long Island. Other times she was said to have been raised in Manhattan, which was true, and educated in the public schools there, which was not. Sometimes she was said to have spent her childhood in Buffalo. Almost always, Buffalo was named as the location of her first vaudeville appearance. That was true, but the descriptions of that first appearance were wildly inaccurate. Usually it was said to have been an amateur contest rather than a professional engagement. Never was there any mention of her having had two partners in her act. Instead, she was said to have performed solo, with the unique exception of one fanciful report that said she discovered her comic talent when she forgot the words to a song while she and her sister were doing their "cornet and singing act" in a small town in Indiana.

One story about Winnie's first vaudeville appearance that was published innumerable times said she intended to be a serious singer but got caught in a rainstorm on her way to the theater. When she stepped out onstage she was muddy and dishevelled. The audience laughed at her appearance and kept on laughing when she sang. She had no choice but to play along. Thus it was that she became a comedian. The tale clearly is nonsense, both because it is implausible that a performer would change career tracks solely because of one unfortunate experience, and also because there is ample evidence that Winnie's comic talent emerged gradually rather than bursting forth all at once on that fateful day in Buffalo. Fictitious though it was, the story contributed to an image of failed femininity that became a key aspect of Winnie's screen persona. Advertisements and publicity releases regularly used phrases like "the rowdy tomboy of the talking screen" to describe her.

It was claimed that Winnie regretted being labelled a tomboy and wished to play roles where she would be taken seriously. Supposedly one of her ambitions was to play Lady Macbeth. Supposedly she also longed for roles in which she could be feminine and sexually desirable. "Evidently I'm not the type," she said resignedly, according to one report. "I'd like a picture in which I could be a lady and have sleek and desirable men bidding for my favor. But the writers and directors seem to be against me." It was even asserted that Winnie pined to be more feminine not just in film roles, but also in real life. The idea that she suffered deep angst over her inadequate femininity was elaborated most fully in a feature article in *Photoplay* entitled "The Tomboy of the Talkies." The article portrayed Winnie as deeply unhappy, "doomed by her type and talents to be a comedienne when her heart of hearts longs for the admiration, love and shelter given her more feminine sister." All her life she had missed out on "the two things that should be every woman's lot—happiness and protection." Left motherless at birth, she had suffered through a childhood filled with "poverty, grief, memories of rough places on life's path." The implication was that Winnie had been emotionally damaged and masculinised by her traumatic childhood. She wished she could be soft-spoken and demure like her sister, but just couldn't help being noisy and aggressive. That explained why she had suffered through three failed marriages and still could not find Mr. Right.

The *Photoplay* article spun an elaborate myth from an artful mix of half-truths, lies, and omissions. It was true that Winnie's mother had died birthing her, but the article neglected to add that Winnie was reared from infancy by foster parents who loved her as their own. While the economic circumstances in which she grew up might be considered poverty by today's standards, they most certainly were not when Winnie was a girl—or for that matter in the 1930s. Winnie did remember being in some rough places, such as the empty lot where she beat up a bully, but she recalled them with amusement rather than grief. She had been a little tomboy in pigtails, but was glad of it. Winnie and her so-called sister must have had a good laugh over the claim that Winnie pined for the happier life that Theo supposedly enjoyed. Winnie had been through three failed marriages, but the article neglected to mention that the first two had been little more than brief flirtations. More importantly, the article omitted the fact that Winnie had by now settled into a happy relationship with Roy Del Ruth.

As Warner Bros. began gearing up for the release of *She Couldn't Say No*, Winnie was scheduled for another radio broadcast, and this time she was to be heard nationwide on the twenty-two stations of the CBS network. A barrage of publicity announced that on the evening of 29 January 1930 the Kolster Radio Hour would feature Winnie Lightner and the Columbia Orchestra doing songs from her new picture, as well as some already released. The broadcast was nearly derailed at the last minute. For years the poorly managed Kolster Radio Corporation manufactured more of its pricey home consoles than it sold. In November 1929 the company went into receivership, and now the receivers decided to pull the plug on the Kolster Hour. Rather than disappoint her expectant fans, Winnie went ahead with the program despite having to forgo the $1,500 that had been promised.

She Couldn't Say No premiered on 14 February 1930 and then played simultaneously at two theaters in Manhattan and one in Brooklyn. At the Beacon Theater, which had opened on Christmas Eve as the new

Warner Bros. showplace on the Upper West Side, *She Couldn't Say No* enjoyed the distinction of being the first film to be held over for a second week. Later on it did reasonably good business elsewhere, at least judging by reports from Washington, Philadelphia, Pittsburgh, and Minneapolis, but it was not among Warners's top ten earners that season. A theater manager in Minneapolis reported, "Male customers didn't seem to care much for this, but feminine comment was all to the mustard and that's what counts mainly. Opening three days big and then trade tapered off. One of the best weeks house has had, however, in several months; several thousand bucks above recent averages."

Critical response to the film was uneven. Many reviewers said that its focus on nightclubs and racketeers was a tired cliché. All of the critics agreed, nevertheless, that it was entertaining and well worth seeing because Winnie's singing was as good as ever. One reviewer said that the best aspects of the picture were Winnie's "use, with a vengeance, of the slang that comes with checkered vests and sparklers," together with the fact that "the author did not seek to prevent Winnie from singing. As if anybody could." (Inconceivable as it seemed at the time, in less than a year Warner Bros. not only could, but would stifle Winnie's singing.)

Where the critics differed most was in their assessment of Winnie's foray into serious acting. Some thought she had done well. One predicted, "Winnie Lightner, the stage's greatest contribution to the screen since the advent of Al Jolson, will win millions of new fans" by proving "she can play on the heartstrings; and, above all, she can hold the undivided interest of even the most restless theater-goer." Another agreed, saying Winnie was "heartsome and convincing. You laugh at and with, and feel terribly sorry for her." Others were less impressed. A writer in *Variety* gave tepid praise, saying that "when called upon to go dramatic" Winnie was "not bad with it." Mordaunt Hall in the *New York Times* said flatly that when portraying "the more serious emotions" she was "not good."

Some thought Winnie simply did not belong in a serious role, not because she could not handle it but because it was a waste of her talent. Harry Evans in *Life* predicted that "there will be lots of very sophisticated people who will be blowing their noses" watching Winnie in the deathbed scene with Chester Morris. Yet to Evans, Winnie's success in moving viewers to tears was beside the point. "Miss Lightner," he said, "is a most entertaining comedienne, but like all comediennes she feels constrained to prove the versatility of her art by going in for torch songs and death scenes. Now don't be silly, Winnie. Anybody who can roll them in the aisles as you do is a nut to aspire to big moments. There are a hundred tear-jerkers in the movies to one consistent fun-maker, so stick to your stuff." Evans's comment was unfair, for Winnie's dramatic role had been thrust upon her by Warner Bros., not chosen by her to show off her versatility. She was under contract and had to do as she was told. She couldn't say no.

Winnie did not attend the premiere of *She Couldn't Say No*. Instead, on that very evening she began the first in a series of personal appearances that occupied the remainder of her stay on the East Coast. Big-time, two-a-day vaudeville was now, strictly speaking, extinct, for even the Palace had added a third show on Sundays. Yet the shrunken but substantial small-time carried on. The Loew's organization still offered performers a solid thirty-nine-week tour of its presentation houses and lesser outposts, and there were many hundreds of other cinemas where the feature film was similarly supplemented by variety acts. In September 1928 Warner Bros. had taken over the Stanley-Fabian chain of 270 theaters. Warners now paid Winnie a reported $4,000 a week to headline vaudeville bills at some of the top Stanley houses in New Jersey and Pennsylvania. It proved a good investment, for Winnie attracted enthusiastic crowds that came to see her rather than the run-of-the-mill films that accompanied her appearances. In Philadelphia the week's takings at the box office reached $57,000. At the first show there were standees six deep who cheered as Winnie belted out "Physically Fit," "Bouncing the Baby Around," and "Singin' in the Bathtub." As always, she gave the audience its money's worth. Benny Ross, a veteran vaudevillian who both emceed and performed in the stage shows, reported cheerfully in *Variety* that Winnie was "banging the stuffins' out of me."

Meanwhile, two thousand miles away in Los Angeles, *Hold Everything* premiered on 20 March 1930. It received excellent notices. Edwin Schallert of the *Los Angeles Times* said, "Joe E. Brown and Winnie Lightner 'tear loose,' and the outcome is a riot." Their comedy delivered a "knockout wallop" as their verbal sparring released "a storm of hilarity." Schallert praised Brown at length, especially for his climactic fight scene, but added that Winnie "is really amazingly good." Harry Burns in the *Hollywood Filmograph* said that Brown and Lightner were like Punch and Judy come to life: "The laughs came like tornadoes, and the audience was tickled pink. . . . At no time have we heard so much laughter in any theater in Los Angeles as we heard at the premiere showing at Warner's Hollywood, for *Hold Everything* just panicked them. Punch and Judy were the whole show." Sid Silverman in *Variety* pronounced the film "probably the best comedy picture Warners has turned out since talkers came in. Certainly the best musical comedy for laughs to date." Silverman said he "wouldn't be surprised if Warners had another *Gold Diggers* in *Hold Everything*. It's a corking laugh picture."

On 18 April *Hold Everything* was the opening attraction at the newly named Warner Theater (formerly the Grand) in Pittsburgh, and four days after that it performed the same function at the sparkling new Hollywood Theater in New York City. Warner Bros. had hoped to premiere *Hold Everything* at the Hollywood but had been thwarted by construction delays. Still, few New Yorkers knew that the film had been showing for a month out on the West Coast, and its first appearance in Manhattan was heralded with all the hoopla of a world premiere. In a radio show heard coast-to-coast on the forty stations of the NBC network, Winnie delivered songs from the movie, and Joe E. Brown joined her in voicing some of the dialogue. At the premiere itself, New York mayor Jimmy Walker joined what *Film Daily* called "as distinguished an audience as has silk-hatted its way into a Broadway playhouse opening in many a moon." Situated on Broadway at Fifty-First Street, the Hollywood was the first picture palace in the city to be designed and built specifically for talkies. It was also the last grand cinema to be built there before the deepening Depression halted such endeavors. Although it sported an art deco facade and lobby, along with state of the art equipment and acoustics, the Hollywood was surprisingly traditional in its interior decor, a lavish French Baroque confection that included fluted columns, gilded cherubs, a five-ton chandelier, and murals of seasonal scenes such as "Birds Nesting," "Fruit Picking," and "Tending the Yule Log." The auditorium also had an enormous stage, even though Warners had no plans to make use of it.

Hold Everything received mostly positive comment from the local critics, although they were more restrained than their West Coast peers. Mordaunt Hall of the *New York Times* said the picture was "a gusty affair" that "aroused many a wave of laughter." Joe E. Brown's fight scenes "afforded no little merriment," and "the Technicolor effects in these scenes are especially good, most of them being in focus." In addition, "there are some pleasing songs and Miss Lightner does her share in her own way to enliven the episodes in which she appears." A reviewer for the *Brooklyn Standard Union* said that *Hold Everything* "has everything to make you laugh and make you like it." The reviewer also remarked that "there are no mammoth production scenes, for which Allah be praised." That was an early hint at what would soon become all too evident to the

Hollywood moguls: The public was becoming overdosed on musicals. More pointed criticism came from the *Wall Street Journal*'s critic, who thought the film's action skipped about too much, and also that "Winnie Lightner and Joe E. Brown try hard to put their comedy over, but they seldom rise to points of real interest." In that reviewer's singular opinion, "Even Miss Lightner's songs are not very effective." The reviewer did join with everybody else in praising the quality of the Technicolor, which he called "the highest point of perfection yet achieved," but pointed out a serious flaw in the sound: "Abe Lyman and his band furnish the music. In one scene the camera is focussed on Mr. Lyman and his drums, but the microphone seems to have been placed elsewhere, for the result of Mr. Lyman's efforts is inaudible, while the music emanating from his fellow-musicians is clearly recorded." The Hollywood Theater had the best cinema sound system then in existence, but Warner Bros. and other filmmakers still had things to learn about sound technology.

Of the eighty-two films that Warner Bros. produced in its 1929–30 season, Winnie appeared in three of the best moneymakers. Only *She Couldn't Say No* failed to place in the top ten. *Hold Everything*, with total earnings of $1,332,000 ranked eighth; *The Show of Shows* at $1,559,000 was fourth; and *Gold Diggers of Broadway* at a spectacular $3,967,000 was number one.

Winnie was in New York when *Hold Everything* premiered in Los Angeles, but she was back in Los Angeles when it opened in New York. Having completed her round of personal appearances in the east, she boarded the New York Central's *Twentieth Century Limited* for the overnight run to Chicago, then changed to the Santa Fe *Chief* for the longer journey to Los Angeles. She arrived home in Hollywood the evening of 30 March 1930. Roy Del Ruth welcomed her back. Soon they were working together again, this time on a movie that eminently suited Winnie's comic talent. It was called *The Life of the Party*.

CHAPTER 9

A Singer Silenced

ON THE AFTERNOON OF THURSDAY 27 MARCH 1930, JUST BEFORE
Winnie strolled down the red carpet to board the *Twentieth Century Limited*
at Grand Central Terminal, a newspaper reporter asked her how she felt
about leaving the great metropolis where she had spent so many years
touring the vaudeville subway circuit and starring in Broadway revues.
"I'll miss New York," she replied, "but Hollywood is a great place. Extras
get seven dollars a day there for doing nothing but sitting around the set
waiting for something to happen. The theater was never like that!" The
following Sunday evening when she stepped down from the *Chief* at La
Grande Station in Los Angeles, she encountered another reporter who
posed much the same question. This time she did not say she would miss
New York. Instead she declared, "Hollywood seems more like Broadway
than Broadway itself. Nearly everybody who made the Great White Way
what it is now claims Hollywood as their chosen abode."

The talkies had indeed drawn a great wave of talent westward. The
four principal supporting roles in Winnie's next picture, *The Life of the
Party*, all went to veterans of Broadway who had shifted their focus to
Hollywood only recently. But a look at what subsequently became of
those same individuals reveals something Winnie did not foresee: Many
of the Broadway people who came to Hollywood in the first flush of the
talkies did not flourish there and soon vanished from the movie business.
Just a year after Winnie said that all of the heavy hitters from Broadway
were now in Hollywood, a columnist would calculate that of the sixteen
most prominent stars of the stage who had come west to work in talkies,
only seven remained. Even Al Jolson, once such a superstar, had seen his
appeal fade. Winnie was among the lucky ones still going strong.

The love interest in *The Life of the Party* was supplied by Irene Delroy
and Jack Whiting. The other chief supporting roles went to Charles

139

Butterworth and Charles Judels. Irene Delroy had appeared in a silent movie released in 1921 but otherwise spent her career on the stage, working throughout the 1920s in Broadway productions, especially revues. Jack Whiting also spent the twenties on Broadway, appearing in a dozen musical comedies. Delroy and Whiting both moved from New York to Hollywood in 1930 but stayed only about a year. Delroy made three movies, but then married a real estate tycoon and quit show business altogether. Whiting made four pictures, but then mostly reverted to stage work. Charles Butterworth was another 1930 arrival from Broadway, and but unlike Delroy and Whiting he stayed on in Hollywood. Over the next fifteen years he appeared in more than forty films, including two more with Winnie. Finally, Charles Judels had been in many Broadway productions in the twenties, including the two editions of *Gay Paree* in which Winnie starred. He had made a handful of film appearances in the years since his movie debut in 1915, but in 1930 his movie career really took off. He appeared in eight features that year, ten the next, and scores of others throughout the following two decades.

All four supporting players, like Winnie herself, were well suited to their roles in *The Life of the Party*. Each had a different style of comic acting, and they bounced off one another with sparkling results. The laughs start coming right after the opening credits and never let up. First comes a title card: "New York was originally purchased from the Indians for six dollars and thirty cents—the thirty cents was for Brooklyn." That sets the tone for the whole picture as pure farce. It also hints at the Manhattan setting and con artist swindling that are to come. The title card gives way to exhilarating images of Broadway by night with theater marquees glowing, electric signs flashing, and vast crowds thronging the sidewalks. The camera zeroes in on a storefront, then moves inside. There Winnie and her pal (Irene Delroy) are at work as sheet-music pluggers. (There is an inside joke here, in that Delroy complains about the lousy songs they have to sell, while the wall behind them displays the actual sheet music from Winnie's hits in her earlier pictures.)

Into the shop comes a volatile Frenchman (Charles Judels), whom Winnie and Delroy know to be the owner of a classy fashion house. Flirting with the girls, he has Winnie do a song titled "Poison Ivy," but then declines to buy a copy. Rebuked by the shop proprietor for wasting the girls' time, Judels flies into a rage. He grabs handfuls of sheet music and throws them into the air (Winnie helpfully hands him one pile), then goes outside and smashes the shop window with a garbage can. The angry proprietor blames the girls for the mayhem and fires them.

Back home in their apartment, Winnie tries to convince Delroy that instead of hunting for new jobs, they should become gold diggers. Delroy is not persuaded until she learns from a newspaper that her boyfriend has dumped her to marry a rich widow. After that she declares her willingness to con the very gold out of men's teeth. Winnie rejoins, "We'll take the teeth too and sell 'em to the Elks as watch charms." (That was a funny quip at the time, but nowadays requires explanation: Fraternal societies flourished during the 1920s, and the use of an elk's incisor as a watch charm became so popular among members of the Benevolent and Protective Order of Elks that the animals were killed in alarming numbers until conservationists persuaded the Elks to discourage the practice.)

Winnie and Delroy attend a lavish fashion show at Judels's establishment and talk him into lending them a pile of expensive gowns with the understanding that they will come to his apartment that evening. When they send a mocking telegram instead of showing up for a hot time, he flies into another rage, this time wrecking his own home. Meanwhile, the two women escape to Havana. There they check into a grand hotel and pass themselves off as wealthy widows. Learning that the hotel guests include a certain Mr. Smith who has made millions from a new soft drink, they resolve to snag him as a husband for Delroy. Unfortunately, there are two Mr. Smiths in the hotel, and the girls have focused on the wrong one. Their quarry turns out to be a male gold digger who thinks he is latching on to a rich widow. Meanwhile, Delroy falls in love with the rich (she and Winnie didn't know this yet) Mr. Smith (Jack Whiting), much to the consternation of Winnie. Winnie's frustration mounts owing to her encounters with an eccentric Kentucky racehorse owner (Charles Butterworth), who shows up at the most inopportune times, such as when Delroy fakes a fainting spell just outside Mr. Smith's door in hopes he will emerge to rescue her. Every time Winnie hollers for help, Butterworth appears with a glass of water. Even worse, Judels arrives on the scene, demanding payment for his gowns and smashing more mirrors and furniture. "I am glad I did not lose my temper," he says, after obliterating a room.

With their gold digging scheme in tatters and the hotel about to evict them, Winnie decides the only hope for her and Delroy is to bet their last dollars on Butterworth's horse, Butterworth having assured Winnie that it is a sure thing. When Butterworth's jockey is found passed out drunk just before the race, Winnie puts on his silks, takes his place at the weigh-in ("You're a little heavy," says the official in charge), and then rides the nag herself. So does she win and save the day? No, she does not. The horse, frightened by a black cat shooed onto the track by some baddies, bolts and runs the wrong way. Winnie is thrown from the saddle, landing in a mud puddle. But of course there has to be a happy ending. Whiting forgives Winnie and Delroy for their deception, pays off Judels and the hotel, and asks Delroy to marry him. Then Butterworth proposes to Winnie with the memorable words, "Ever since I met you I can't think of anything else. I'm wondering if you'd marry me so I can forget you. . . . I think we could be very happy. I'm away a lot. Occasionally I might drop in at night." Thus Winnie, too, lands the man of her dreams.

Thanks to Roy Del Ruth's superb direction, this ludicrous story unfolds at a brisk pace, and the talents of the splendid cast are fully exploited. Delroy's feminine restraint balances Winnie's garrulous aggressiveness, while Judels's slapstick demolitions contrast with Butterworth's deadpan inanities. The script is studded with good lines, including a great pre-code one delivered by Judels in the scene at his fashion emporium where he shows his creations to Winnie and Delroy. Pointing out one gown, he explains that it was made for a princess. The one next to it, he then declares, "the prince wants to wear, but his mother will not let him." Even the script's bad lines often are delightfully bad. In one scene, Smith the gold digger tries to impress Winnie and Delroy by extolling the beauty of Venice. Their dialogue surely must have been poached from some ancient burlesque routine:

SMITH. Do you know Venice?
WINNIE. You mean the girl with her arms cut off?
SMITH. I love Venice. It's so easy to get around.
WINNIE. Yes, such a wonderful streetcar system.
SMITH. And the gondoliers! Did you like the gondoliers?
WINNIE. Oh, they were gorgeous. We had one growing in our
    backyard, only the frost killed it.
SMITH: Have you ever been on a Cook's tour?
WINNIE: Us on a cooks' tour? My dear, we can't even boil water
    without burning it.

The Life of the Party was filmed in Technicolor, which Roy Del Ruth put to especially good use in displaying the beautiful gowns of the fashion show, as well as the colorful decor of the hotel in which most of the later action occurs. The picture also just missed employing an important technological innovation in that Warner Bros. planned originally to film it on

65 mm stock so that it could be projected onto a doublewide screen. Had that been done, *The Life of the Party* would have been one of Warners's earliest widescreen features, a concept Fox had already pioneered with its 70 mm "Grandeur" system. Falling revenues led Warners to shelve the idea, however, and by the end of the year all of the studios had abandoned their experiments with widescreen (and also television).

While it narrowly missed displaying the new technology of widescreen, *The Life of the Party* was one of the last films to employ the old technology of sound-on-disk. The quality of sound-on-film had improved so much that it was pointless to continue using the cumbersome Vitaphone process of capturing only the visuals on film while recording the sound separately. Warner Bros. had long been distributing all of its films in both formats but still obstinately insisted that direct recording to disk was "by far the best method." While there no longer was any real justification for that claim, it was true that the Vitaphone system, too, had seen much improvement. Multiple cameras could now be synchronized, and films and disks could be edited simultaneously without difficulty. The camera and its operator no longer had to be enclosed in an airtight box weighing half a ton. Now the camera was merely covered by a "blimp" that weighed just thirty-seven pounds. That meant filming could easily take place outdoors. Consequently, some scenes of *The Life of the Party* were shot not on the Warner soundstage in Burbank, but fifty miles to the east in Riverside, where that community's mission revival architecture stood in for Havana. For the dramatic horserace sequence, the entire cast, along with a whole trainload of "atmosphere" (the cheapest category of extras), were taken even farther afield, to the Agua Caliente hotel and racetrack in Tijuana, Mexico. There the filming was plagued at first by an abundance of insects. The problem was solved with an equal abundance of insecticide sprayed onto carpets, furniture, and even clothing. "Boy, oh boy," Winnie later said, "there are sure no flies on me in *The Life of the Party*."

Although moviemakers always try to work expeditiously, it is inevitable that actors spend much of their time waiting around between takes. During one such lull, Winnie, Delroy, Whiting, and Judels gathered around a piano that happened to be on the set and began singing corny old songs like "Get Out and Get Under." That led to a good-natured competition to see who could remember the oldest song. Winnie won when she came up with "You Can't Play in My Back Yard," a tune from the 1890s she said she had learned from her Irish aunt. Before anybody else could think of an even older one, the command "Quiet on the set" rang out, and filming resumed. Shooting, which began on the first of May, was not finished until July.

The studio lights had scarcely cooled before Winnie faced them again. While *The Life of the Party* was in production, *Hold Everything* became a huge hit. Consequently, Warner Bros. announced that Winnie and Joe E. Brown would be paired again in another comedy to be called *Sit Tight*. Churned out quickly and at a third less cost than *Hold Everything*, partly because it was in black and white rather than Technicolor, *Sit Tight* shamelessly repeated the formula that had worked so well the first time. The main difference now was simply that the sporting milieu in the movie was switched from boxing to wrestling.

Brown again plays a cowardly braggart, this time a wrestler who boasts about the fancy holds he learned via correspondence school. That he is actually a big sissy is underlined by the pansies that decorate his apparel. He tries to woo Winnie, but she spurns his overtures. He works at Winnie's gymnasium, where both shapely young women and ill-proportioned old men exercise. The storyline closely parallels *Hold Everything*. This time Winnie trains a handsome young man (Paul Gregory) to become a champion wrestler, over the objections of his girlfriend (Claudia Dell). The story climaxes with Brown and Gregory each winning both his wrestling bout and the hand of the woman he loves. The final bouts were filmed outdoors, apparently just because it was now easy to do so. The story, to belabor the obvious, lacks originality. And the scriptwriters did little to enhance the proceedings. When Brown asks, "What are you trying to do, make a monkey out of me?" Winnie replies, "No, nature beat me to it." That is about as witty as the dialogue gets. Pretty much the only thing that saves the picture from becoming a snore-fest is its plentiful supply of slapstick comedy performed by Winnie and Brown.

Winnie is named first in the credits, but it is more Brown's picture than hers. Her best moments come in the first reel as she supervises the guys working out in her gym. She slaps them around both physically and verbally, yet also uses feminine charm to sweet-talk them into doing her bidding. The rest of the movie consists largely of Brown running around trying to escape from various assailants while falling over furniture or blundering into the ladies' dressing room. Winnie does come to the fore again in a scene where Brown, having been knocked unconscious, dreams that he is a sultan surrounded by his harem within a magnificent palace. Into this setting comes Winnie, dancing sensuously. When the camera lingers on her derriere, the sultan picks up a telephone and orders his broker to buy a thousand shares of American Can. The scene is so elaborate that one might wonder why Warners was willing to pay for it. The answer is that it cost virtually nothing. The set and costumes were left over from *Kismet,* a high-budget production that Warners had completed just as *Sit Tight* got underway. Ironically *Kismet* no longer exists, so the dream sequence in which Winnie wiggles her posterior offers a rare echo of a lost film once celebrated for its lavish production values.

While Winnie was making *The Life of the Party* and *Sit Tight* and for years afterwards there was much discussion in the press about her efforts to control her weight. Female readers evidently were keenly interested in the matter, or at least were thought to be. Gossip columnists vied with one another to tell the inside story. Some said Winnie shed pounds by means of a miracle diet whereby she consumed only buttermilk for lunch and soup for dinner. As one writer put it, "Diet continues to be a favorite subject of Hollywood conversation. The Eighteen-Day diet is dead and buried. Lamb chops and pineapple are as out-of-date as last year's hat. All you hear about now is—soup and buttermilk. Winnie Lightner introduced this one, I believe. Anyway, whoever introduced it, soup and buttermilk is the last word in weight-reduction conversations." Three years later another writer noted, "Interwoven in Hollywood's history is a chronicle of diets for the sake of slimness. Nita Naldi started it all, I believe, with some freak menu. There was the era of the baked potato, when stars lived for weeks on nothing but tubers. To Ethel Barrymore is accredited the hard-boiled egg and tomato one. Winnie Lightner led the buttermilk brigade." In 1939 columnist Jimmy Fidler, in recounting "memories that bless and burn," included the time when "Winnie Lightner started a frenzied reducing vogue by announcing that she had lost twenty-eight pounds on a straight diet of bean soup and buttermilk."

Whether Winnie ever followed any such wacky diet is unclear. Perhaps the idea that she did was just a hoax dreamed up by the Warner Bros. publicity department. For one thing, the reports that she was subsisting on soup and buttermilk are at odds with simultaneous reports that she enjoyed preparing good meals when she felt like it or when her cook had the day off. Many outlets printed Winnie's prize recipe for what she called Italian salad. The main ingredients of its dressing were a tin of sardines, two hard-boiled eggs, an onion, and a clove of garlic. The instructions for preparation were: Mash the sardines and finely chop everything else; add one tablespoon vinegar and two tablespoons oil; mix and then chill thoroughly; serve over quarters of head lettuce.

It appears certain that Winnie initially lost weight by working out at Jack O'Brien's gym in New York. Then, after returning to Hollywood, she reportedly was among the many stars who came under the care of Sylvia Ulback, a masseuse and fitness guru. Gossip columnist Patricia Dillon quoted Winnie as saying, "I never did diet, Sylvia did it all." According to Dillon, "Sylvia goes out to Winnie's house, night after night, and pounds her," and Winnie says, "It isn't fair that after all that hard work, Sylvia didn't get the credit." There was, though, another report saying, "Winnie Lightner's figure is the storm centre of a lively fight these days. The star ascribes her new-found slimness to clear soup and buttermilk, but Philadelphia Joe [sic], a gymnasium expert, wants the credit for exercising the pounds off Winnie, while Sylvia, a Hollywood masseuse, threatens a lawsuit because her hard work in rubbing the pounds off Winnie was not mentioned." Later on Winnie was reportedly among the clients of Nate Slott, a former boxer and occasional actor who had become a personal trainer to the stars. That might explain a report of Winnie sparring with a boxing partner and working out with a punching bag. Still later Winnie was quoted as saying, "Each morning before breakfast I combine the juice of one medium-sized lemon with one tablespoon full of honey and drink it. This mixture seems to have qualities that aid in reducing the weight and assist one in keeping the figure, no matter if one eats three square meals a day." Despite all of this confusing and contradictory information, what can be said with considerable confidence is that Winnie worked at keeping her weight in check but found doing so a challenge. "One of my ambitions in life," she was quoted as saying, "is to get rich enough to retire and grow as fat and comfortable as nature intended me to be."

Another preoccupation of Winnie's that received press attention was her alleged reliance on fortune-tellers. One columnist said that during the making of *Gold Diggers of Broadway* Winnie's relatives back east informed her that her foster mother, Margaret Hansen, was ill but expected to recover. However, a psychic told Winnie that Mrs. Hansen would soon pass from this world. Then a telegram arrived saying Margaret had died. There were repeated reports that Winnie consulted clairvoyants and heeded their advice. After Los Angeles prohibited fortune-telling as a commercial activity, a columnist wrote, "Winnie Lightner doesn't think so much of Hollywood since that city ordinance banished the soothsayers and fortune tellers. The comedienne admits she has abided by their dicta and spent a small fortune having her fortune told. Hollywood without them is just no place to live at all." Winnie needn't have worried. The town's plentiful swamis and mystics evaded the law by organizing churches where devotees could still come to be counseled—and of course make a voluntary donation to support the faith.

Related to Winnie's alleged faith in fortune-tellers was her supposed belief in ghosts. She was said to have spent a sleepless night at a hotel in Riverside in fear that she would encounter a specter reputed to haunt the establishment. The most outlandish story connecting Winnie to the supernatural was a terrifying tale she herself allegedly told. "Sudden gusts of wind are dreadful to me," she was quoted as saying. "They bring to me the ghost of a man who was always fleeing from the wind, a man who one night, in the middle of a vaudeville skit, confessed to me that he was a murderer." She explained that this man, whose name was Sloe, was supposed to deliver the line, "You wouldn't go back on a chap like me, would you?" One night he said instead, "You wouldn't go back on a murderer like me would you?" He then turned white and ran from the stage. Hours later the police came to tell Winnie that Sloe had committed suicide, leaving behind a written confession that he had murdered his young wife and buried her body in the backyard of their house on the outskirts of a little town in Illinois. His confession ended with the words, "The wind blew all night." There is no evidence that anybody named Sloe ever performed with Winnie in vaudeville, nor that any person she ever worked with anywhere was exposed as a murderer. Most likely the story came from the fevered imagination of a Warner Bros. publicist. It is possible that all of the reports about Winnie's reliance on fortune-tellers also were fabricated, although that is less clear. Many Hollywood personalities did consult such people, and it would not be particularly surprising if Winnie had been among them.

Between October 1930 and January 1931, Warner Bros. ceased all production. There had always been a break between the company's filming seasons, but this time Warners was especially eager to curb spending in the face of falling revenues. Half the personnel of the publicity department was laid off for the duration, and the company's twenty-four stars and feature players, as well as many directors and writers, were given vacation time. Winnie used the hiatus to make another foray to the East Coast, this time bringing along her two-year-old son, Richard. They arrived in New York City on 29 October. One of the stories about Winnie and the fortune-tellers held that she never rode in airplanes because a mystic had warned her to avoid them. Perhaps that explains why she made her journey entirely by train. On the other hand, in 1930 one did not necessarily have to be clairvoyant to decide that flying might not be the safest way to travel from Los Angeles to New York. Planes flew only during daylight and landed frequently to refuel. The quickest way for Winnie to get to New York would have been to fly from Los Angeles to

Clovis, New Mexico, landing four times enroute; then sleep overnight on a moving train; then fly the next day from Waynoka, Oklahoma, to Port Columbus, Ohio, landing five times; then sleep overnight on a train to New York. The entire trip would have taken about forty-six hours, or thirty-four hours less than was required to make the trip entirely by train. Whether the time saving would have been worth spending all those hours aloft cradling a two-year-old in a twelve-seat prop plane—not to mention taking off nine times and landing nine times—was another matter.

When Winnie reached Manhattan, *The Life of the Party* was already showing in Detroit and probably some other cities. In Los Angeles it opened on 2 November and played simultaneously at both the Warners Downtown Theater and the Warners Hollywood Theater, the first time any picture had done so. To promote the event Warner Bros. launched a barrage of newspaper ads and radio spots, plastered the city with billboards and posters, distributed fifty thousand flyers to households, and sent a "ballyhoo truck" out to roam the streets. A few days later the New York opening was heralded with an even grander flourish. The entire facade of the Winter Garden Theater above the marquee was covered with an immense cloth banner thirty feet high and 155 feet long. Spelled out on it in letters ten feet high were the words, "Winnie Lightner in 'The Life of the Party'—Gold Diggers of Broadway in Havana." Winnie did not attend the New York premiere, although she did provide some advance publicity for it by singing on NBC radio the day after her arrival in the city. The night after the premiere she was guest of honor at a gala ball for Warner Bros. employees held at the Hotel New Yorker.

The Life of the Party won high praise from the great majority of reviewers in both trade and popular periodicals. *Film Daily* said the picture offered "boisterous deluxe screen fun reel after reel" thanks to "a cast which gets laughs out of every inch of material," including Winnie, who "clowns through the show in big league style, shooting a load of personality along with her lines." *Picture Play* described the movie in similar terms, saying it was "rollicking, boisterous fun," that "a funnier film hasn't been seen in a blue moon," and that Winnie's antics "take an added bounce—if you can believe that!—and yield more laughter than before. Strenuous as she is, with her mugging, wisecracking and bumptiousness, she has the virtue of spontaneity and sincerity." Edwin Schallert in the *Los Angeles Times* wrote that Winnie's comedy was "surefire" and the picture "hilarious enough to justify the claims that are being made for her popularity." Mordaunt Hall in the *New York Times* said "the audacious Winnie Lightner" was "no more restrained" in this film than in her earlier ones, and that it was "a bright and merry production, with especially enjoyable quiet comedy contributed by the inimitable Charles Butterworth." There were a few dissenters, however. *Variety's* reviewer said the film was "anemic hokum," and Harry Evans of *Life* called it "trash." Evans said Winnie had ceased to be amusing now that she had "started screaming all of her lines at the top of her voice, and accompanying each whoop with a grimace of some sort."

The general public sided overwhelmingly with the positive reviewers. *The Life of the Party* was held over for a second week at both Los Angeles theaters, and in New York it played for a month at the Winter Garden before moving on to the neighborhoods. When it reached Brooklyn, a review in the *Brooklyn Standard Union* hailed the film as "an unusually successful, exceptionally diverting venture" that released "a hurricane of laughter." The review added, "The exuberant Miss Lightner has never been better. Her vigorous deviltries, her robust spirited style light up the production with a glowing atmosphere. And she receives splendid assistance. . . . The production does not let go for a minute. Surprisingly insane adventures rapidly unfold with a mad felicity. It is one of the best comedies of the year, bound to please almost any fan."

Neither the critics nor the thousands of regular folks who flocked to see *The Life of the Party* knew that the picture they were viewing was not the picture that Warner Bros. had intended to make and in fact actually made. *The Life of the Party* had been planned and in due course completed as a musical comedy. By the time the movie was released, however, the public had tired of the musicals that had gushed forth in such abundance since the birth of the talkies. There had been more of them than anybody wanted to see, and many had been of poor quality. As one British critic lamented, "Personally, during the last eighteen months I have heard more films than was good for me, and have emerged from the ordeal dazed, as if slipping uncertainly from a gin palace into the cool night. When I look back there is the glare of brutal extravagance, of utter falseness, of hideous voices saying and singing unintelligible things, of crude colours, of chorus girls in mechanical exhibitions." Consequently, shortly before *The Life of the Party* was released Warner Bros. decided to remove almost all of the music and convert the picture into a straight comedy. How many songs it originally had and who sang them is unknown, but clearly there were several. Their loss now seems deeply regrettable.

Just one song remained in the film when it was shown in Los Angeles and New York. Reviewers there mentioned explicitly that the picture contained a single tune, "Poison Ivy." Warners had to retain that one because it was essential to the unfolding storyline. It will be recalled that the movie begins with Winnie working as a plugger in a sheet music shop. Charles Judels comes in and asks her to sing "Poison Ivy." She does, but then in rapid succession Judels declines to buy a copy, the shop owner upbraids him, Judels wrecks the place, and Winnie gets fired. It would have been impossible to excise the song without leaving the film audience thoroughly confused. While "Poison Ivy" would have been kept in the picture whether or not it was any good, it is actually quite funny and was tailor-made for Winnie in that it embodies her customary irreverence toward gender norms. In the song a wife boasts gleefully that she has turned out to be "poison ivy," rather than the "clinging vine" that her husband expected. The lyrics include such lines as, "He thought I'd save his money but I took him for every dime," and "He thought I'd stay at home nights singing lullabies, but all I did was roam nights with fifty other guys."

Probably the picture was shown everywhere else in the United States with only the one song, although that is not entirely certain. Newspaper blurbs and advertisements in some locations claimed that Winnie "sings several brand new numbers in her inimitable style," and some of them mentioned specifically a song titled "You Ought to See the Horse," which Winnie presumably would have sung following the race sequence in which she ends up in a mud puddle. The most likely explanation for these curious references to one or even several additional songs is that they derived by mistake from publicity material that Warner Bros. had prepared prior to the last-minute decision to delete most of the music. Still, it is strange that such statements appeared as late as April 1931.

Even greater uncertainty surrounds the question of what music was included in *The Life of the Party* when it was exhibited in foreign markets. It is sometimes said that outside of North America there was no backlash against musicals, and that consequently *The Life of the Party* was shown abroad with all of its music intact. The same thing is said about three of Winnie's later films as well. Such claims hold out the tantalizing possibility that intact versions of the pictures might surface someday. It seems more likely, however, that these claims are erroneous. In the first place, there is no good reason why foreigners should have become any less fatigued than Americans by the surfeit of musicals. It was, after all, a British critic who made the comment about being dazed by the ordeal of sitting through so many of them. Also, when *The Life of the Party* was shown in London, a writer in the *Daily Mail* described it as having "a theme song entitled 'He got poison ivy instead of a clinging vine.'" That the writer heaped praise on the film's excellent acting and sumptuous color, yet gave no hint that there were any musical numbers other than the so-called theme song, implies there were none.

The notion that *The Life of the Party* was distributed abroad with its music intact may have arisen from the same sort of faulty publicity that cropped up in the domestic market. In Australian newspapers, blurbs for the picture sometimes contained statements like "Winnie Lightner sings several brand new numbers," but never specified what those numbers were. Today when lost films surface, they often turn up in Australia. Once a print made it to that faraway outpost of the empire, its British distributors sometimes perceived it as having no more commercial value and did not require that it be returned. In the 1990s an almost complete reel from *Gold Diggers of Broadway* surfaced in just this fashion. It would be wonderful if a version of *The Life of the Party* with all of its original music were to come to light, but it seems unlikely that Warner Bros. ever distributed such a film either at home or abroad.

At present the only surviving version of the picture not only has just the one song, it also exists only in black and white. That, too, is a grievous loss, for the original Technicolor added a good deal to the film's appeal. Critics unanimously praised the quality of the color, some of them saying it was the best they had ever seen. Many commented on the gorgeous scenes set within a grand hotel, and some described the colorful fashion-show segment as a highlight of the picture. Today, when watching the movie in black and white, the hotel decor is mostly just obscure background, and the fashion show comes across as a needlessly prolonged interruption of the action. Some idea of how different the impact of the fashion show was when seen in its original Technicolor may be gleaned from reading that a single gown shown just briefly near the end of the scene had cost Warner Bros. nearly $3,000. Made of white velvet heavily embroidered in silver thread and studded with rhinestones, it was banded around the bottom with a wide swath of red fox fur. Uninteresting in black and white, it must have been stunning in the original color.

While *The Life of the Party* was drawing crowds to the Winter Garden, Winnie was vacationing and visiting with relatives. No doubt she was happy to have family at hand, for while she was in New York her little boy had to have his tonsils removed. Winnie was reported to be deeply worried that the toddler might not be entirely well before she had to leave town, but he recovered quickly. Then Winnie enjoyed herself. A bemused columnist wrote that Winnie's favorite recreation was riding around on the city's elevated transit lines. The columnist appeared mystified by her choice of amusement, but obviously it was a great way to recall her good old days on the subway circuit and see how the streetscape had changed. She must have especially enjoyed taking the "el" that ran along Columbus Avenue with its stop at Sixty-Sixth, the street she lived on as a child. Back then every time she stepped out the front door of her tenement and glanced eastward she could see the elevated trains rattling by, but she rarely if ever had the nickel needed to board one. Now she could ride to her heart's content.

Another columnist told of an incident that occurred one day when Winnie emerged from the Palace Theater after attending its vaudeville matinee. Probably it was on a Monday, as that was when show-business insiders traditionally came to see the new bill. The usual cluster of impoverished boys selling newspapers outside the Palace had been joined recently by a contingent of impoverished men selling apples. Thousands of the latter had appeared suddenly all over Manhattan as a result of an arrangement between the fruit growers of the Pacific Northwest and the City of New York. Stuck with a surplus crop for which there was no market, the growers had arranged for the city's unemployed to be supplied with boxes of apples for which no payment was due until after they were sold. When confronted by the hawkers outside the Palace, Winnie purchased neither fruit nor papers but presented each and every apple seller and newsboy with a dollar bill. Then, as she climbed into a taxi, one small newsie ran up and asked for her autograph. The little guy didn't really know who Winnie was but hoped that flattery might be rewarded. Winnie knew what he was up to but didn't mind. She sent him happily on his way with both her signature and a five-dollar bill.

Perhaps Winnie would not have been quite so generous if she had known that even she would soon feel the sting of the collapsing economy. On 10 December a rumor spread that the Bank of United States, one of New York's biggest financial institutions, was in trouble. Frightened depositors began crowding into the BUS branches and withdrawing their money. The next day the bank, faced with even bigger crowds and with its cash vaults empty, closed its doors. It was the worst bank failure in the city since 1907 and shattered public confidence in the entire banking system. A relatively minor run already underway on weak banks now snowballed into a widespread panic. Across the nation more than three hundred banks failed in the month of December alone. Winnie was among the thousands of people who lost savings. According to columnist

O. O. McIntyre, Winnie deposited $18,000 in the BUS just before it tottered and crashed. Unlike many depositors, however, Winnie had plenty of other assets to fall back on. Moreover, she had earning power that most people could scarcely dream of.

After a month at leisure, Winnie put her earning power to use by making lucrative personal appearances at some of the leading Warner presentation houses. Her fame bolstered by *The Life of the Party*, she was now an even bigger draw than she had been back in February. At the Stanley in Pittsburgh, where she topped the bill of five live acts accompanying the feature film, a local critic described her performance as "slambang, uproarious." The general public agreed. *Variety* reported the Stanley's take for the week as "$36,800; biggest figure here since 'Singing Fool'; sensational gross, with all credit going to Lightner."

During her week in Pittsburgh, Winnie participated in an effort to help those residents hit hardest by the economic crisis. The municipal government had appropriated $100,000 to help the unemployed survive the winter, but already the money was almost gone. The president of the city council reported that seventy-five hundred families had already applied for relief, adding, "No one knows when this depression will end." An organization of former newsboys decided to help out. On 8 December the ex-newsies, some of them now prominent citizens, returned to their old street corners and peddled a special edition of the *Pittsburgh Press* with all proceeds going to the aid of destitute families. Meanwhile "a flying squadron of entertainers aboard trucks went singing from one strategic corner to another, selling papers from the trucks. . . . Ed Lowry, master of ceremonies at the Stanley Theater, with Bernie Armstrong at the piano, auctioned off papers autographed by Winnie Lightner. . . . Papers sold thick and fast as Miss Lightner pleaded the cause of the Hundred Neediest Families." The stunt raised a total of $5,334. That sum may have provided vital assistance to some of the neediest, but it was a drop in the bucket compared to what would have been required to help all seventy-five hundred families desperate for food, coal, and rent money. If the $5,334 had been apportioned equally among them, each family would have received just seventy-one cents.

After the Stanley in Pittsburgh, Winnie played the Earle in Washington, DC. *Variety* commented that even though the film on show at the Earle had been panned by the local critics, so many fans flocked to see Winnie that "the place isn't big enough to hold them." At admission prices of thirty-five, fifty, and sixty cents, the week's takings reached $23,000, "a new box office record at the scale." Winnie left Washington to spend Christmas with family in New York, and then it was time for her and Richard to head back to Hollywood. On the way they stopped off at Indianapolis where, at the Indiana Theater, Winnie put in one more week of personal appearances. As usual, she proved a huge draw, with local railroads announcing special excursion fares so that out-of-towners could take in the show. Neither the throngs that filled the Indiana's more than three thousand seats nor Winnie herself knew that they were witnessing the last stage performances she would ever make. She would continue to make movies, but never again would she step out in front of a live audience to belt out tunes and slay 'em with her mugging and wisecracks.

With her usual knack for missing premieres, Winnie had returned to Hollywood by the time *Sit Tight* debuted back east. The film was shown first at the Stanley in Pittsburgh, where Winnie's brother Fred was featured as a comedian in the accompanying stage show, and then opened on 18 February at the Winter Garden in New York. Critical reaction was mixed, but there was more positive comment than might have been expected given the derivative character of the picture and the slapdash manner in which it had been put together. All commentators agreed that whatever entertainment value the film had was entirely due to the antics of Winnie and Brown, although there was much disagreement as to which of the two deserved more credit. In their overall judgment of the film, reviewers for sophisticated publications like the *New Yorker* and the *Wall Street Journal* were dismissive. The *New York Times* said the picture had "the artificial humor and synthetic situations of a rather sad comedy," except for "the one completely happy burst of comedy" provided by Brown's wrestling match near the end. In contrast, the *Brooklyn Standard Union*, addressing a more down-to-earth audience, said the film was "a familiar but not unamusing affair," thanks to its stars' ability to "endow any comedy with a carefree and good-natured air." All of the trade papers predicted that the picture would succeed at the box office. *Variety* said it had "enough laughs to stand up fairly well in big houses" but was "especially good for the neighborhoods." *Sit Tight* drew enough patronage to the Winter Garden to play there for six weeks before moving on to other New York theaters, and it was held over in several cities. The *Los Angeles Times* began a report on the film's West Coast opening with the headline, "Rough Byplay Hits Bullseye. . . . 'Sit Tight' Wins Jubilant Audience Reception."

Sit Tight, like *The Life of the Party*, was completed as a musical comedy, but then had all but one of its songs cut shortly before release. In *Sit Tight*

WINNIE LIGHTNER

VITAPHONE #1118
REL. NO. 2591.

At the dawn of the talkies era, Winnie appeared in three one-reel short subjects. Belying her pious pose in this publicity still for *Winnie Lightner, the Song a Minute Girl* (1928), her risqué lyrics made her the first person in motion picture history to be censored for spoken words. (Courtesy Ron Hutchinson/The Vitaphone Project.)

Winnie's hilarious antics as a plump, rambunctious chorus girl determined to land herself a man in *Gold Diggers of Broadway* (1929) catapulted her to instant stardom as the first great female comedian of the talkies. (The Shubert Archive.)

One of the few surviving images of Winnie in the mostly lost *Gold Diggers of Broadway* is this fragment in which she woos Albert Gran. No sound track is visible because the sound was on a separate disk. (Courtesy Brian Pritchard, Motion Picture and Film Archive Consultant, Staffordshire, UK.)

Although scores of Warner Bros. stars appeared in *The Show of Shows* (1929), Winnie's drawing power was so extraordinary that some exhibitors named only her in their advertisements.

In the tearjerker melodrama *She Couldn't Say No* (1930), Winnie persuades Chester Morris (right) to stop working for gangster boss William Tully (left), but then Morris returns to crime and ends up dying in her arms. Winnie proved she could play a serious role, but public reaction was tepid.

Winnie had determinedly worked off her excess weight before she strong-armed Joe E. Brown in the hit musical comedy *Hold Everything* (1930).

The two stars promoted *Hold Everything* in a radio broadcast heard coast to coast on 19 April 1930. (Courtesy Ron Hutchinson/ The Vitaphone Project.)

Warner Bros. teamed Winnie and Brown again in *Sit Tight* (1931), but most of the picture's songs were deleted because the public had tired of musicals. The pansies on Brown's robe accentuate his portrayal of a boastful wrestler who is really a big sissy.

The Life of the Party (1930) is a rollicking farce in which Winnie and her pal Irene Delroy are ruthless gold diggers out to snag a millionaire. They flee New York for Havana after conning a fashion designer out of a pile of expensive outfits.

The Life of the Party was filmed in Technicolor but survives only in black and white, dulling the impact of its gorgeous sets and costumes. It also had songs cut prior to release.

In a rare glimpse of Winnie's private life, she and son Richard depart for New York in June 1931. While happy to talk to journalists about her little boy, Winnie did not want him photographed. Her intimate relationship with film director Roy Del Ruth was by then well known to Hollywood insiders but not publicized.

In *Gold Dust Gertie* (1931) Winnie terrorizes ex-husbands Chic Johnson (left) and Ole Olsen (right), but pretends to be prim and ladylike in order to seduce their fusty old boss, Claude Gillingwater.

As the Great Depression deepened, desperate exhibitors tried to entice customers with give-aways and gimmicks. Here a Milwaukee theater stages an elaborate publicity stunt to promote *Gold Dust Gertie*, even though it will be showing there for only three days. (Milwaukee Polonia Collection, digital i.d. kw000268, University of Wisconsin-Milwaukee Libraries.)

the single song retained was "Face It with a Smile." Winnie sang it to Paul Gregory, encouraging him to "bear up and grin" and "cheer up and win." Although Winnie delivered it with her usual verve, the song was neither first-rate nor essential to the storyline. It is therefore curious that Warner Bros. did not jettison it along with the others. That Warners had been wise to cut most of the music—and might have been wiser to cut all of it—can be inferred from the commentary of the *Wall Street Journal's* reviewer, who objected vehemently and at length to the one number that was kept. "Now that Hollywood has decided musical films are not wanted by the public," he wrote, "it would seem almost incredible to expect a film to be produced in which one of the stars suddenly bursts into song without the slightest provocation in plot or situation. Yet that is precisely what Miss Lightner is allowed to do in the present film." The reviewer scolded,

> In two years of experimenting, nothing seems to have been learned about the technique of introducing music into films. We had thought it was clearly established by now that a song can be brought in successfully only when it fits clearly and realistically into the framework of the scenario. Better still, at this juncture in the development of sound films, it would appear desirable either to make pictures entirely devoid of songs or completely dependent upon music throughout their entire length.

Sit Tight was the sixth best moneymaker out of the sixty films that Warner Bros. produced in the 1930–31 season. *The Life of the Party* did even better; it was the company's second best earner. It was first in domestic revenues but lost out in total receipts to *Viennese Nights*, a lavish operetta, because of the latter's exceptional foreign earnings. While both of Winnie's features did well relative to others, they could not escape the devastating impact that the nationwide economic meltdown was having on the entire motion picture business. In the 1929–30 season every one of the top ten Warner pictures had earned over a million dollars, but in the 1930–31 season not a single one yielded that amount. *Viennese Nights* came closest with $950,000, and *The Life of the Party* was next at $897,000. Warner Bros. made a profit of over $14 million in 1929, but only $7 million in 1930. Then, despite fierce cost cutting, Warners lost $8 million in 1931. All of the other Hollywood studios were reeling, too. Fewer and fewer people could afford to go the pictures, and those that could were generating less and less revenue. Theater managers tried desperately to attract custom by reducing admission prices, changing their programs two or three times a week instead of just once, and offering double features. All three of those stratagems helped some theaters remain open, eluding the fate of the many hundreds that had gone dark, but they also meant less revenue for the studios.

In February 1931 Winnie started work on a new picture called *Gold Dust Gertie*. Its production had been scheduled for the previous July but then postponed, at first because *Sit Tight* was shoehorned into the schedule and later because Warners slowed output in order to slash spending. Winnie received top billing in *Gold Dust Gertie*, but was supported by Ole Olsen and Chic Johnson as featured players. Olsen and Johnson had been a top vaudeville duo for many years before Warner Bros. signed them to a contract to make movies, of which this one with Winnie was their third and last.

Gold Dust Gertie is a comedy revolving around the multiple marriages of the character played by Winnie. The film opens with the title card "1925," followed by a brief scene depicting Winnie marrying Olsen. Next comes the title card "1927," followed by a scene that is identical except that this time Winnie marries Johnson. Finally the title card "1931" appears, after which the story proper begins. Olsen and Johnson have each married one of a pair of twins. They did so mainly to keep their jobs at a bathing suit company, where the ultraconservative owner (Claude Gillingwater) is a staunch advocate of enduring matrimony. He also insists that the firm's products refrain from revealing the female form, which means that sales are poor.

Winnie now arrives on the scene, demanding from her ex-husbands the stipends they promised to pay her when she divorced them. The new wives of Olsen and Johnson are furious to learn that their husbands have been married before. Winnie begins wooing Gillingwater by pretending to be a delicate, sensitive young woman of deep moral conviction. He falls for her ruse, and she persuades him to let her design a new swimsuit to be entered in a contest in Florida. Winnie, Gillingwater, Olsen, and Johnson sail to Florida in a yacht, with complications arising en route when the captain of the yacht turns out to be yet another of Winnie's ex-husbands. Upon arriving in Florida, Winnie shows her swimsuit design to Gillingwater. He is horrified by its lack of modesty. Then he sees Winnie in it and decides that revealing the female form is not so bad after all. The suit wins first prize in the competition. Winnie is about to marry Gillingwater when the preacher remembers having presided over her previous marriages and spills the beans. Winnie, Olsen, and Johnson flee in a speedboat. Gillingwater pursues them in another boat, and Winnie fears he has a gun. The boats run aground. Gillingwater catches up with Winnie, only to tell her that he still wants to marry her no matter how many times she had been married before. The happy ending is not shared by Olsen and Johnson. Their angry wives show up in a rowboat, clobber them with the oars, and chase them into the sea.

This ridiculous storyline could have been the basis for a picture just as ebullient as *The Life of the Party*. Winnie was in her element playing the familiar part of a gold digger in hot pursuit of her quarry. Her demure and ladylike masquerade provides a novel twist, being a comic reversal of her usual loudmouthed aggressiveness. She also makes her usual shambles of gender convention by making light of marriage and divorce and, more subtly, using a bathing suit not just to satisfy male expectations, but also as a means of her own empowerment. *Gold Gust Gertie* is a profoundly feminist movie. All of its male characters are steamrollered by this formidable woman who does as she pleases and gets what she wants.

Unfortunately, the finished picture did not live up to its potential. Much of the blame for that shortfall must fall on the director, Lloyd Bacon, who failed to imbue the film with anything like the zest and spontaneity that Roy Del Ruth had brought to *The Life of the Party*. Whereas the opening sequence of *The Life of the Party* brilliantly set the stage for the farce that followed, the opening of *Gold Dust Gertie* is lackluster. The two brief wedding scenes are puzzling rather than amusing, and they do not deliver a clear message that everything to follow is to be taken as pure farce. Consequently, Winnie's initial berating of Olsen and Johnson comes across as shrewish and unpleasant, an impression exacerbated by the fact there is nothing witty in what she says. All of the picture's dialogue sorely lacks funny lines, despite being written by the same Arthur Caesar who had peppered *The Life of the Party* with corkers. The Hollywood studios were becoming increasingly fearful of lobby groups clamoring for censorship. Until *Gold Dust Gertie* was in mid-production it was called *Red Hot Sinners*. The substitution of a less provocative title makes one wonder if perhaps the dialogue, too, was toned down, with funny but risqué lines expunged.

Some of the physical comedy in the picture is similarly uninspired. Olsen alternately opens the transom above an office door in order to eavesdrop on what is going on next door, or closes it to keep from being overheard. Lloyd Bacon evidently thought that action would provoke more and more laughter with each repetition, but it is scarcely funny the first time and downright tiresome after that. All through the movie

Olsen and Johnson have little opportunity to display the qualities that had made them vaudeville headliners. On stage they practiced a unique style of anarchic comedy in which literally anything could happen, from sudden explosions to bizarre props falling from the flies. In the movies, though, they were confined by scripts and storylines that made them come across as eccentric but not particularly entertaining.

Still, *Gold Dust Gertie* has its moments. It even includes a few bits that might not have been allowed under the strict production code introduced in 1934. For example, Olsen on his honeymoon recites a love poem to his bride. She asks, "Do you really feel that way?" He replies, "Last night I felt every way." There is also a scene in which a young woman wearing the prototype of a new bathing suit turns around to reveal a tag that reads, "Model to Be Made." Good physical comedy includes a shipboard scene in which Winnie shoves Olsen and Johnson out a porthole so they will not be seen by Gillingwater, who is knocking at her cabin door. Then she tells Gillingwater that the shrieking he hears is the romantic cry of a lonesome seagull pining for its mate. When Olsen and Johnson are hauled back on board, Olsen sports a giant lobster attached to his backside. A second round of sea-creature slapstick shows up during the speedboat sequence at the end of the picture. After their boat dives underwater, Olsen and Johnson resurface festooned with assorted fish and an eel. Winnie, although dunked along with them, curiously escapes similar embellishment. Perhaps that means she was telling the truth when she later told a columnist that she flatly rejected Lloyd Bacon's suggestion that she take the eel down the back of her neck. The speedboat chase also features another gag in which the trio gets their faces blackened by engine oil, at which point Winnie strikes an Al Jolson pose and exclaims, "Mammy!" That joke can either be condemned as blatantly racist or perhaps defended on the grounds that it merely ridicules the cliché of blackface performance.

Gold Dust Gertie premiered in New York City on 29 May 1931, playing simultaneously at three Warners theaters. The *New York Times* dismissed it as "an abortive affair" comparable to "a conventionally mediocre two-reel comedy of the chair-throwing school." Most other reviews were more balanced. One critic said, "Laughs in this farce may be far between, but when a laugh does come along, it is a hearty one." Another said the film suffered from "a rather weak story. . . . However, Winnie succeeds in keeping the fun going, and she is her usual riot in several of the high spots." Edwin Schallert of the *Los Angeles Times* delivered a remarkably favorable assessment. "It's a wild and raucous hour that that gay soul

Winnie Lightner provides in her newest comedy," Schallert wrote. "If you very much want to laugh here is your chance to laugh." Reports on the picture's performance at the box office were as spotty as the reviews. In Pennsylvania, for example, it was held over in Philadelphia but flopped in Pittsburgh. When released in the United Kingdom under the title *Why Change Your Husband?* it was well received. In London it played for two weeks at the Regal Theater and long afterwards at lesser houses. The *Daily Mail* described it as "a talking picture which moves at great speed and seems to include every known comedy situation. It is a gay and irresponsible affair with a wealth of slapstick and with more than a suggestion of vulgarity in its dialogue."

It is sometimes rumored that *Gold Dust Gertie* originally included songs that were deleted from the domestic release but retained in foreign markets. The modest running time of the movie, only a little over an hour, might be explained by the deletion of musical numbers. Also, several of the publicity photographs for the film include a miniature horse or pony. In one image Winnie, straddles the animal while Johnson holds its head and Olsen its tail. Another photo depicts Olsen and Johnson feeding it castor oil. A third shows them attempting to weigh the pony by planting its hooves on a scale. No such scenes occur in the movie, implying they were removed shortly before its release. Also, one advertisement said the movie included a depiction of Winnie at a knitting mill where bathing suits were made. Again, there is no such scene in the film. Thus some last-minute cutting apparently was done, whether or not it involved any songs. The first Warners publicity release about plans for the picture said that it "is naturally to have some musical features." All later publicity, however, referred to it simply as a comedy rather than a musical comedy, and no contemporary accounts of the making of the film mention anything about songs. Warners had cut the songs from *The Life of the Party* only about three months before *Gold Dust Gertie* went into production, and then did the same thing to *Sit Tight* at about the same time *Gertie* was filmed. It seems unlikely that Warners would have expected the backlash against musicals to subside before *Gertie* was ready for release. Therefore, the likeliest conclusion is that Warners did originally plan for *Gold Dust Gertie* to include songs, but then decided before filming began to make the movie a straight comedy instead. Anybody searching foreign archives for a print of the film that is complete with songs is most likely pursuing something that never existed.

In *Gold Diggers of Broadway*, the feature in which Winnie first burst into motion picture stardom, and in the three films that followed close on

its heels—*The Show of Shows, She Couldn't Say No,* and *Hold Everything*—
Winnie's singing was a huge part of her appeal, just as it had been all
through her years in vaudeville and on the Broadway stage. Nobody
could put over a comic song better than Winnie. Millions of moviegoers
had laughed with delight when she voiced her longing for a mechanical
man or celebrated the simple joy of singing in the bathtub on Saturday
night. She could and did perform serious songs too, plaintive ballads and
sorrowful laments that deeply touched her listeners. It is unfortunate
that the deluge of inferior musicals unleashed by Hollywood in 1930 and
1931 alienated the vast public that had been so thrilled by the arrival of
movies that could be heard as well as seen. It is tragic that the backlash
against musicals caused Winnie's wonderful singing voice to be all but silenced. *The Life of the Party* was a splendid comedy that would have been
even more splendid had it not lost most of its songs. *Sit Tight* and *Gold
Dust Gertie* were lesser efforts, but certainly they, too, would have been
more pleasing if only Winnie had been permitted to make full use of her
musical as well as comedic talent. Musicals would come back into favor
within a few years, but by then it was too late for Winnie to resume her
rightful place as a doyenne of the genre.

Winnie's natural gifts were about to be suppressed in another way as
well. In all but one of her movie roles she had been a comic caricature
of what we now regard as an ardent feminist. Nobody called her that at
the time—they called her a tomboy instead—but from our perspective a
feminist is certainly what she was. In film after film, she blithely ignored
gender convention by being loud and aggressive and by treating men
not as superiors to be deferred to, but as weaklings to be dominated and
exploited. That behavior had gone over well with audiences in 1929 and
1930, but it was far less popular by 1931. As the Great Depression worsened, public sentiment turned increasingly hostile to feminism. Even in
the prosperous 1920s, feminists had made little progress in challenging
traditional sex roles. The great majority of Americans continued to assume that men should be family breadwinners, while women should
concentrate on homemaking rather than careers. When confronted with
the catastrophic unemployment crisis of the 1930s, Americans clung still
more firmly, indeed desperately, to that traditional model of family life.
There were concerted efforts to drive married women out of the work
force so that men could have jobs. School districts fired women who
married. The federal Economy Act of 1932 declared that government
employees with working spouses should be the first to go when there
were layoffs.

Husbands and wives who were struggling to feed their children and keep a roof over their heads did not want to see movies in which traditional gender roles were challenged or reversed. Nor did they want to see marriage ridiculed or divorce treated as a lark. Both marriage and divorce rates plummeted in the early 1930s. Tens of thousands of young men and women fell in love but could not afford to marry and start a family. Tens of thousands of married couples ceased to love each other but could not afford to set up separate households. There were 1,233,000 marriages in the United States in 1929, but only 982,000 in 1932. There were 206,000 divorces in 1929, but only 164,000 in 1932. In that troubled social climate, audiences that once had laughed at stories about care-free flappers, gleeful gold diggers, and fire-breathing feminists no longer found such tales amusing. *Gold Dust Gertie* was the last movie in which Warner Bros. would allow Winnie to spurn gender convention and to lampoon marriage and divorce with the glorious abandon that was her trademark. Instead, Warners now tried to foster a new screen image for her, one that was in tune with the changing times.

CHAPTER 10

Feminism Restrained

FOLLOWING THE STOCK MARKET CRASH OF 1929 THE AMERICAN economy went into a steep decline that lasted until 1933. Winnie Lightner's film career spanned the years of ever-deepening depression and ended just as the first green shoots of recovery started to emerge. While she made movies Warner Bros. struggled to survive by slashing production and promotion budgets, and by closing or selling off many of the theaters and other assets that the company had acquired during its heady expansion in the late 1920s. Warners also tried to cater to the changing public appetite by churning out a series of gritty urban dramas, especially crime and gangster stories, that brought to the fore new stars like James Cagney and Edward G. Robinson. Those films were cheap to make and generated a good return. Neither the gangster pictures nor anything else, however, could outweigh the impact of the economic crisis. Warner Bros. suffered a staggering net loss of $14 million in 1932. The situation then began to improve, though slowly. Warners lost $6 million in 1933 and $2.5 million in 1934. The bleeding stopped in 1935 when the company eked out a meager profit of $674,000, but it was not until 1943 that Warners dug its way out from under the mountain of debt the company accumulated during the Depression.

In the spring of 1931 it was rumored that Warner Bros. would not exercise its option to renew Winnie's contract, "partly on account of salary, and partly on account of musicals being on the wane." The rumor proved false, however, for Warners did not drop Winnie from its roll of stars. Instead, the company tried to reposition her by toning down the strident feminism that had marked all but one of her earlier roles. She would continue to display female capability and empowerment, but no longer would she treat virtually all men as either fools to be spurned or suckers to be milked. Neither would she target marriage and divorce as subjects for easy ridicule.

The studio publicity department now portrayed Winnie as more feminine and sexually appealing than in the past. For example, a fashion spread distributed to newspapers featured Winnie along with four other female movie stars: Loretta Young, Dorothy Jordan, Madge Evans, and Doris Kenyon. All except Winnie wore sumptuous evening gowns, but she was clad in an alluring ensemble described as "silken pajamas for hostess or lounging." Another similar montage depicted six actresses, and again Winnie's outfit was sexier than the others. Lilyan Tashman, Conchita Montenegro, Bebe Daniels, Loretta Young, and Anna May Wong all wore gowns, while Winnie sported a provocative number that fully exposed her well-proportioned legs. The caption read, "Winnie Lightner favors black lace intimate apparel, and throws a negligee of black velvet trimmed with embroidery about her when the phone rings unexpectedly." Actually, the ringing might have stopped by the time Winnie donned the rather cumbersome item, which featured voluminous drooping sleeves and a floor-length cape at the back.

The most egregious example of the effort to rebrand Winnie as a sex symbol was her appearance on the cover of *Police Gazette*, a periodical devoted mostly to articles about sports and crime, accompanied by advertisements for loaded dice, marked cards, and bottled concoctions said to make homemade hooch look and taste like fine spirits. There was nothing at all about Winnie inside the magazine, but the cover showed her wrapped in a fur jacket and nothing else. The caption read, "Here's something very, very nice in a fur jacket. We could crack wise, too, and say the jacket is okay as fur as it goes, but we'll just tell you that the shapely lady is Winnie Lightner. Miss Lightner is giving her idea of what the woman's costume of the future may shrink to. Ho hum! It's all right with us."

Of course the attempted alteration of her public image did not mean Winnie had changed her own opinions about feminism and the place of women in society. She rarely commented publicly on such matters, but on one occasion a journalist recorded a lively conversation in which Winnie, Charles Butterworth, and Dolores Costello discussed whether it was men or women who got more fun out of life. Butterworth took the position that women could enjoy life as much as men because they were now free from the strictures that had confined them in the past. They could take up jobs and professions that had once excluded them.

They could become actresses without being judged immoral. They could play sports and fly airplanes. He admitted that women still could not play football or drive locomotives, but regarded those as minor exceptions. (The idea of women becoming combat soldiers evidently was inconceivable to Butterworth—and, for that matter, the other two participants in the discussion.) Costello agreed with Butterworth, pointing out that women enjoyed some pleasures that men were denied. In centuries past men had adorned themselves with powdered wigs, fine silks, and colorful apparel, but could not do so now, whereas many women derived much enjoyment from following fashions. She also thought it obvious that homemaking was a woman's most important function and naturally took precedence over career.

Winnie disagreed. She said women faced far more constraints than Butterworth supposed. A woman still could not travel unaccompanied without having to contend with "the advances of every Tom, Dick and Harry. She's like a hen that's strayed too near a family of hawks." Any woman who entered the business world, Winnie added, "is hedged with conventions that men are free from. She has to watch her step every moment. And in spite of all the statements that women have freed themselves from the false modesty of the past, she still has to be more modest than she would like to be." Nor was that reality likely to change. "I still think women don't get the same fun out of life that men do," she concluded. "They're handicapped by the conventions that men have built for them. And I see no way out." Butterworth then took a new tack. He suggested that how much people enjoyed life was mostly up to them. Some men, he said, "never get any fun out of life no matter how much leisure or income or opportunity they have. And others can enjoy life no matter how little money they've got. The same with women. Getting fun out of life is a matter of temperament, not of being either male or female." Butterworth thought Winnie would have to concede the point, but she did not. "Why is it, then," she replied, "that nine women out of ten will tell you that they wish they were men? And why not one man in a million will say he wishes he were a woman?" Neither Butterworth nor Costello had an answer to that one, leaving Winnie with the last word.

Winnie had a less roseate view of women's lot in life than did the other two discussants partly because she came from a less advantaged background. Left motherless at birth and brought up by foster parents, she was a working-class girl who never had worn a fashionable dress until Newton Alexander and Theo Lightner hired her for their vaudeville act. Then three failed marriages made her all too aware that it was not easy for a woman to combine matrimony with a career. Dolores Costello, in contrast, was always in a position to indulge an interest in fashion without worrying about the cost. As the daughter of Maurice Costello, a matinee idol in the early days of cinema, she played children's roles in her father's pictures and eventually rose to stardom of her own. As the wife of John Barrymore, she was about to put her career on hold for five years while caring for the couple's infant daughter. Charles Butterworth was already privileged simply by being male, but he also benefitted from a background of relative affluence. He was the son of a physician and earned a law degree before becoming an actor. While in his conversation with Costello and Winnie he trumpeted the alleged freedom of women to pursue careers, he later expressed a less positive view. In a 1936 interview he acknowledged that his wife, actress Ethel Sutherland, had stopped working after they were married. "Thank goodness, she's gotten over acting," Butterworth said. "Matrimony is enough problem without ambition butting in." By ambition he meant of course female ambition.

The first movie to display the shift toward Winnie's new persona was *Side Show*. Filmed in May 1931, it consists of two contrasting storylines. Both center on Winnie, but otherwise could not be more different. One story features the aggressive, tough-as-nails, and always comical character that her fans had come to know and love. The other revolves around a less familiar Winnie, who is stereotypically feminine and emotionally vulnerable. Of the seven feature films in which Winnie had appeared, *She Couldn't Say No* was the only one in which she had played the latter sort of role. The two stories in *Side Show* unfold in alternating scenes. The setting for both stories is a traveling circus complete with big top, sideshow, Ferris wheel, caged animals, and concession stands. Most scenes take place either in and around the sideshow tents where various "freaks" and other attractions are displayed, or else on board the private train that moves the show from one town to another.

The first story is based on the premise that the circus is in financial difficulty and its owner (Guy Kibbee) drunk most of the time. Winnie steps into the breach and strives heroically to keep the show going by persuading employees to keep working despite not being paid. When some of the performers quit, she fills in for them herself. That provides the pretext for a series of scenes that are undeniably funny, if sometimes deplorably racist. In one, Winnie is covered head to toe in black makeup and body stocking. With a top hat over a fright wig, a white dickey on her chest, an alarm clock dangling from her grass skirt, and a huge club in her hands, she is exhibited in the sideshow as a "cannibal chief." When a fight breaks out between the circus folk and some local rubes, she wades in with her club to help quell the riot. She also receives a custard pie in the face—something she had once said she would never do—for the first and only time in her career.

Winnie also appears in two other versions of male drag. First she briefly replaces the sideshow barker, who is otherwise occupied. Then she substitutes for "The Great Santini," a high diver who has quit the show. She dons the departed Santini's bulky coveralls and further disguises herself by pasting a handlebar mustache to her upper lip. Lest her voice give her away, she pretends to be deaf and dumb, using fake sign language that includes flashing a middle finger at the local sheriff. Then, to the applause of a vast crowd, she nervously ascends a 110-foot tower, is set on fire, and plummets into a tank of water, the surface of which is engulfed in burning gasoline. Winnie later explained that she had gamely agreed to climb halfway up the tower, but after that a stunt double took over. The double really did perform the dive exactly as seen in the movie, but emerged unscathed because his asbestos clothing kept him from being burned on the way down, and then the splash that he made put out the flames on top of the tank.

In another episode a male audience crowds into a tent to see "Lady Beautiful, a Picture That Lives." Curtains draw aside to reveal a large picture frame with Winnie inside it in tableau. She wears a body stocking simulating near-nudity (although not very successfully) and tries to appear glamorous and alluring, which is difficult because she is reclining and at the same time pouring a glass of champagne from a bottle she holds high in the air. The audience takes in the scene for a moment, but then somebody blows a loud raspberry. Winnie scowls but holds her pose. Then a kid with a peashooter scores a direct hit on her bum. Winnie bolts upright, crying, "Who did that?" The curtains close quickly, but not before the champagne bottle, swinging on a wire, bops Winnie on the nose.

This classic display of failed femininity contrasts with another scene, one in which Winnie appears as exotic dancer "Princess Mauna Kea, the only living descendant of Hawaiian royalty." Clad in hula skirt and lei, Winnie sings a raunchy number about a "high-brown hoochie-coocher" who mesmerizes men with her "red-hot lips" and "ball-bearing hips." Matching her movements to the lyrics, she invites the audience to "take a look at this, and take a look at that." Her exaggerated moves provoke laughter from the viewers, but she is laughing, too. Although it seems at first that she may fail again, this time she wins over her audience and finishes her performance to a storm of applause.

Henry Jenkins, the only scholar to give Winnie anything like the attention she deserves, hails her Mauna Kea act as an outstanding example of her ability to subvert gender conventions: "At once excessively feminine and awkwardly mannish, Lightner adopts and exaggerates the traditional demeanor of the burlesque queen, glorying in the exhilaration of self-display and self-mastery while ridiculing the norms by which such erotic performances are judged." She makes a spectacle of herself, but it is not the one her audience expects. On the contrary, she "asserts her right to determine the meaning of her performance and to direct the male spectators' attention. She proclaims the attractiveness and desirability of flesh that otherwise falls outside traditional standards of beauty. . . . She becomes a spectacle on her own terms and makes her audience enjoy it."

Another scholar, M. Alison Kibler, points out that while Jenkins rightly celebrates Winnie's spurning of gender norms, he overlooks her stereotyping of brown-skinned island people as exotic, over-sexed primitives. Her Mauna Kea performance undermines gender hierarchy, but supports ethnic hierarchy. Kibler's point is well taken. And it is notable that the filmmakers gave no hint that it was odd for a former Hawaiian princess to be a cooch dancer, thus implicitly endorsing the imperialist assumption that the lesser races have naturally been subjugated and displaced by the superior Anglo-Saxons.

Neither Jenkins nor Kibler mentions that the Mauna Kea episode comes before the Lady Beautiful segment. That ordering lessens the effectiveness of Winnie's challenge to male expectations and gender norms. While Mauna Kea buoys feminist spirits, Lady Beautiful soon dashes them with the unequivocal message that it is males—with or without peashooters—who rule, and that a woman who fails the femininity test must suffer the consequences. Because *Side Show* is a poorly structured film, the ordering of the two scenes may have been merely accidental. On the other hand, the filmmakers may have deliberately dulled the impact of Winnie's feminist assertiveness.

Most moviegoers, of course, did not trouble themselves about sexism, racism, or any other ideological concern. They just wanted to be entertained. Winnie's sideshow antics provide many laughs, and so do her interactions with an eccentric employee (Charles Butterworth) who has a trained seal act. The film contains only one brief glimpse of Butterworth with his seals (with his usual ineptness he drops a ball, whereupon a seal applauds), but in two extended scenes he tries to court Winnie, who bats away his botched efforts. In the first scene, set just outside a circus wagon, their conversation begins as follows:

WINNIE. What do you want?
BUTTERWORTH. Oh, there was something I wanted to ask you. Sorta slipped my mind right now. Oh, do you roll and toss very much at night?
WINNIE. I don't know. Sometimes. Why?
BUTTERWORTH. I was thinking of proposing marriage to you.
WINNIE. You'd be better off if you didn't think at all.

Butterworth, undeterred, gets down on his knees, removes his derby, and declares that he loves Winnie and has decided that he would be "a dandy catch" for her. Winnie enters the circus wagon and slams the door. An elephant trudges by. Following the elephant is an attendant with a broom and shovel who sweeps Butterworth's derby into the shovel and walks on.

In the second scene Butterworth tries again, this time in an even more bizarre manner. He announces to Winnie that he has composed a poem in her honor. "Well, let's have it," she says resignedly. Butterworth then recites his free verse composition, which mainly describes his preference for a plain lettuce salad made without tomatoes, as opposed to a plain lettuce salad made without cucumbers, but ends by declaring that he cannot live without Winnie. She responds, "What a pity you have to die so young" and walks away. Butterworth, apparently not overly upset, muses to himself, "I hope I can sell this poem someplace so it won't be a total loss."

If *Side Show* were made up entirely of those comedy scenes and more like them, it would be a better movie. Unfortunately, the comic element is only half the picture. The other half presents an entirely different storyline, one intended to be taken seriously. In the second story Winnie is in love with the show's barker (Donald Cook), but it is glaringly obvious that he does not care much about her. When, after frantically running around dealing with an emergency, she returns at night to their train compartment, where he is just lounging around playing solitaire, he asks her to fetch him a cup of coffee. "Sure I will, Honey," she replies, and sets off on the long trek to the kitchen car, passing through sleeping cars with curtained bunks and then plain coaches where she has to climb over the sprawling legs of low-level employees. From the start this storyline is hard to swallow. Are we really to believe that a woman who dives through fire and practically holds a whole circus together with her bare hands is so besotted with her layabout boyfriend that she can't tell him to go get his own fucking coffee? The segment does lead to a pretty good joke, though. In the kitchen car Winnie encounters Butterworth. He tells her that he wouldn't ask her to fetch him coffee like that. Winnie's face brightens until Butterworth adds, "I'd have you wear an overcoat."

The plot thickens when Winnie's younger sister (Evalyn Knapp) shows up and wants to join the show. Winnie, although determined that Knapp should finish school and have a better life than the circus, reluctantly agrees to let her stay just for the summer. Winnie then persuades Cook that they should conceal their intimate relationship by not sharing quarters so long as Knapp is around. (That Cook and Winnie have been shacking up is treated quite matter-of-factly, which shows clearly that this is a pre-code picture.) In short order, as any soap opera fan could have predicted, Cook and Knapp fall for each other. Bitter confrontations ensue, and then the two of them run off together. Winnie is devastated. She announces to Kibbee that she can't take it anymore and is going to quit the show. Kibbee pleads with her to stay, urging her to consider the examples of the sideshow's three-legged boy, who can do nothing but sit, yet still gets on with life, and the armless boy, who learned to overcome his disability by using his toes.

The story might have come to a fairly believable conclusion if Winnie had taken courage from Kibbee's remarks and resolved to persevere. Perhaps then the movie could have closed with scenes of a triumphant Winnie being applauded after swinging on a trapeze or being shot out of a cannon. Unfortunately, the scriptwriters came up with a different scenario. Kibbee does not succeed in persuading Winnie to stay. But then Cook and Knapp suddenly reappear, accompanied by Knapp's aunt and her high school boyfriend from back home. Cook explains that no sooner had he and Knapp left than they realized they were making a terrible mistake, so he immediately escorted her home to her auntie. Cook declares that he loves only Winnie and that Knapp wants to go home with her high school sweetheart. The only thing that mitigates the impact of this ludicrously implausible turn of events is that before it can sink in, the movie quickly ends with a final joke. Butterworth rushes in, exclaiming, "The bearded lady's drunk again!" Winnie tries to shoo him away, until he explains that the bearded lady is *shaving*. "What?" exclaims Winnie. "Holy mackerel!"—and rushes out to confront the latest crisis.

Saddled with its storyline of a love triangle that vanishes unaccount-
ably, *Side Show* would have been a flawed picture even if it had been
well constructed. Perhaps it was originally well constructed, given that
Roy Del Ruth directed it, but then between being filmed and being released it was altered so much that it became a hodgepodge of scenes that
seldom segued smoothly from one to the next. One alteration was the
deletion of songs. Warners had hoped that the backlash against musicals
would be over by the time *Side Show* was complete but decided it was
not. How many songs the film originally included is unknown, but when
previewed to the trade press in early July at the Forum Theater in Los
Angeles, it still had two. One was "Cannibal Cafe," which Winnie evidently sang in her blackface role as a cannibal chief, and the other was
"She Came from a South Sea Isle," which she delivered as cooch dancer
Mauna Kea. A contemporary report said that at the preview both numbers "drew long rounds of applause."

To some Hollywood journalists the inclusion of the two songs was
enough to suggest that a sea change was underway. One noted, "Winnie
Lightner warbles twice in her new production" and therefore proclaimed, "Songs are coming back into motion pictures again. That means
that New York's Tin Pan Alley crowd will soon be hitting the iron train
for Hollywood once more." Another declared, "Maybe you have felt it
coming—this return of music to the screen? And did you notice that
Winnie Lightner put across two songs (no less) in *Side Show*? A year ago
Hollywood would have had a violent attack of the shudders if you had
so much as mentioned musical pictures." When *Side Show* premiered in
New York City on 19 September, however, it contained only the "South
Sea Isle" number. The decision to cut "Cannibal Cafe" must have been
made at the last minute, because only a few weeks before the premiere
Winnie sang it on a nationwide radio broadcast obviously intended to
publicize the forthcoming picture.

Despite its defects *Side Show* received fairly positive assessments in the
trade press. *Motion Picture Daily* said the Los Angeles preview received "an
approving, if not a rousing reception." *Variety* said the picture's laughs
and slapstick made it "a safe bet for Miss Lightner's fans to put it over in
a moderately big way" despite its "muddled" storyline about "a shabby
three-cornered affair." *Film Daily* called the film "good popular entertainment" thanks to Winnie's hard work, Butterworth's absurdity, and
the plentiful action scenes. *Photoplay* complained that some of the dialogue was insipid, but credited Winnie and Butterworth with doing "the
best they can with impossible situations and lines," and added that there

were at least "a few funny gags and a very naughty song." In the popular press, comment was less sympathetic. Many local reviewers remarked on the weakness of the picture's melodramatic storyline. A Wisconsin critic wrote, "Everything gets straightened out in the end, and even then it doesn't matter." Furthermore, he added, "Winnie Lightner, in a straight role, is like a fish in strange waters. She should have been given lots and lots of songs." An Iowa reviewer said the picture was "just another talkie . . . neither good nor bad," except for Winnie's hula dance, which was "as low and senseless an exhibition of depravity as we have witnessed in the movies for a long time." These two and many other reviewers also grumbled that a movie about circus life was no novelty, which certainly was true. There had been so many that an entrepreneur named Al Copeland had long specialized in providing the Hollywood studios with everything necessary to produce them. Having furnished the goods for forty-eight previous circus movies, Copeland had required only a day's notice to supply Warner Bros. with the myriad tents, animals, and circus performers that were on view in *Side Show.*

Mordaunt Hall of the *New York Times* said *Side Show* had little to offer beyond some of Butterworth's funny bits and added, "Miss Lightner can scarcely be congratulated on her performance." Hall did admit, however, that at the screening he attended "the audience howled with glee at the high dive scene," and that the gag at the end about the bearded lady shaving also was "really funny." John Scott of the *Los Angeles Times* agreed that *Side Show* held "little interest," blaming it on the filmmakers' inexplicable decision to have Winnie play the contradictory roles of both comedian and serious actress. "Few players," Scott said, "can clown one minute and go dramatic the next." The *New Yorker*'s critic was less scathing. He described *Side Show* as one of those minor pictures that "may reconcile you to life for a while if you wander in on them." He seemed almost embarrassed to confess that he had been "a little bit diverted at times by the roughneck performances of Miss Lightner (Winnie) in the circus scenes of *Side Show*," adding, "I suspect that I must have been in a lenient and amiable mood."

While making *Side Show*, Winnie experienced a personal scare. For years her brother Fred and his wife Roscella had toured vaudeville and presentation houses. Their travels occasionally brought them to Los Angeles. They were there on 10 May 1931, when Fred had a near-death experience. He was among the guests at a swimming pool party hosted by Esther Ralston, an old friend from vaudeville who was now acting in films. Ralston was proud of her ability to swim underwater for long distances, and Fred decided to demonstrate that he could do likewise. Repeatedly he held his breath while doing laps. It was just a bit of harmless showing off, but a few hours later Fred lapsed into unconsciousness as a result of acute heart dilation. Fortunately, he recovered and the incident had no long-term impact upon his health.

Another personal concern may have led Winnie to make a quick trip east after completing *Side Show*. On 13 June she and her son Richard arrived in New York City. On 1 July they were back in Hollywood. Given the long train journeys each way and the brevity of their stay, the trip appears to have been a matter of some urgency. What made it urgent is unknown, but one possibility is that Winnie wanted to persuade George Holtrey to agree to an amicable divorce. If so, she failed. She did not launch divorce proceedings against Holtrey until the following year, and the process then was far from amicable.

Winnie hurried back to Hollywood because she was scheduled to begin work on her next picture, *Big-Hearted Bertha*. It was to star Winnie as the kind-hearted keeper of an actors' boarding house. Warner Bros. was already advertising the film in the trade press, claiming it would give Winnie "the biggest role she ever had" in "one of the most novel comedies Warner Bros. have ever produced." It turned out, however, that Winnie need not have raced home. Despite all of the preliminary promotion, Warners cancelled *Big-Hearted Bertha* because of the urgent need to reduce spending in the face of falling revenues. The entire studio shut down in June and did not start up again until September. Winnie did not face the cameras until mid-October. When she did, it was to make an entirely different movie.

Warner Bros. had acquired the film rights to a Broadway play called *She Means Business*. The show flopped, closing in only a week, but Warners thought its storyline could work in a film if the setting were changed. While the play was set in a women's handbag factory, Warners substituted the more propitious milieu of a theatrical costume company. Warners originally used the same title the play carried, but before filming began the movie was rechristened *Manhattan Parade*. The change was odd, in that the original title accurately reflected Winnie's role in the picture, while the new one had so little relevance to the content of the film that *Variety* thought it must have been "picked out of the hat." It seems likely the title change was made because *She Means Business* was too evocative of the aggressive, feminist Winnie that Warner Bros. was now trying to play down.

In the movie Winnie's husband (Walter Miller) owns a costume company, but Winnie is the brains behind the business, skillfully juggling the myriad demands of customers, suppliers, and employees. Miller suddenly announces that he wants Winnie to give up working and stay home with their little boy because, he says, "Running a business is a man's job; running a home is a woman's job." Winnie meekly acquiesces. (Obviously this is the new, non-feminist Winnie that Warners was promoting; despite being a super-competent businesswoman, she accepts without question that her proper work is motherhood and homemaking.) Months later Winnie learns that Miller wanted her out of the way because he is carrying on an affair with a seventeen-year-old secretary (Greta Granstedt). After letting the business slide, he absconds to Europe along with Granstedt, having promised her that he will divorce Winnie and marry her. Facing up to this challenging situation, Winnie takes charge of the company again and hauls it back from the brink of disaster. Miller then reappears. He has dumped Granstedt and wants to get back together with Winnie. She tells him to get lost. He points out that he still owns the company. Soon sheriff's deputies arrive, instructed to seize all of the costumes and other assets unless Miller receives $35,000. Winnie thwarts him by getting Granstedt to threaten a breach-of-promise suit unless he signs the business over to Winnie. So Winnie triumphs in the end.

This melodramatic storyline is more plausible than the one in *Side Show* but still rather banal. What saved the film from becoming a flop just like the earlier play was Warners's decision to tack on an additional plot packed with comedy. Like *Side Show*, the film has two parallel storylines, one serious and the other comic. The comic story was a response to *Once in a Lifetime*, a Broadway play by Moss Hart and George S. Kaufman that had satirized Hollywood and the talkies. In the play a failed vaudevillian goes west, becomes a film director, and makes a hopelessly botched movie that is hailed as a masterpiece by journalists who mistake stupidity and incompetence for artistry. The comic storyline in *Manhattan Parade* was an attempt by Warner Bros. to spin a similar yarn, but this time satirizing Broadway productions and implicitly arguing that mounting them was every bit as crazy as making movies.

At the start of *Manhattan Parade*, Winnie's clients at the costume company include a pair of business partners (played by the veteran vaudeville team of Joe Smith and Charles Dale) who are former cheese makers turned Broadway producers, and who bicker constantly in Yiddish accents. ("You vas tellink *me*? Say, I vas tellink *you*.") Later on, when

Winnie struggles to revive the company, she is visited by a mad Russian (Luis Alberni), who says he is going to put on a spectacular show and wants to order a vast quantity of costumes. Winnie is thrilled until Alberni reveals that he cannot make a down payment because his personal assets total $6.43.

It dawns on Winnie that she can salvage Alberni's big order if she can persuade Smith and Dale to back his show. She succeeds in doing so because Alberni has such outlandish ideas that Smith and Dale believe he is a genius. Preparations for the production ensue, with Alberni constantly announcing ever more bizarre innovations, such as ripping out the theater's main floor seating to make room for an underwater ballet (with *hot* water), and placing the house orchestra in the balcony, where the musicians are to hum rather than play instruments. Alberni also wants elephants, later switched to ostriches, then back to elephants again. In one scene a couple of elephants are painted with strange designs, one of the beasts sporting a giant question mark on its face. In another scene one of Winnie's employees (Charles Butterworth) walks in leading an enormous ostrich decked out in a frilly costume.

With Alberni's production obviously shaping up as an utter catastrophe, the astute moviegoer can guess how this comic story will end: The zany show will become a surprise hit, and Smith and Dale will profit handsomely on their investment. One of the best things about *Manhattan Parade* is that its makers anticipated that moviegoers will anticipate that surprise ending, and so they supplied instead an ending that is a much better surprise. Alberni's show is not a hit. It is an utter catastrophe. A workman seen clearing letters off the marquee the day after the opening remarks that it was the first show that hadn't made it past the prologue. Then comes the final scene of the film, a sort of epilogue: Smith and Dale, washed up on Broadway, are back running their cheese factory, bickering as always. Business is terrible. A secretary comes in, announcing a potential customer, who turns out to be Alberni. "I want fifteen tons of your finest imported Swiss cheese," he cries. "But I don't want it full of little holes, I want one great big hole!" Smith and Dale leap on Alberni and begin pummelling him.

This entertaining story is punctuated by funny lines, but only one of them is given to Winnie. It occurs near the start of the movie, when she explains to a customer just which costumes are available. "Charlie Chaplin will be in at 6:00," Winnie says. "Cleopatra's out with Lindbergh. I can let you have Madame du Barry, but that will cost you $3.00 extra. You know, Madame du Barry is generally $10.00 a night." Aside from that sly joke, Winnie plays it straight while others put over the comedy. Smith and Dale are extensively featured, and Alberni is effective as the demented impresario. Butterworth delivers some good lines in his usual deadpan manner. Many more laughs are supplied by Bobby Watson, who plays the role of Paisley, an effeminate costume designer. Paisley minces about waving his hands and gushing over fabrics and colors. He throws a hissy fit when Winnie insists he make some costumes in the cerise that the customer ordered instead of the maroon Paisley prefers. "But cerise is vulgar!" he protests. "Maroon is so fluffy. It has such a tender glow." Winnie mollifies him by promising that he can have new drapes for his windows.

While fleeting allusions to homosexuality were ubiquitous in pre-code comedies, including Winnie's, Watson's Paisley is the most blatant portrayal of a gay man that had appeared thus far. It is, it need hardly be said, an outrageous stereotype. Just as African Americans were routinely portrayed as stupid and subservient Uncle Toms, gay men were depicted as frivolous, limp-wristed fairies. The only unusual aspect of the Paisley character is that, although ridiculous, he is not worthless. On the contrary, his talent is critical to the success of Winnie's business. He is, she says, "the best costume designer in New York City," to which he responds that he is "the best costume designer in the whole wide world." Also worthy of note is that when *Manhattan Parade* was released, nobody anywhere objected to Paisley. It is understandable that gay people as a persecuted minority were in no position to complain about being stereotyped, but one might suppose that at least some defenders of public morality would have been affronted. Yet *Film Daily* reported the remarkable fact that *Manhattan Parade* was passed by every state and local censorship board in America without a single cut. There appears to have been a universal public acceptance that homosexuals, like African Americans, were part of the social fabric, like it or not. Beginning in 1934 strict enforcement of the Motion Picture Code would prohibit any portrayal of "sexual perversion." After that, there could be no more Paisleys in American cinema until the 1960s when the code at last released its icy grip.

Although *Manhattan Parade* was made on a constrained budget of around $225,000 (less than half what had been spent on *The Life of the Party*, for example), its sets and costumes were perfectly adequate. Moreover, it was filmed in Technicolor. For about a year most studios, including Warners, had shied away from color, partly because of the Depression's impact on company finances, and partly because of musicals having fallen out of favor. But in the closing months of 1931 color began a modest revival. In early September a new contract between Warner Bros. and the Technicolor company called for several new color films, of which *Manhattan Parade* was the first. Although the color was still of the two-filter type that could not reproduce the full spectrum, it was produced via an improved process that resulted in richer tones and a less grainy image. One cinema projectionist was so impressed he wrote an open letter to a trade paper praising *Manhattan Parade* as "a distinct surprise, not so much in the color itself as in the matter of sharp definition and register. The entire picture is clean-cut and sharp. It is a God-send to every projectionist whose hair is slowly turning gray in the attempt to get good focus in projecting color prints." Better color combined with other factors to make Winnie look prettier and more feminine, in line with her new image. Ruth Morris, a *Variety* columnist, took particular note of the change: "Winnie Lightner looks better in 'Manhattan Parade' than in any of her previous films. Her new strawberry blondness is pressed into even waves that soften the plump roundness of her face. Her eyes are softened with careful make-up. Conscientious dieting has brought her figure down to a smart outline that need not apologize to well cut frocks and ensembles bordered deeply with lustrous furs."

While Winnie's newly glamorous appearance elicited comment, nobody remarked on the fact that *Manhattan Parade* contained not a single song. Preliminary reports had said the picture would be a musical, but Warners decided the time was still not ripe. Winnie was originally slated to do at least two numbers, "Temporarily Blue" and "I'm Happy When You're Jealous." Whether they were cut before release or never filmed is uncertain, but when *Manhattan Parade* was exhibited it contained no music other than an orchestral version of "I Love a Parade" that was played over the opening and closing credits. Winnie's vocal talent, reduced to a single number in *Side Show*, was now suppressed altogether.

Manhattan Parade premiered at the Winter Garden in New York on 24 December 1931 and was the attraction over the holidays both there and at the three Warner theaters in Los Angeles before going into national release in early 1932. Critical reaction was positive, although not overly enthusiastic. Reviewers in both trade and popular papers invariably said the picture provided enough laughs to make it worth seeing. Mordaunt Hall in the *New York Times* wrote the most tepid of the major reviews, yet even he acknowledged that there were funny scenes, especially those involving Smith and Dale. Hall's principal complaint was that the satirical treatment of Broadway lacked even a hint of subtlety. In contrast to Hall,

Muriel Babcock in the *Los Angeles Times* hailed the picture as "mad, merry enjoyable fun, played at a rapid pace." Few of the reviews paid attention to the movie's serious storyline, regarding it as insignificant compared to the comic one.

There were mixed reactions to Winnie playing a straight part and leaving the comedy to others. Muriel Babcock praised her performance, declaring, "Winnie Lightner is excellent. You will probably like her better than ever before." Mordaunt Hall, on the other hand, said Winnie "cannot be said to arouse much sympathy during the unfortunate moments when the narrative takes itself more or less seriously." *Variety*'s critic said that Winnie had been "badly miscast" and that her yielding pride of place to Smith and Dale meant that "the pair is coming in while Winnie goes out, as far as the Warner part of pictures is concerned." That observation proved to be only partially right. Smith and Dale were not on their way in at Warner Bros., which dropped them after just one more movie. The suspicion that Winnie was on the way out, however, proved true.

Even before *Manhattan Parade* had its premiere, *Variety* published two reports, the first datelined 30 November and the second 21 December, saying that Warner Bros. would not be renewing Winnie's contract. Soon gossip columnists Robbin Coons and Louella Parsons said the same thing. With no denial forthcoming from either Winnie or Warners, the news was more or less official by early 1932. Winnie was not alone in facing the axe. In February a columnist in *Photoplay* said that at all the studios "salaries are being cut, options are not being renewed. Honestly, the poor stars don't know where their next caviar canapé is coming from." John Barrymore's remuneration had been slashed from $200,000 per picture to $125,000. Adolphe Menjou had departed for Europe rather than accept similar indignity. "There's not enough box-office to carry Winnie Lightner's salary," the columnist said, and added that the same was true of Anna May Wong.

The decision by Warner Bros. to drop Winnie was undoubtedly based on economics, but Hollywood insiders offered varied explanations as to why Warners not only was dissatisfied with the earnings of *Side Show*, but also saw no prospect that *Manhattan Parade* or any other Winnie Lightner vehicle could do much better. *Variety* blamed the continued backlash against musicals. The hope that inclusion of two songs (later cut to one) in *Side Show* might be a harbinger of better days had been dashed. The complete absence of songs in *Manhattan Parade* showed that Warners had no faith that allowing Winnie to sing again would win favor with the moviegoing public. "With the return to popularity of musical pictures apparently just a song writers' castle in the air," *Variety* said, "Warners has decided to unload Winnie Lightner."

Hollywood columnist Robbin Coons suggested that Winnie's stout figure was another factor in her descent from stardom. Although she had slimmed down remarkably for *Manhattan Parade*, she could not shed the bone structure that Mother Nature had given her. In profile she was wispy thin, but viewed head on she still had hips. "Many a husky corn-fed lass has come to Hollywood and departed in despair," Coons said, "but clinging vines, delicate, dainty little ladies of ethereal weight and negligible waistline have remained to triumph. The camera is kind to them." As examples he cited "doll-like Mary Pickford, diminutive Gloria Swanson, frail Constance Bennett, tiny Janet Gaynor." Coons lamented that if Winnie Lightner left Hollywood "this town will be without a prominent exponent of strong-armed femininity on the screen. . . . Miss Lightner's toughness for comedy purposes in her films made the term 'the weaker sex' ridiculous."

It apparently did not occur to Coons that Winnie's strong-armed femininity might itself have played a role in her departure from Warner Bros., but clearly it did. In both *Side Show* and *Manhattan Parade* the studio had tried to craft a new Winnie, one who was in tune with the social atmosphere of the 1930s. She remained strong-armed in the workplace but was no longer rigorously feminist in her relationships with men. Gone were the days when she shamelessly exploited poor old Albert Gran in *Gold Diggers of Broadway*, or slapped around hapless fiancé Joe E. Brown in *Sit Tight*, or terrorized ex-husbands Olsen and Johnson in *Gold Dust Gertie*. The new Winnie of *Side Show* and *Manhattan Parade* was emotionally dependent upon and submissive to her male partner, an incompatible combination of strength and weakness. Winnie was not convincing as a woman who ran a circus yet slavishly fetched coffee for her boyfriend, or as a corporate Godzilla who nevertheless meekly consented when her husband ordered her to stay home with their kid. No actress could have made such contradictory behavior believable. Warner Bros. could have avoided the conflict by giving Winnie roles in which she either was a full-time homemaker, or else was as submissive to male authority in the workplace as she was in her domestic relationship. But then what scope would there be for her comic talent? What had made her hilarious were her "masculine" assertiveness and her cheerful disregard for conventions of gender and morality.

Faced with a public uninterested in musicals and unsympathetic to feminism, Warners could not star Winnie in any more movies featuring either her superb singing or her gift for gender-bending comedy. No such film had any chance of becoming a hit, and the studio was in dire need of hits as it fought to survive. The attempt to reshape Winnie's image so as to make her more feminine and sexually appealing had achieved some success, but not enough to prolong her stardom. Glamorous and attractive as she was in *Manhattan Parade*, she still did not have the breathtaking beauty of face and body sufficient in and of itself to sustain a career. She was, after all, in her thirties—"old" by the cruel standards of Hollywood—and could not compete with the dewy freshness of a teenager like Loretta Young.

Winnie's career was not over, but it was entering its final phase. She now shifted from starring roles to supporting parts. Doing so enabled her to revert to being more like the good old Winnie who had resisted male domination and thumbed her nose at moral norms. So long as the female star of a picture was stunningly beautiful, unambiguously feminine, and happily acquiescent to male supremacy, the public did not mind if she had a girlfriend who lacked those attributes. Winnie was that friend. In her final four pictures she played the role of an older, cynical, and loud-mouthed roommate of Loretta Young, Joan Crawford, or Mona Barrie. The audience was not put off by her presence because she was there just for comic relief, and her antics merely accentuated rather than detracted from the "correct" behavior of each picture's star.

CHAPTER 11

Best Friends Forever

WHEN WARNER BROS. DECIDED TO DROP WINNIE FROM ITS ROSTER OF stars, she still had one more picture to make before her contract expired. That final feature, *Play-Girl*, was filmed in January 1932. As specified in her contract, Winnie's name comes first in the picture's credits. The real star, however, is Loretta Young. The storyline focuses on Young's rocky relationship with the male lead (Norman Foster). Young marries him and only afterwards finds out he is a gambler. That leads to their breaking up, leaving Young pregnant and alone. No prize for guessing that by the end of the movie they are reconciled just in time for the birth of their baby and all set to live blissfully ever after. Young is a most agreeable leading lady, both dazzlingly beautiful and delightfully feminine. Although she is not totally submissive to her man, her temporary rejection of him is acceptable because she is merely insisting that he fulfill his proper gender role as family provider.

With Young serving as the female paragon that moviegoers desired, Winnie is free to be less conventional. At the start of the film the two women share an apartment and work as salesclerks in a department store. Winnie flirts with the boss (Guy Kibbee) in the hope that he will transfer her to the cane department, where she can meet lots of affluent older gentlemen. When he instead puts her in plumbing supplies, she is furious until she realizes that he did so in order to keep her for himself. In her scenes with both Young and Kibbee, Winnie gets to deliver many amusing lines in her own inimitable style. For example, while at home with Young one evening, Winnie washes her undergarments in the bathtub (accompanied by an orchestral background that includes a few bars from her old hit "Singin' in the Bathtub") and then hangs them outside the window to dry. When a gust of wind sweeps them away, the following dialogue ensues:

WINNIE. Oh! There goes my last panties!
YOUNG. Well, now what are you going to do?
WINNIE. Keep off of stepladders.

When Kibbee takes Winnie for a ramble in the countryside, he happily charges up a hill. Winnie lumbers along behind, hating every minute of it. When at her insistence they stop to rest, Kibbee seeks her counsel on a momentous decision. He confides that he plans to build "a little nest in the country" and wants her advice regarding "the most important room in the house." Winnie, pleased but also slightly scandalized by his broaching so intimate a matter, exclaims, "Oh you!" and pokes him with her elbow. Kibbee then unfurls a catalog of bathroom fixtures. "And you made a mountain goat out of me just to ask me that?" cries Winnie, and storms off down the hillside.

While Winnie is once again a gold digger out to land herself a man of means, this is a relatively subdued version of that familiar role. She does not initially choose Kibbee as her matrimonial target, and when she does end up marrying him, their union results from him pursuing her rather than the other way round. When they return from their honeymoon, Winnie explains to Young that she accepted Kibbee's proposal because "I'm getting kinda old and I gotta find out what it's all about before it's too late."

Although the filming of *Play-Girl* was scheduled to take six weeks, it was finished in only four thanks to some new technological kit. Elaborate theatrical productions had long used revolving stages. Warner Bros. now applied the idea to moviemaking. The filming of *Play-Girl* used two such stages, each containing two complete sets. A scene using one set was filmed, and then a quick revolution brought the other set in front of the lights, cameras, and microphones, all of which had remained in place and required only minor adjustment. Once the second scene had been filmed, the cast and crew moved over to the other revolving stage and shot two more scenes. The elimination of the usual sitting around between set changes saved a great deal of time, and time was money.

Play-Girl premiered in Los Angeles in March and received moderately favorable reviews. Muriel Babcock of the *Los Angeles Times* said the picture's main storyline was hokum, but added that it was "good, honest hokum—to be devoured with greedy eyes by those who like such tales." Most critics praised Loretta Young's melodramatic acting, but many of them regarded Winnie's funny antics as a greater contribution to the entertainment value of the film. *Variety* declared that the picture's main plot was "turgid" and "tediously drawn out," but that it was "saved as mild program material mainly by its gags." *Film Daily* said, "Winnie Lightner's comedy, much of which is pretty broad and snappy, is the chief item of enjoyment." The *New York Times* reviewer implicitly agreed, saying that the picture's "excellent dialogue, particularly as interjected during the more comical scenes," had saved it from "the pitfalls of sentimentalism" and that "a word of praise might well be said for the interpretation of one of the secondary rôles—that of Winnie Lightner."

One especially perceptive reviewer, Frederick James Smith of *Liberty* magazine, observed that in the prevailing social climate "film fans like their heroines to be serious, sexy, and sentimental—but never wise-cracking." Consequently, eccentric comic actresses like Louise Fazenda, Charlotte Greenwood, and Winnie Lightner had to dial back their former exuberance. While Winnie still came across as decidedly tough and outspoken compared to Loretta Young, she no longer was the feminist amazon that she usually portrayed in her starring roles. Smith lamented, "Winnie Lightner, rough-and-ready comédienne, turns mild in Play Girl. She is just a great big sister to the heroine, and the most unladylike thing she does is to take a sock at a sarcastic saleswoman who sneers at her pal." Nevertheless, even Winnie-light was too much for some sensibilities. In Kansas the state board of censors expunged some of her "indecent" remarks from the film's first reel.

When she had completed her contractual obligation to Warner Bros., Winnie was free to use her time as she pleased. It was rumored that she would embark upon a tour of vaudeville and presentation houses, but she did not. Rather, she took on the job of extricating herself from another, more vexing contractual arrangement. The first oblique reference to what she was up to appeared in mid-February when columnist Walter Winchell reported, "Winnie Lightner is having matters rearranged so that she will have more elbow room." Winchell evidently had an advance tip on a story that broke four months later when in a New York courtroom Winnie formally filed for divorce from George Holtrey.

Considering that Winnie and Holtrey had been leading separate lives since she left for Hollywood three years earlier, it might be supposed that either of them could easily obtain a divorce on grounds of desertion. That was emphatically not the case, however, for New York State had one of the most restrictive divorce laws in the nation. Astonishing as it may seem, from 1787 until 1967 the sole grounds for divorce there was adultery. That meant that couples who wished to end their marriage for any other reason nevertheless had to convince a court that at least one partner had been unfaithful. It was an open secret that many husbands and wives, with advice from cooperative attorneys, conspired to fake evidence and perjure themselves in order to persuade the court that adultery had occurred.

There was no chance that Holtrey would collude with Winnie in that way, for he vigorously opposed her divorce action. It appears likely he did so because Winnie was still paying the rent on his Manhattan residence. That seems a reasonable inference, based upon a 1935 newspaper report that Winnie was being sued for $1,016.68 in "rent assertedly due for five months in 1933 on an apartment which Miss Lightner and her husband, George Holtrey, are declared to have leased." Holtrey did everything he could to delay and obstruct Winnie's divorce suit. First he demanded that the case be tried before a jury. Then he launched a separate legal action of his own, suing Roy Del Ruth for "alienation of affection" and asking $250,000 in damages.

Fortunately, Winnie did not require any cooperation from Holtrey in order to press her case. Holtrey was not overly discreet about his extramarital activities. Probably with the help of a private detective, Winnie produced evidence that Holtrey had "misconducted himself" with three different women on a total of eight occasions. Regarding one of those occasions, the evidence was dramatic. According to a newspaper report, Winnie, "aided by her foster father and a crowbar, found her husband, George Holtrey, broker, with a showgirl, Joyce Haley, in a suite in the Dearborn Apartments here early last June." (Most reporting on the case said Holtrey was a stockbroker, but Walter Winchell pointed out, correctly, that he actually was a stagehand.) Holtrey realized it was game over and decided to make the best of the situation. On 23 November the court awarded Winnie her divorce. In announcing the outcome of the case, her attorney said the couple had parted amicably. "They have decided they are going to remain friends," the attorney said, "sharing the affection of Richard (a son of 4) between them, and Mr. Holtrey has discontinued all charges against Roy Del Ruth." In fact, Winnie and Holtrey never had anything to do with each other after the divorce, and Richard grew up using Lightner as his surname and never meeting his father.

Although Winnie had extricated herself from her marriage, she still could not regularize her relationship with Roy Del Ruth. That could happen only if Roy divorced his wife, Olive, but doing so was a daunting prospect. The exhausting months of legal wrangling that had accompanied Winnie's case and the eagerness with which the press reported the lurid details can only have increased Roy's reluctance to begin a divorce proceeding of his own. It was all too evident that Olive would be no more willing to go quietly than Holtrey had been. Moreover, the judicial system was oftentimes less sympathetic to a man who wished to divorce a woman than to a woman who wished to divorce a man. It was considered normal for a woman to be dependent upon a man, whereas a man was expected to fend for himself. Roy therefore remained married to Olive, and she continued to burn through his money. Roy and Winnie continued as before, maintaining separate residences and never calling public attention to their relationship. Whenever Winnie attended social events or show-business functions, she went by herself, or at least that was what the press reported.

Winnie and her son Richard continued to share their home with her old vaudeville partners Newton Alexander and Theo Lightner. When all four of them moved to Hollywood in 1929, Theo already managed Winnie's business affairs. Soon she began taking on other clients as well. In June 1930 she opened her own theatrical agency in the Taft Building at Hollywood and Vine. Her most notable client besides Winnie was swimming champion and actor Johnny Weissmuller. In December 1931 Theo sued Weissmuller, alleging that she was entitled to 10 percent of his earnings from a motion picture contract. Apparently the case was settled out of court, as there were no further reports about it. Whether coincidentally or not, Theo gave up her agency business around the time Winnie left Warner Bros. Afterwards Theo and Newton reportedly became involved in movie production in association with Sol Lesser. (In the 1940s Lesser would become well known as the producer of several popular RKO features starring Johnny Weissmuller as Tarzan.)

As for George Holtrey, after his divorce from Winnie he was able to fend for himself, but his standard of living was a far cry from what it had been when he resided in a luxurious $350-a-month apartment paid for by Winnie. When the enumerator for the 1940 federal census came calling at one of the flats at 53 West Seventy-Second Street in Manhattan, the door was opened by a young woman named Emily Baker. She told the census taker that she and one other person resided there. The other resident was George Holtrey. Baker identified Holtrey as head of the household and herself as a friend. Holtrey, age forty-one, was a stage electrician. He had been employed for twenty-five weeks during the calendar year 1939 and earned $2,500. Baker, age twenty-one (so she said anyway), was a showgirl. She had worked forty weeks in 1939 and earned $600. Neither of them had any other income. The rent on their apartment was $55 a month.

Soon after Winnie won her divorce case, Warner Bros. signed her to appear in a new picture. Winnie's last film under her former long-term contract had done reasonably well at the box office. While no blockbuster, *Play-Girl* earned enough to persuade Warners to make another inexpensive feature along similar lines. The title of the new movie was *She Had to Say Yes*. Winnie and Loretta Young again starred, but this time Young's name precedes Winnie's in the credits. Again they play characters who share both a flat and a workplace. This time they are secretaries at the headquarters of a garment manufacturer. Young's boyfriend (Regis Toomey) is a salesman for the firm. The storyline has more twists and turns than a bowl of linguini.

Toomey gets the bright idea of having the secretaries double as "customer girls" who provide evening companionship to out-of-town buyers. Young is keen to take part despite Winnie's warning that the clients may be expecting more than just conversation. Ostensibly so that he can receive a sales commission but really so that he can see another woman, Toomey allows Young to entertain one of the out-of town buyers (Lyle Talbot). The buyer tries to rape her but backs off after realizing that her innocence is not just a pose. She promptly forgives him, saying (believe it or not), "Oh, I guess it was my fault. I suppose you do feel cheated. I'm just not a good sport, that's all."

After learning from Winnie that Toomey is two-timing her, Young breaks up with him. Toomey, jealously thinking Young has "gone all the way" with Talbot, shows up drunk at her apartment and would have raped her but for the timely arrival of a neighbor. Young begins dating Talbot. He is trying to conclude a lucrative business deal and asks Young to entertain the other party (Hugh Herbert), promising her $1,000 if she can get him to sign the contract. Young does so by luring Herbert into a compromising situation and then blackmailing him. Talbot mistakenly assumes Young landed the deal by having sex with Herbert. After paying Young the $1,000, Talbot lures her to an isolated house where he intends to rape her, but then at the last minute decides not to.

Toomey, who follows them, meets Young as she exits the house. He and Young are seemingly on the brink of being reconciled when Young drops her purse, which falls open. Toomey bends down to pick it up and spies the $1,000 check from Talbot. Toomey angrily accuses Young of having been used, paid off, and discarded by Talbot. Emerging from the shadows, Talbot slugs Toomey and makes him apologize to Young. After Toomey leaves, Talbot apologizes to Young for having doubted her virtue and asks her to marry him. Young accepts, saying (believe it or not), "I suppose it's just a matter of choosing the lesser evil." Talbot says he will drive her back to town, and they will get married in the morning. She whispers in his ear. He smiles, picks her up, and carries her back into the house. The End.

From this convoluted story it may be inferred that: (1) men are inherently unfaithful, manipulative, violent, and possessive; (2) because men are that way it is okay for women to trick and blackmail them; (3) it is okay for men to rape women who are not chaste; and (4) it is reasonable for a woman to marry a man who has twice tried to rape her, if at the time of the assaults he was under the mistaken impression that she was not chaste. All in all, the bizarre storyline makes it rather understandable that public demand for censorship was on the increase.

Winnie's role in *She Had to Say Yes* is limited in that she is assigned no love interest of her own. She just stands up for her pal and makes wisecracks. Some of her one-liners clearly reflect the impact of the Great Depression. When Young says that her unfaithful boyfriend "was different once," Winnie replies, "Yeah, so was the Republican Party." When Winnie then exits their apartment, she quips that she is going out "to see if there's a Depression on at the Automat." Winnie has only one major scene without Young, but it is the picture's comedy highlight. Having spent an evening as a customer girl, Winnie is escorted home by a portly and inebriated client. As she unlocks her apartment door, he crowds against her. She promptly thrusts back her rump, nailing him in the groin. "This is where you get off," she announces. "We don't go any further." He protests, "You mean you ain't even gonna let me say goodnight to you properly?" Winnie responds, "I *am* gonna let you say goodnight to me properly, and *this* is where you say it." There are further exchanges, including one in which Winnie says, "Now you be a good little boy and take your little kiddie-car and go on home before your wifey finds out, see?" The conversation ends with the client saying, "I'm from Missouri," and Winnie replying, "Oh yeah? Well I'm from the Virgin Islands." With that, she slaps his hat on his head, kicks his butt, and shoves him down the staircase. Obviously Winnie could have taught Loretta Young a thing or two about how to handle men. But then, if Loretta had handled men the way Winnie does, the movie would have been over almost before it began.

The first critical response to *She Had to Say Yes* appeared in the April issue of *New Movie Magazine*, which evidently previewed the film well before its release. The brief report was quite positive, saying the picture "goes rather a long way to prove very little but it certainly results in

As societal attitudes turned conservative, Warner Bros. curbed Winnie's feminism by assigning her to contradictory roles in which she is a powerhouse in the workplace, yet submissive to the man in her life. In *Side Show* (1931) she keeps a struggling circus alive by substituting for unpaid employees who have quit. Disguised as "The Great Santini," she performs a high dive after being set on fire by Charles Butterworth.

After being exhibited as a "cannibal chief" she wields her club to help quell a riot.

As cooch dancer Mauna Kea, Winnie sings a raunchy number after being touted by the show's barker, Donald Cook, who is also the lazy boyfriend on whom she dotes.

Warner Bros. tried to foster a more glamorous and feminine image for Winnie by featuring her in fashion spreads in which she modeled "silken pajamas for hostess or lounging" (left) and "a negligee of black velvet trimmed with embroidery" (right). (Courtesy Ron Hutchinson/The Vitaphone Project.)

In *Manhattan Parade* (1931) Winnie runs a costume company with impressive competence, yet is meekly subservient to husband Walter Miller—until he runs off with a young secretary.

Because Winnie's new screen persona did not attract big box office, her stardom ended. In her final four movies she plays the roommate and best friend of the female lead. She tops the cast list one last time in *Play-Girl* (1932), but the real star is Loretta Young.

No longer striving to appear svelte and glamorous, Winnie in *Play-Girl* washes out her ample undergarments to the strains of "Singin' in the Bathtub."

In *Play-Girl* Winnie is a salesgirl in a
department store. She wants to work
in the cane department so as to meet
affluent older gentlemen, but boss
Guy Kibbee assigns her to bathroom
fixtures instead.

In a rare informal shot, Kibbee
and Winnie relax between takes.

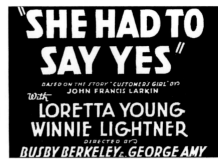

Warner Bros. teamed Winnie and Loretta Young again in *She Had to Say Yes* (1933), but this time Loretta came first in the credits.

Winnie is Joan Crawford's vociferous roommate in MGM's *Dancing Lady* (1933), one of the first in a new wave of musicals. Unfortunately, no studio chose to bring Winnie's singing talent to the fore again in this new wave.

Winnie's last film was *I'll Fix It* (1934) for Columbia Pictures. As roommate and best friend to Mona Barrie, she was named third in the credits but ignored in the advertising.

Snapshots from the retirement years: With son Richard on the boardwalk at Jones Beach, Long Island, during their visit to New York City, 1941. (Courtesy Richard Lightner.)

With Roy Del Ruth and son Tom, 1945. (Courtesy Thomas Del Ruth.)

In her garden, 1955. (Courtesy Thomas Del Ruth.)

With Tom, 1961.
(Courtesy Thomas Del Ruth.)

With her grandchildren, Christmas 1963. (Courtesy Richard Lightner.)

some brisk entertainment. . . . For Miss Lightner it is a throw-back to the old days of 'Gold Diggers of Broadway' and she is funnier than she has been of late. Miss Young is delightful." Most subsequent reviews were negative, however, sometimes scathingly so. The *Hollywood Reporter* said, "Between you and me and the box office, 'She Had to Say Yes' is just so much waste matter." The storyline, complained the *Reporter*, "goes round and round," giving the audience "repetitive blues." After the film's premiere on 28 July, the *New York Times* grumbled that the repeated suspicion of the obviously innocent Young by her boyfriends became irksome: "No sooner has one cloud of doubt been dispelled than another clatters across the horizon, like a creaking movable set in a village opera house." That was unfortunate, added the *Times*, because "the picture has some bright lines and threatens, here and there, actually to become amusing." Although the *Christian Century* condemned the film's "cheap situations" and "vulgar, suggestive 'humor' from Winnie Lightner," most reviewers were not bothered by the portrayal of company girls. *Liberty* magazine commented rather blandly that the film's complicated plot was bewildering but showed "how sex rears its pretty head in competitive business." No reviewer found it weird that Loretta Young consented to marry a man who had twice tried to rape her, which must say something about how social attitudes have changed since the 1930s.

The critics had little reason to mention what now seems a notable fact about *She Had to Say Yes*: It was the first movie directed by Busby Berkeley. How that came about is a tale that began the previous autumn, when Winnie was in the throes of her divorce case. Warner Bros. suspected that the public aversion to musicals might at last have subsided. Warners decided to find out by making a picture called *42nd Street*. A conventional backstage story, it was directed by Lloyd Bacon, but Busby Berkeley was hired to produce three big musical production numbers, which were cautiously positioned toward the end of the film so they could be cut if audiences hated them. Berkeley already had a reputation for imaginative camera work, such as his kaleidoscopic overhead shots of dancers in the first-wave musical *Whoopee!* (1930). Now he was given a budget big enough to create song and dance extravaganzas that ostensibly took place in a theater, but in actuality could scarcely have been contained in Times Square. Pleased with Berkeley's contribution to *42nd Street*, Warners afterwards granted him the opportunity he had long sought to direct a picture of his own. That picture was *She Had to Say Yes*. To be on the safe side, Warners appointed George Amy, an experienced film editor, as co-director. The two men got along well and finished shooting the movie in record time. They made a fair job of it, too, considering that they were saddled with a tortuous storyline and a miserly budget of around $110,000. In the completed picture the clearest evidence of Berkeley's genius is a scene that opens with the whole screen occupied by a pair of shaking maracas. The maracas pull away to either side revealing a violin being played by a person unseen except for his arms. The violin moves aside affording a distant, fuzzy view of a female dancer. The camera moves closer, bringing the undulating dancer into focus. The camera draws back to reveal an elaborate nightclub setting. Finally, the camera pans sideways and then zeros in on Young and Talbot seated at a table.

As soon as Berkeley finished *She Had to Say Yes* he was assigned another project. Instead of waiting to see what the public reaction would be to *42nd Street* when it was released, Warner Bros. made the bold decision to get started on another musical. Again Berkeley was asked to create the production numbers, and this time they were not clumped together at the end of the film. The picture was *Gold Diggers of 1933*. It was a remake of the 1929 talkie that had made Winnie a star, but the new version was adapted to a social and economic climate that had changed beyond recognition. Whereas *Gold Diggers of Broadway* was saturated with the sparkling hedonism of the Roaring Twenties, *Gold Diggers of 1933* embodied the grim realism of the Great Depression. Winnie's movie had ended with an explosion of laughter as she raised her Liberty torch and then forgot her lines. The new version ended with Berkeley's gut-wrenching production number "Remember My Forgotten Man" lamenting the fate of the First World War veterans now standing in breadlines.

The gamble that the public might again be receptive to musicals paid off in spades. *42nd Street* premiered in March. *Gold Diggers of 1933* followed in May. Both were hits. *42nd Street* racked up total earnings of $2,281,000, while *Gold Diggers of 1933* earned $3,231,000. To be sure, even the latter figure was far below what *Gold Diggers of Broadway* had achieved, but it was a spectacular sum for a film released when the national economy had hit bottom and the movie business was on its knees. Of the five biggest studios, only MGM was not losing money. RKO, Paramount, and Fox had all gone broke and were in receivership. The success of the new musicals saved Warner Bros. from following them into bankruptcy by convincing creditors that Warners still had a chance of recovery.

Unlike the musicals, *She Had to Say Yes* made no significant contribution to saving Warner Bros. Opening at the Strand Theater in Manhattan on 28 July, it played there for just a week and brought in an unimpressive $12,000 at the box office. Over the next six months it made the usual rounds, generally showing as part of a double feature, and then quietly disappeared. It gave Warner Bros. no incentive to make any more movies pairing Winnie with Loretta Young. Less understandably, Warners also made no place for Winnie in the new series of musicals that it began churning out in rapid succession. Fortunately for her, however, competing moviemakers immediately plunged into making musicals, too. In June the most prestigious studio of them all, MGM, gave her an opportunity to participate in the emerging second wave of musicals by signing her to appear in *Dancing Lady*.

Dancing Lady was MGM's response to *42nd Street*. It starred Joan Crawford and Clark Gable in yet another backstage story. Winnie again plays the female star's roommate and best friend. As usual Winnie is tough, loud-mouthed, and deficient in femininity. This time, though, the contrast between star and friend is less clear-cut than it was when Winnie was paired with Loretta Young. Joan Crawford is, as expected, more feminine, less assertive, and more respectful of social norms than Winnie, but in her own way she is every bit as tough.

At the start of the picture Crawford and Winnie dance in a burlesque show, and Winnie sings "Hold Your Man." (Oddly, Winnie is satirizing a performance by the star in one of MGM's own movies; "Hold Your Man" was both the title and the theme song of a recent MGM picture with Jean Harlow.) Then the women sashay out a runway that projects from the stage. With vociferous encouragement from the mostly male audience, they begin removing their clothing. Suddenly there is pandemonium as policemen pour in, raiding the theater. The showgirls are hustled outside and into a van. Crawford is mortified, but not Winnie. "Oh, goody, goody!" she exclaims. "We're going on a bus ride. I'm glad I don't have to walk home."

Soon the women are standing in night court, wrapped in blankets and charged with giving an indecent performance. After a police sergeant testifies that he witnessed them doing a striptease, Winnie is called before the judge. She gives her occupation as "hip swinging." Asked to explain "just what constitutes a striptease," she snappily replies, "a good constitution and a couple of zippers!" She cheerfully offers to provide a demonstration, but is hustled away before she can shed her blanket. Next up is Crawford. Unlike Winnie, she is subdued and does not sass the judge. But when asked why she performed a striptease, she is defiant: "If you'd walked the streets looking for a job and hadn't eaten for a week, you'd do a striptease too." The judge pronounces sentence: thirty dollars or thirty days.

Sitting dejectedly in a cell, Crawford is surprised to learn she is free to go. A handsome young upper-class gentleman (Franchot Tone) who had been slumming by attending the burlesque show had taken a shine to Crawford. He followed her to court and paid her fine. After springing her from jail, he takes her to dinner. When Crawford gets home, Winnie eagerly interrogates her and is consternated to learn that her friend does not intend to take full financial advantage of her new admirer. Crawford opens and reads a note that Tone had given her. It criticizes her grammar ("Don't say 'them things'") and encloses a fifty-dollar bill ("to buy yourself a dress without a zipper"). Crawford angrily rips up the note. She is about to do the same with the fifty when Winnie grabs it, exclaiming, "Don't get so noble with the groceries! There's enough in this to eat for a month!" Crawford acquiesces but then says she now owes Tone $80.00 and intends to pay him back. Winnie is beside herself. "Oh, how can you pal around with me and still stay so dumb?" she cries.

Despite her initial resistance, Crawford begins dating Tone. She also tries out for a Broadway show being cast by a top-notch director (Clark Gable). Tone secretly backs the show and arranges for her to be given a place in the chorus. Gable soon recognizes Crawford's exceptional talent and makes her the star. Determined to pursue her dancing career, Crawford rejects Tone's proposal of marriage. She says, however, that she will marry him if the show fails. Tone then withdraws his backing for the show, causing it to be cancelled. Tone's scheme is derailed when Gable resolves to finance the show with his own money. In the end Gable and Crawford realize that they have fallen in love. As in most backstage stories the film climaxes with what supposedly are scenes from the show's opening night. In an obvious attempt to outdo Busby Berkeley, a series of elaborate production numbers appear. In one of them Crawford and her dance partner rise into the sky and then descend in—of all places—Bavaria. The final, surreal production scene features Crawford riding a gigantic art deco carousel with plunging horses and flashing mirrors.

While prominent in the first two reels of *Dancing Lady*, Winnie is glimpsed only sporadically after that. MGM packed the film with so many members of its huge talent pool that there probably just wasn't room for any more Winnie. *Dancing Lady* includes the motion picture debut of Fred Astaire (dancing), early appearances by both Nelson Eddy (singing) and The Three Stooges (jabbing fingers into eyeballs), as well as lesser roles for May Robson, Robert Benchley, Ted Healy, Grant Mitchell,

Sterling Holloway, and Eve Arden. Among the songs in the picture are the memorable "Everything I Have Is Yours" and "Rhythm of the Day." There also are some clunkers. "Heigh-Ho, the Gang's All Here" is both the title and first line of one of them. The second line is "So let's have pretzels and let's have beer." It does not get better after that. Then there is "Let's Go Bavarian," which includes such lyrics as "Here in Bavaria they take good care of ya" and "Get yourself a sweet fraülein, she can help you drink a stein." Not to mention that Germany is a peculiar choice of setting for jolly musical numbers, considering that the Hitler dictatorship was established there while the film was in its early planning stages.

Released in November, *Dancing Lady* scored with both critics and public. Mordaunt Hall of the *New York Times* described it as a backstage story that, although predictable, was more entertaining than most because of praiseworthy acting by most of the cast. He singled out Winnie, however, as "one of the players who is not particularly good." Hall did not explain why he thought her performance below par, and nobody else seems to have shared his negative opinion. *Photoplay* named Winnie among the principals who had done "fine work" in a picture that afforded "top-notch entertainment." The *Hollywood Filmograph* said, "Winnie Lightner makes a decided hit as the companion and adviser" of Joan Crawford in a "marvelous production" that was "bound to be a hit in any theater." *Filmograph* added that MGM "will make a barrel of money." That prediction proved correct. With worldwide earnings of $2,406,000, *Dancing Lady* was MGM's top domestic moneymaker that year. (It was second overall, being edged out by the Greta Garbo drama *Queen Christina*, which earned only a little more than half as much as *Dancing Lady* in the home market, but over twice as much abroad.)

After the release of *Dancing Lady* a whole year went by before Winnie's fans got to see her in another movie. It would be her last. In her contract for *Dancing Lady*, MGM had included an option to use her in additional films but chose not to. That decision may have been a mistake, for moviegoers still enjoyed her comedy. Reporting on his customers' response to *Dancing Lady*, a theater manager in Montpelier, Idaho, wrote, "I wish they had given our old friend Winnie Lightner a break. She is one of the best stars in Hollywood and gets more laughs per minute than the rest put together. They didn't give her much of a part, but she surely had them laughing every time she appeared." Another manager, this one from the little village of Fort Plain in upstate New York, said, "Glad to see Winnie Lightner again in this one. Hope she still stays in pictures. Folks like her."

Cast aside first by Warner Bros. and now by MGM, Winnie began shopping for opportunities elsewhere. In March 1934 the trade press reported that producer Lou Brock planned to team Winnie with Pert Kelton, an actress with a somewhat similar screen persona, in an RKO comedy called *The Great American Harem*. Brock did make the picture, but with its title changed to *Bachelor Bait* and with Kelton but without Winnie. It was just as well that Winnie was left out, because the movie flopped and RKO lost money on it. Then in August Columbia Pictures signed Winnie for a feature called *I'll Fix It*. Winnie's descent from the heights of MGM down to second-tier Columbia was an unmistakable sign that her career was on the wane. Still, she evidently decided that working for a lesser studio beat not working at all.

I'll Fix It starred Jack Holt and Mona Barrie. Holt had been in pictures for decades, whereas Barrie was a newcomer from Australia in her first starring role. In the storyline Barrie is a schoolteacher. Holt is a real-estate wheeler-dealer who is accustomed to getting anything he wants. Winnie, Barrie's roommate and best pal, earns her living giving singing lessons to snotty little girls. Holt has a kid brother (Jimmy Butler) on whom he dotes. When Barrie flunks Butler on a math test, barring him from playing on the school baseball team, Holt persuades her to give the lad another chance. She does, but then catches him cheating. Holt does not believe his angelic little brother would do such a thing, and is determined to get him back on the baseball team. Holt showers Barrie with expensive gifts, but she promptly returns them. After he apologizes for his crude attempt at bribery, she laughs it off and begins dating him. She still will not let Butler play baseball, however, so Holt pulls strings and gets her fired. Barrie's fellow teachers support her with a protest parade, but to no avail. Meanwhile, Holt gets into hot water over a piece of land he allegedly bought because he had inside knowledge that it was to be the site of a new school. Holt was going to skip town, but after Butler bravely confesses to having cheated on his math test, Holt decides that he, too, will face up to his accusers. The story reaches its climax with a public hearing at which Barrie saves Holt's bacon. First she and Winnie destroy a document that would have compromised him. Then Barrie testifies that Holt acquired the land not in order to profit from reselling it, but rather as the site for a splendid playground that he intends to donate to the community. That was news to Holt, but of course he then confirms that he is indeed donating the land. The film ends with Holt and Barrie driving off to start a new life together.

Winnie has little involvement in the main plot beyond serving as Barrie's wisecracking confidante. Because the stringent new Motion Picture Code had come into effect in July, the month before *I'll Fix It* went into production, none of Winnie's remarks is anything like the risqué ones in her earlier films. The only hint at sexual innuendo comes when Barrie announces she has been fired, and Winnie responds, "Who'd you say no to today?" Still, some of Winnie's wisecracks are funny. The best one is her response after Barrie explains that she lost her job for failing Butler on his math test. Winnie declares that if she were Butler's teacher, "He'd have passed so fast he'd have thought last season's Ford was a '35 Duesenberg!"

Winnie's character is given additional scope by a subplot in which she pursues a romantic interest of her own. Early in the movie Holt is accompanied by a faithful but stupid assistant (Edward Brophy), who follows him around like a cocker spaniel while constantly chomping on an apple. When Holt takes Barrie out on a date, Winnie latches on to the clueless Brophy to stop him from tagging along with the courting couple. Winnie forces Brophy to sit down at her piano and sing a duet with her. Their joint performance of "The Moon Does Things to Me" is funny but also charming, as it reveals their growing attraction to each other. It is believable, too, for Brophy obviously is just the sort of dim and docile man who would be compatible with a bright and bossy woman like Winnie. When the song ends, Winnie takes a big symbolic bite out of Brophy's apple. Soon he is marching alongside her in the teachers' protest parade. Winnie and Brophy's reversal of conventional gender stereotypes affords a comic contrast to the "proper" relationship between Barrie and Holt, in which Barrie is feminine and submissive, while Holt is ultra-masculine and domineering.

While the subplot involving Winnie and Brophy is plausible, the main storyline has holes big enough to drive a Duesenberg through. How has Holt become the guardian of his little brother, and why is there such a vast age gap between them? The film gives no clue. (When the movie was made Holt was forty-six, while Butler was thirteen. Few middle-aged men have brothers who are young schoolboys.) How is it that Holt has supposedly done nothing really wrong, and yet is in big trouble because of the land purchase? The movie provides no clear explanation, but at one point seems to suggest that Holt is blameless because the initiative came from other people who were party to the deal, as if that somehow exonerates him. Above all, why is Barrie so astonishingly inconsistent?

First she is the paragon of righteousness who will not bend even at the cost of her job. Then she treats Holt's blatant attempt at bribery as a mere peccadillo, warming to him instead of excoriating him. Finally, she destroys evidence and perjures herself in order to shield him. Why doesn't she tell the truth? The closest the movie comes to an explanation is in its closing scene when Holt says, "For a guy that's turned over a new leaf you sure made a swell liar out of me," and Barrie responds, "I had to do it . . . When you decided to return and face things, I simply couldn't go through with it." The most that can be said for this messy storyline is that the acting is sufficiently skillful and the plot development so rapid that moviegoers might not notice how illogical it all is.

I'll Fix It premiered at the RKO Palace in New York on 9 November 1934. It played there for just one week. The following week it was at the Strand in Brooklyn, paired with a Joe E. Brown comedy. After that it was in wide release, virtually always as part of a double feature. It received mixed reviews. The most enthusiastic assessment came from *Film Daily*, which described it as a "very entertaining, amusing and suspenseful comedy-drama" that was "satisfying fare for any audience." In contrast, *Variety* said that the movie "doesn't quite make the grade." Nevertheless, after critiquing Mona Barrie's looks and wardrobe, Cecilia Agers, whose *Variety* column was aimed at female readers, remarked with seeming approval that "Miss Lightner, besides having no end of pep, gives singing lessons to little girls. Also, Miss Lightner is quite a card. Also, when Miss Lightner registers something, she registers it with every muscle in her face." The *New York Times* review was unambiguously negative. Cruelly headlined "In Need of Repair," it sarcastically described the film's ending: "The schoolmarm decides at the last minute that the fixer is honest at heart, perjures herself with the greatest of ease and she and the fixer—presumably—live happily ever after. Colossal!" The film's premiere engagement was accompanied by five live stage acts, ranging from comedian and headliner Ben Blue down to the Six de Cardos performing on teeterboards. According to the *Times* critic, the picture was "running a definite second to the vaudeville bill."

Winnie had come full circle. In October 1915, only three months after beginning her career, she played the Palace. It was an extraordinary feat, for vaudeville was then the preeminent form of mass entertainment in America, and playing the Palace was the epitome of vaudeville success. By 1934 the entertainment industry had been transformed. Big-time vaudeville had disappeared, and the talkies reigned. Even the Palace had gone to a film-only policy in 1932, although by 1934 it had reverted temporarily to a film-plus-vaudeville format. Winnie had been part of the sound revolution that shifted the center of the entertainment industry from the stage of the Palace to the sound stages of Hollywood. It seems fitting that her last movie premiered in the theater that had been the summit of vaudeville. In 1934 the Palace was no longer a venue of any importance. Major pictures did not premiere there. When *I'll Fix It* opened, it had been a while since the Palace had hosted even a first-run movie, much less a premiere. Winnie's career, too, had waned. Once she had been a vaudeville headliner, a Broadway showstopper, and the toast of Hollywood. But after starring in eight Warner Bros. features, she was relegated to secondary roles. Now even the secondary roles had ended. At age thirty-five Winnie still had half her life ahead of her, but she would never be seen again on stage or screen.

CHAPTER 12

I Never Cared a Hang for Fame

EVEN BEFORE THE RELEASE OF HER LAST MOVIE, COLUMNISTS AND fans were starting to ask what had become of Winnie Lightner. They continued to do so for years, and every once in a while a journalist would seek Winnie out and write about her. Early on she was briefly back in the news when one of her neighbors, an oil millionaire named William F. Gettle, was kidnapped and held for ransom. The police managed to crack the case and rescue him unharmed. Thousands of well wishers welcomed him home. His wife wore a corsage, which, she explained, was a gift from Winnie Lightner. It had arrived along with a card reading, "An orchid to you, Mrs. Gettle, for your courage and bravery." There was also another orchid, addressed "to Mr. Gettle, for your safe return home." A year later a reporter who had covered the case published a note scribbled down while Gettle's fate was still unknown: "Sunday, May 13, 1934. No late sleeping today. Working on Gettle case, assigned to stake home, Beverly Hills. Camped all day in backyard with other reporters, photogs, etc. Mysterious figure suddenly climbed over back fence, landing with a thud in geranium bed. It was neighbor Winnie Lightner. Said she was lonesome."

Winnie no doubt regretted flattening the geraniums, because gardening was one of her retirement hobbies. According to an article in a fan magazine, she enjoyed tending her plants and possessed an impressive collection of implements like trowels and lopping shears. The article went on to offer some of her gardening tips, such as soaping the fingernails before getting busy in the dirt so as to make cleaning up easier afterwards. Winnie also had a flair for home decoration, especially at Christmas time. In 1938 her outdoor display, always one of the most elaborate in town, included a snow-covered cottage surmounted by a jovial Santa Claus. Gossip columnist Jimmie Fidler estimated that the whole set-up must

have cost a thousand dollars. The police were keeping a close watch because a year earlier some Grinch had made off with Santa.

Shortly before Santa was kidnapped, Fidler had written extensively
about Winnie. He said that he had chatted with her and came away
believing she was "that rarest of all living creatures, a completely happy
person." She decided to retire simply because she had "enough." Movie
studios repeatedly offered her contracts, and a tobacco company made
her a lucrative offer to star in a weekly radio program, but she turned
them all down. Winnie said, according to Fidler, "Why should I spend
the rest of my life grubbing for more money and more success? I have
enough to live on comfortably—and I never cared a hang for fame."
She was living contentedly with her nine-year-old son, her sister, and
her brother-in-law. She liked hosting barbeque dinners for close friends,
but had no interest in going to nightclubs or attending film premieres.
"What does she do with her time?" asked Fidler rhetorically. "Well, for
one thing, she cans fruit—a basement full every fall—and anyone who
has tasted her preserves will remember their flavor far longer than he
will remember the average motion picture."

At the time of Fidler's conversation with Winnie, she may have been
as happy as he said she was, but his claim that her retirement was entirely of her own volition is contradicted by the testimony of her brother
Fred a year earlier. When an interviewer asked Fred if it were true that
Winnie was "washed up" in pictures, he replied, "Yeah, washed up the
same as Marie Dressler was. She might make a big come-back. She's sort
of figuring on it, I think. You might say that she has retired temporarily,
but not through any wish of her own. The trouble was that she had a
three-year contract to make three pictures a year, and they didn't have
any good stories for her, so her pictures were busts at the box office. That
gave them the idea that the public didn't want her, I suppose." Fidler's
claim that the movie studios still courted Winnie is also open to question.
A whole year had elapsed in between her last two pictures. The final one
was *I'll Fix It*, and Fidler said she regretted making it. Her stardom was
long over, and playing the secondary role of "best friend" in four successive pictures had typecast her in a way that limited her opportunities.
Another impediment was the introduction of the strict Motion Picture
Code. Filmmakers now had to approach sexuality subtly if at all. There
had never been anything subtle about Winnie, and many of the best moments in her films had been decidedly pre-code in character.

Still, even if her Hollywood prospects were dim, Winnie could have
remained in show business had she been so inclined. That is evident

from a glance at the career of her brother Fred. He never acquired anything like the star power Winnie had, yet he remained active as a comedian, actor, and singer decades after she retired. While Winnie made movies, Fred and his partner Roscella played vaudeville, often touring on the Loew's and RKO circuits. Critics usually praised Fred's comedy and sometimes remarked that his talent would be more appreciated if he were not always identified as Winnie's brother. Fred was prosperous enough in 1932 to buy a commodious house in his hometown of Greenport, Long Island. His father, Chauncey Reeves, and Chauncey's second wife thereafter resided in the house year-round, while Fred and Roscella made it their permanent address and spent breaks there whenever their schedule permitted. Later on they also acquired a cottage at nearby Sandy Beach. Besides having a good income, Fred evidently felt secure enough in his employment to quit a job over a matter of wounded pride. When he and Roscella arrived for a weeklong engagement in Toronto, they found themselves placed first on the bill, rather than in the next-to-closing spot they had expected. They immediately obtained a release from their contract and returned to New York.

Until the late 1940s Fred worked primarily in the theaters that still presented live acts along with films. As late as 1946 there were around thirty such theaters in New York City alone, although by 1949 only a handful remained. Fred also entered other branches of show business. He performed on radio, most notably in 1937 when he was the summer substitute for Jack Benny. He had roles in musical comedies both in successful road shows and in a couple of short-lived Broadway productions. He appeared in nightclubs, and he even dipped a toe into the movie business by acting in four two-reel comedy shorts made by Educational Pictures at their Astoria, New York studio. Perhaps the most memorable facet of his career came during the Second World War, when he made two extensive USO tours aimed at boosting the morale of Allied soldiers in the European theater. On his second tour he partnered with Marlene Dietrich in a USO unit that followed close on the heels of the troops that liberated Paris and then pushed on into Germany. The 5 March 1945 issue of *Life* contained a photo spread in which Dietrich displays her famous legs, teases a blushing young GI, and exchanges quips with Freddie Lightner.

If Fred's career demonstrates that Winnie could have remained in show business, it also makes it understandable that she chose not to. Big-time vaudeville was no more, and life in the surviving small-time was no picnic even for a headliner like Fred. He and Roscella nearly always gave at least three shows a day, often four or five. Fred sometimes served also as master of ceremonies, which meant he had to be present not only for his own act but throughout all of the other ones as well. On top of that came the wearisome travel between engagements that lasted a week at best, but often only three or four days. In an article titled, "Saddest Jump Known to Show Biz," *Variety* reported that every week ten acts had to travel from New York all the way to Florida to play the Loew's and RKO houses in Miami. The circuits provided only the price of a bus ticket, and most performers could not afford the added cost of making the trip by other means. By train it was possible to leave New York at 9:00 a.m., spend one night in a comfortable Pullman berth, and arrive in Miami by 8:00 p.m. the following day. By bus the same journey took three days and three nights. It is difficult to imagine what it must have been like for a performer to emerge dirty and exhausted after three grueling days and three even more miserable nights aboard a cramped bus, and then immediately plunge into the usual grind of three or more shows a day, followed by the equally excruciating bus trip back to New York.

Fortunately, Fred never had to undergo that ordeal. He was successful enough to refuse any contract that included it. He did not make even short trips by bus or train, because he was prosperous enough to own his own automobile. Then again, driving nonstop through the night, gas pedal to the floor, could be arduous enough. The actress June Havoc recalled in her memoirs that she got her first big break when Fred hired her in 1936 to substitute temporarily for Roscella, who was sickened by a difficult pregnancy. Fred, Roscella, and June all piled into Fred's car and left for Atlantic City in a blizzard. On another occasion Fred, Roscella, and their friend Esther Ralston drove all the way from Los Angeles to New York before recuperating at the family homestead in Greenport.

Even in the glory days of the two-a-day, incessant travel took its toll on vaudevillians. Small wonder Winnie had no desire to return to an itinerant lifestyle. Since arriving in Hollywood she had put down roots that would remain firmly in place throughout the second half of her life. A big part of that rootedness was her congenial relationship with Roy Del Ruth. During the years that Winnie made movies, Roy's career also flourished. A profile of Roy in *Variety* credited him with making James Cagney a star by directing him in *Blonde Crazy* (1931) and *Taxi!* (1932). Because Roy reliably turned out pictures in record time and on budget, he was the one director that Warner Bros. never loaned out to other studios. Perhaps he chafed under that constraint, however, because at around the same time Winnie retired, Roy left Warners. Thereafter he rotated among the big studios, but continued to display his accustomed skill and versatility. He turned out an array of musical comedies ranging from *Broadway Melody of 1936* with Jack Benny and Eleanor Powell, to *Happy Landing* (1938) with Sonja Henie and Don Ameche, as well as off-beat items like the drama *It Had to Happen* (1936) with George Raft and Rosalind Russell, and the fictionalized biography *The Star Maker* (1939), in which Bing Crosby impersonated vaudeville kingpin Gus Edwards. In the 1940s Roy's output slowed to just a picture or two annually for MGM. Then toward the close of the decade, he not only directed but also produced independently three movies, beginning with the heartwarming classic *It Happened on Fifth Avenue* (1947) and ending with the film noir *Red Light* (1949). In between came the sugarcoated sports biography *The Babe Ruth Story* (1948). William Bendix played the Babe, but Roy tried to give Fred Lightner a leg up by casting him as Yankees manager Miller Huggins.

Although the critics acclaimed Fred's fine performance in *The Babe Ruth Story*, he received no more offers in Hollywood and had to return to the stage. Opportunities there were becoming sparse, however. In 1950 Fred settled down in Elyria, Ohio, where he hosted a morning disc jockey show on radio, but soon he was performing again, with bit parts in at least one film, *Fourteen Hours* (1951), and in some radio and television dramas. Then in the summer of 1953 Fred was one of the principal performers in impresario Mike Todd's spectacular production *A Night in Venice* at the mammoth Jones Beach amphitheater on Long Island. Every evening as many as eight thousand spectators looked across a real Grand Canal, complete with swimmers and gondolas, to an enormous revolving stage populated by literally hundreds of musicians, singers and dancers. That was the last big success of Fred's career. In July 1954 Walter Winchell disclosed, "Freddie Lightner (former two-a-day headliner) is a clerk at the Taft Hotel." In December Fred was back on Broadway with a role in the musical comedy *Hit the Trail*. Unfortunately, both critics and the public decided the show should do as its title suggested. It closed after four performances. That appears to have been pretty much the end of the line for Fred.

If there ever was a time when Winnie was tempted to emulate Fred and return to the stage, it might well have come during the Second World War, when many veterans of vaudeville considered it their patriotic duty to swell the ranks of the USO. Winnie could not even remotely consider joining them, however, because a few months prior to America's entry into the war she became pregnant. Knowing she soon would be tied down caring for an infant, this time without the assistance of servants, Winnie decided to make a nostalgic visit to New York City. She took along her thirteen-year-old son, Richard. In addition to the usual tourist sites, she showed him the tenement on West Sixty-Sixth Street where she had grown up amid surroundings very different from those in which he had spent his formative years.

Winnie gave birth to her second son on 1 May 1942. She and Roy named him Thomas. It was also the second round of fatherhood for Roy. His firstborn, Richard Del Ruth, was now twenty years old and about to enlist in the army, so if his presence had been a reason for Roy to continue residing with his estranged wife, Olive, that was no longer a consideration. Roy decided to bite the bullet and begin the process of extricating himself from his lifeless marriage. In July 1944, he quit the house he had shared with Olive and moved in with Winnie. Olive then sued Roy for "separate maintenance." Normally separate maintenance was requested in situations where spouses wanted to live apart but not entirely rule out the possibility of a reconciliation. Yet Olive and Roy had been alienated for many years, and neither entertained the slightest thought of ever resurrecting their marriage. Why then did Olive not simply sue for divorce? The answer seems to be that she acted out of sheer vindictiveness. If she divorced Roy, he would be free to marry Winnie. If, on the other hand, Olive were awarded separate maintenance, then Roy would remain married to Olive and could not legally marry anybody else.

Roy countered Olive's action by filing a cross-complaint asking for a divorce. Each charged the other with "extreme cruelty." The case came to trial in spring 1945. Olive and Roy each testified to numerous acts of cruelty allegedly committed by the other. Olive said Roy called her nasty names, once gave her a black eye, hired private detectives to entrap her in misconduct, spent his evenings either away from home or else shut up in his room, and refused to have anything to do with her when she tried to be affectionate. Her attorney introduced into evidence a letter dated 13 April 1944, addressed to Roy and written by his niece, evidently in response to Roy telling her about his intentions. It read in part, "Roy, I am so very happy over the grand news about you and ———. I am so anxious to meet her and I know I will love her, as she looks like such an understanding and gifted girl. She is what you should have had many years ago." Olive testified that she found the letter in the mail, opened and read it, and then confronted Roy with it. Although Olive did not explicitly charge Roy with adultery, she did say that in 1929 Roy had an "association" with an actress that caused the actress's husband to sue

Roy for alienation of affection. Olive did not say that Roy had fathered a child by Winnie. Because Winnie and Roy had kept the birth of their son Thomas very quiet, it is possible that Olive did not know about it. Alternatively, perhaps Olive knew but decided that bringing it up in court might weaken her case for separate maintenance.

When it was his turn to take the stand, Roy said that Olive had refused to have sexual relations with him for many years, had been unfaithful to him, and had cursed and abused him. She stayed out late, and when she came home slammed doors, turned on lights, and played the radio. She never did any housework, refusing even to make up beds when the help had a day off. She had a terrible temper. Once she struck a household maid for making a mistake. The blow broke the maid's glasses and blinded her in one eye. Olive's spending habits were wildly extravagant. On the day Roy moved out she spent $800 on clothes. A few days later she spent an additional $1,100.

The judge tried to expedite matters by asking both parties to draw up a list of the specific acts of cruelty that they intended to prove. Olive came up with a list of fourteen; Roy listed twenty-five. The judge decided to disregard everything that had occurred prior to the year 1941, on the grounds that by continuing to reside under the same roof the parties had condoned each other's earlier misbehavior. The judge also excluded the letter to Roy from his niece because, although written in 1944, it was connected to Roy's association dating back to 1929. The judge then sent word to Olive that he wished to speak with her in his chambers. At that meeting he asked her if there was any possibility of reconciliation between her and Roy. She said there was not. The judge than told her that he would be reluctant to award separate maintenance. He suggested that she ask instead for a divorce. He pointed out that if she obtained a divorce she could request alimony, whereas if Roy won a divorce no alimony could be awarded her.

Olive's lawyer surely must have told her that when the judge who decides your case recommends a particular course of action, it is wise to take the hint. Olive nevertheless continued to press for separate maintenance. On 20 June 1945, the judge rendered his decision. He ruled that Roy had not inflicted extreme cruelty upon Olive, but that Olive had inflicted extreme cruelty upon Roy. Therefore the judge rejected Olive's demand for separate maintenance and awarded Roy the divorce that he had sought. The judge ordered that Olive receive a $75,000 share of the couple's community property but no other support. The remaining community property of $25,000 went to Roy. Considering that Roy reportedly earned a salary of $1,750 a week, it is remarkable that the community property totaled only $100,000. Evidently Roy's complaint about Olive's extravagant spending was well founded. Roy and Winnie must have been elated at the outcome of the case. If Olive blew through her $75,000 and ended up broke, that would be her problem. Roy was free at last.

Only he wasn't. Olive appealed the court's decision. Another protracted legal battle ensued. It climaxed in August 1946, when the California Second District Court of Appeal declared that the judge in the original case had erred when he excluded all evidence relating to offenses committed prior to 1941. Because Olive had not been allowed to present all of her evidence, she had not received a full and fair trial of her case. Therefore the court of appeal reversed the decision granting Roy a divorce. One year after the first court decision, and two years after Roy moved out on Olive, it was back to square one. Another round of legal maneuvering began. This time Olive sued for divorce rather than separate maintenance, and Roy did not contest her action. In August 1947 the divorce was granted. Olive was awarded a residence, furs, jewelry, and alimony to a total of $32,400, payable at $900 per month.

Although Roy was stuck paying alimony for the next three years, he could rejoice that his marriage to Olive was ended at last and he could get on with his life. On 14 August 1948, Roy Del Ruth and Winnie Lightner were married. The ceremony was held at the Mission Inn at Riverside and attended by the couple's relatives and close friends. On 1 September 1950 Roy made his final alimony payment to Olive. She had received every penny of the $32,400 to which she was entitled. Roy was free at last.

Only he wasn't. In January 1951, Olive initiated a lawsuit asking that her $900 monthly alimony be reinstated and that it continue for the rest of her life. She alleged that the settlement that she agreed to in 1947 was "grossly unfair and unjust," and that she was "ill and emotionally upset" when she accepted it. The outcome of Olive's new lawsuit was not reported in the press, but it appears she was unsuccessful, because a year later she launched yet another legal action. This time she sought to recover community property funds that Roy allegedly had spent supporting Winnie between 1930 and 1947. Winnie testified that she had received no money from Roy. Instead, she had supported herself using her own resources, including the $249,462 that she earned working in the motion picture industry between 1929 and 1932. In an effort to show that Winnie had not been paid that money, Olive sought testimony from

Cy Wilder, a Warner Bros. financial officer. It seems obvious that Wilder can only have confirmed that Winnie was remunerated as called for in her lucrative contract. Olive's new case was scarcely in progress before Roy faced yet another lawsuit, this one initiated by Roy's son, Richard. Claiming that he was unable to work because of "war disabilities," Richard Del Ruth sought $400 a month from Roy for support and medical expenses. Richard said Roy had been giving him $300 a month up until the previous October, but nothing since then. Richard said he received a pension of only $75 a month from the government.

The outcomes of the two lawsuits were not reported in the press. Possibly they were settled out of court. It is hard to see how either suit could have succeeded at trial. Trying to prove that Winnie had not been paid a fortune during her years of stardom seems so quixotic as to raise questions about Olive's mental state. As to Richard, it is hard to see how a father could be required to support a son who was in his thirties. Also, Richard's disabilities did not prevent him from working later on as an assistant director in film and television. Of course, whether or not Roy had to pay anything to settle the two suits, he still was saddled with more legal expenses, adding to those he had accumulated since he first decided to divorce Olive. He had known at the outset that disentangling himself from her would be difficult, but he could not have imagined that it would involve one courtroom battle after another over the course of seven years. This time the long ordeal was really and truly over. There were no more lawsuits, and Olive was not heard from again.

That Roy's freedom had come at a high price is evidenced by an advertisement that appeared in the *Los Angeles Times* in June 1952. It announced an auction on behalf of "Miss Winnie Lightner, famous motion picture personality, et al." On offer was a vast assortment of furniture, as well as "antique bric-a-brac; cut crystal, ruby, and amber crystal overlay pieces; fine table lamps, singles and pairs; imported crystal stemware; English, German, Viennese and Bavarian china; sterling and Sheffield silver hollow ware" and "hundreds of other items too numerous to mention." There were so many lots that the sale took place over two consecutive evenings. Winnie and Roy were not destitute, but they were doing some serious downsizing. Neither of them minded much. Winnie's adult son, Richard, was away serving in the army, and her old friends Newton and Theo had moved out to an abode of their own, so there was no need for furnishings beyond the requirements of two adults and a child.

That is not to say that Winnie and Roy became reclusive. It is true they were far more likely to be found patronizing the little bookshop on Ventura Boulevard run by former vaudevillians Vivian Oakland and John T. Murray than joining the beautiful people at the latest trendy nightclub, but they continued to entertain guests at their home both formally and informally. Fred and Roscella visited occasionally, and Winnie's stepfather, Andrew Hansen, sometimes stayed for several months at a time. Winnie and Roy gave occasional parties. Winnie, always much more gregarious than Roy, liked having company and constantly invited people she liked to drop by. Many of them were actors. Jack Carson was a good friend and frequent visitor. Dane Clark, Tyrone Power, and Clark Gable lived up the street. Gable, who shared Roy's keen interest in automobiles, would come by to see Roy's latest chrome-laden behemoth and chat about how it compared to others.

In 1949 Roy had returned to his old studio home at Warner Bros. There over the next five years he made eight movies. Many of them were musicals, but there were also dramas and comedies. The last one was the horror picture *Phantom of the Rue Morgue* (1954). It was filmed in 3-D, which Hollywood had embraced as part of its panicked effort to compete with television. Adapting to new technology had never been a problem for Roy, and the 3-D process was no exception. The completed film was filled with startling 3-D effects that all but blew the uncomfortable cardboard spectacles off the moviegoers who wore them.

For reasons now difficult to fathom, neither Warner Bros. nor any other major studio chose to employ Roy after 1954. After directing seventy-five feature films over the course of thirty-five years, he suddenly fell out of favor. Perhaps it had something to do with the crushing impact of television, which caused the frightened studios to make changes, rational or not. Roy had no choice but to go over to the dark side. For four years he devoted himself exclusively to television work, directing episodes of several shows, including *Meet Corliss Archer* and *Zane Grey Theater*.

During those lean years, Winnie was tempted to help out the family finances by going back to work. With her son Thomas old enough to no longer require mothering, there was no need for her to stay home. Consequently, when approached in 1957 about the possibility of starring in a television series called *Tugboat Annie*, she was seriously interested. The character Tugboat Annie had originated in a series of short stories published in the *Saturday Evening Post*. A film adaptation had been released in 1933, with sequels in 1940 and 1945. Annie was a loudmouthed, rough-and-ready female tugboat captain who engaged in endless rivalry with the equally crusty and combative male captain of a rival boat. It is easy to see why Winnie was attracted to the role. In the end, though, she did not take it on. Possibly the producers decided she was too pretty, for the part ended up going to Minerva Urecal, whose coarse features had long made her the actress of choice for any Hollywood director in need of a hatchet-faced housemaid or landlady. An alternative and probably more likely reason Winnie did not become Tugboat Annie is that the producers decided to save money by filming the series in Toronto instead of Los Angeles. It was one thing for Winnie to consider accepting a day job close to home. It was quite another to ponder leaving her family and sunny Hollywood for a lonely stay in frosty Toronto. It does seem a shame, though, for if Winnie had starred in the thirty-nine episodes of *Tugboat Annie* she might have acquired a whole new generation of fans, especially if the producers had been smart enough to let her belt out some songs.

Not long after Winnie toyed with the idea of reviving her career, Roy Del Ruth directed his last two movies. Both were low budget pictures made by poverty row studios. *The Alligator People* (1959) is a horror film based on the familiar theme of a scientific experiment gone wrong. Roy had not lost his touch. Despite meager funding, he succeeded brilliantly in building up an ever more eerie and threatening atmosphere, as a woman searches for her mysteriously vanished husband in an isolated plantation along a Louisiana bayou. Indeed, for anybody who adores a film that climaxes with a key character running around a swamp wearing a rubber alligator head, *The Alligator People* must rank as one of the best of the genre. Roy's final picture was *Why Must I Die?* (1960), a crime melodrama about an innocent woman facing the electric chair. Roy was still earnestly seeking work right up until he died in his sleep on 27 April 1961. Only afterwards did Winnie learn that he had consulted a physician about symptoms of heart trouble. Not wanting to worry her, he had not mentioned it

Winnie lived on quietly in Hollywood for another ten years. One of the rare occasions when her name surfaced in the press occurred in May 1968, when she was among the guests at a gala party thrown by retired actor Jack Haley in honor of his close friend Jackie Gleason, the great television comedian then at the height of his fame. Haley had known Winnie for close to fifty years, ever since he joined her vaudeville act as a juvenile. Nevertheless, the impetus for putting her name on the guest list came from Gleason. He urged Haley to invite not just current stars but also older ones, adding, "You know who I mean, Jack, greats like Charlie Ruggles and Winnie Lightner, people like that." At the party Winnie and Ruggles mingled with George Burns, Cary Grant, George Jessel, Groucho Marx, Pat O'Brien, Gene Raymond, Jane Wyman, and many others. The party was a blast and went on into the wee hours. As it was breaking up, Winnie's son Tom arrived to drive her home. While Winnie was out of earshot, Tom thanked Haley for inviting her, saying she had not been to a party in years. When Haley replied that the invitation had been Gleason's idea, Tom was surprised. He said it was sometimes difficult for him to comprehend that the housewife he saw cooking breakfast in the morning had once been so renowned that even the mighty Gleason knew about and admired her work. Haley, who had seen Winnie perform hundreds of times both in vaudeville and on Broadway, replied with feeling that she had been an extraordinarily gifted performer. She was, Haley said, "an Al Jolson-sized talent—nothing less."

The party was a merry occasion, but the next time Haley and Tom met was a somber one. It was Winnie's funeral. Like so many of her contemporaries, she succumbed to a heart attack. She died on 5 March 1971. At her requiem mass Haley was one of the pallbearers. In his diary he wrote of his dismay that only family and friends had come to mourn "a superstar who thrilled millions of people and made their hearts a little lighter." Winnie herself would not have shared Haley's melancholy over the absence of adoring fans and paparazzi. She disliked crowds, and she never cared a hang for fame.

No doubt Winnie would not have been so forgotten by the public if she had, like her husband Roy, kept working right up until the end of her life instead of ending her career at age thirty-five. Her obscurity is a reminder of how much of the history of show business is lost to us. Much of Winnie's finest work was on the vaudeville circuits and in the great Broadway revues, where inevitably it was evanescent. From the scraps of evidence that survive in critics' remarks, in sheet music, and in a few posed photographs, we can recover only a shadowy impression of those marvelous entertainments that once thrilled audiences in their thousands. It is all too easy to forget that mass popular entertainment did not begin with motion pictures and electrical recording.

Even when the arrival of the talkies made it possible to capture a record both visual and auditory of a performance, that record often turned out to be less than permanent. Films wore out and were discarded. Many were lost in fires or simply through slow chemical decomposition. The current status of the movies in which Winnie starred is fairly indicative of the early talkies as a whole. She began her motion picture career by singing in three short subjects. The first of these is entirely lost, and of the other two only the sound disks exist. The latter preserve the songs that gave Winnie her niche in cinema history as the first person to be censored for spoken words. Winnie's first feature film, the pioneer musical comedy *Gold Diggers of Broadway*, was once thought entirely lost, but then, disk by disk, virtually all of the sound was rediscovered. Then miraculously, first one and then the other of the two final film reels came to light, nearly complete and with their original color still in fairly good condition. Unfortunately, Winnie is glimpsed only briefly in the surviving reels, and of the climactic closing minute of the movie when she famously raised her Liberty torch and forgot her lines, only the sound survives. Of the subsequent movies in which Winnie starred, one has vanished entirely, and only the sound of another remains. Almost everything she ever did that was in Technicolor survives only in black and white. It is a race against time to find and preserve the undiscovered talkie treasures that are still moldering away in forgotten attics and cellars. Since 1991 the dedicated volunteers of the Vitaphone Project have tracked down thousands of sound disks and, where possible, matched them up with complementary film reels. That effort has allowed modern audiences to thrill to performances unseen and unheard for the better part of a century.

Winnie's career casts light not only on the imperfectly remembered history of show business, but also on how that business reflected changing attitudes about women in society. Winnie started out in vaudeville as a model of Victorian propriety. She and her female partner advertised themselves as "dainty and attractively costumed." They promised that together with the male member of the trio they would offer "refined songs, cleverly and delicately sung." It was not long, however, before Winnie morphed into a raucous comedian who was anything but dainty, and whose repertoire increasingly shifted from sentimental ballads to lively ragtime numbers that she belted out in a manner that was anything but delicate. Victorian concepts of womanhood were fading, and Winnie was in the vanguard of that change. After the First World War the ideal of women as paragons of domesticity and morality gave way, at least in sophisticated circles, to the ethos of the flapper, the "new woman" who was free to make her own choices and enjoy life. Nowhere was the new spirit more alive than in the great Broadway revues of the 1920s. One of the quintessential moments of the Jazz Age occurred when Winnie introduced the world to George Gershwin's immortal jazz anthem "I'll Build a Stairway to Paradise." As a parade of beautiful young women ascended staircases at either side of the stage, Winnie urged her listeners to dance their way upward to happiness "with a new step every day."

That same spirit carried over into Winnie's films. Her 1928 short subject *The Song a Minute Girl* unabashedly celebrated sexual enjoyment for men, women, and even underage boys. A year later *Gold Diggers of Broadway* captured perfectly the popular image of the 1920s as a time of progress, prosperity, and female liberation. In that and subsequent films Winnie was the comic epitome of a strident feminist. Aggressive and outspoken, she cheerfully dominated and exploited men, uttered loud-mouthed wisecracks, and gleefully spurned conventional morality. As the Great Depression deepened, however, social attitudes turned against feminism. Moviegoers struggling to survive amid a collapsing economy no longer found it amusing to see the institution of marriage ridiculed, divorce treated as a joke, or conventional gender roles undermined. Warner Bros. tried to adjust to the new climate by glamorizing and feminizing Winnie, and by casting her as a woman who could run a business with an iron will and yet be meekly subservient to the man in her life. It didn't work, and Winnie's stardom ended. In her final pictures she reverted to a muted version of her earlier, feminist incarnation. She could get away with it because she was a secondary character, whose comedy only accentuated rather than challenged the behavior of a female star who was stereotypically feminine and respectful of moral norms.

Winnie Lightner was an exceptional talent. No one could put over a popular song with greater zest. Few could match her ability as a comedian, especially when she was cast in a total farce like *The Life of the Party*, where her mugging and deliberate overacting kept audiences in stitches. She was remarkable in other ways as well. She knew she had gifts and worked hard to make the most of them, but she never developed the bloated ego so typical of stars. She never needed or even wanted to be worshipped by movie fans or anybody else. That attitude accounts for the remarkable fact that, so far as one can tell from the surviving evidence, everyone who ever knew her liked her. Whether it was a humble stagehand in Pittsburgh recalling how kind and helpful she was to the chorus girls in her show, or a celebrated film star like Joe E. Brown remembering how readily she agreed to share equal billing with him in a picture, everybody in show business who ever worked with Winnie was impressed by her generous spirit. Early in her vaudeville days, critics began saying she was the whole act and her partners Theo Lightner and Newton Alexander were superfluous. There are few show-business personalities who would not at that point have gone off to seek stardom on their own, citing "artistic differences" and leaving their erstwhile colleagues behind in the dust. Instead, Winnie not only stuck with her partners in vaudeville, she brought them along with her to Broadway and then to Hollywood. She welcomed them into her home, where they remained for many years even after her career was over. That was typical of Winnie, a most atypical star.

Wild and wonderful Winnie Lightner, the tomboy of the talkies, deserves to be remembered not only for her place both in show-business history and in women's history, but also for having been that rarest of things, a great entertainer who never took herself too seriously. Winnie and her times are long gone, but her admirers may be permitted to hope that her soul is where she once said she longed to be: "out in the open spaces alone . . . with the blue sky stretching to an infinity above . . . with the millions of stars twinkling their eternal message, and with just enough moonlight to read *Variety* by."

ACKNOWLEDGMENTS

FIRST AND FOREMOST I AM GRATEFUL TO MY MOTHER, THE LATE EDITH Kass Lightner, for starting me off on the long journey that has ended in publication of this book. Both of my parents grew up in the little town of Marysville, Pennsylvania. When I was a child, my mother told me about a woman named Winnie Lightner who had been in movies in the 1930s. My mother said that Winnie and her show-business friends had vacationed at Marysville, and that although not a blood relative, she was connected to my own Lightner family. I know now that the connection was via Winnie's vaudeville partner Theo Lightner, who had spent her early years in the vicinity of Marysville. I also know that an uncle of mine was among the guests at a party that Winnie, Theo, and their male vaudeville partner, Newton Alexander, hosted at their Marysville vacation home on 28 June 1917. Almost certainly I am related to Theo, although I still do not know exactly how.

My next encounter with the name Winnie Lightner occurred when I was in high school. One day a classmate showed me a piece of old sheet music, joking that my relative was on the cover. Finally, a decade after that when I was in graduate school, a local television station aired the film *The Life of the Party*. I thought the movie hilarious and was surprised to see that Winnie Lightner not only was in it, she got top billing. From then on I longed to learn more about her. What was her background, and how had she become a film star? What other movies did she make? When and why did she quit making them? What became of her after that? It was not until I retired from my long career as a history professor that I had the leisure to satisfy my curiosity. Fortunately, by that time the emergence of the Internet, with its abundance of digitally searchable newspapers and other sources, had made it feasible for me to answer my questions with a thoroughness that would have been unattainable at any earlier date.

In exploring Winnie's personal life I received invaluable assistance from her relatives. My first contact was Kathy Jewel, a grandniece. Kathy provided me with essential information about the Reeves and Touhey families. She also put me in touch with Bill Touhey, a son of Winnie's older brother, Joseph, and with Winnie's two sons, Richard Lightner and Thomas Del Ruth. All three of those gentlemen supplied essential information that I could not have obtained anywhere else. I am especially grateful to Richard, whose memories stretch back the farthest. Richard and I have had so many delightful telephone conversations, I have come to regard him as a good friend as well as a priceless informant. I also thank both Richard and Tom for supplying family snapshots from Winnie's retirement years.

I am indebted to many other individuals. Charles Conrad, who is writing a book on circus music, shared with me his research on Russell Alexander. Gary Flannery, who is both an accomplished dancer and the preeminent authority on the great Broadway revues, permitted me to reproduce a rare item from his spectacular collection of memorabilia. Andrew Glover, chief operating officer of the C. L. Barnhouse Company, supplied copies of important documents, as well as a splendid photograph of the Exposition Four vaudeville act. Ron Hutchinson, the guiding genius behind the Vitaphone Project, provided several illustrations and also commented on my preliminary manuscript, saving me from some embarrassing errors. Brian Pritchard, a motion picture and film archive consultant based in the UK, supplied a rare frame from the mostly lost visuals of *Gold Diggers of Broadway*. I also thank Eddy Janis both for offering a wonderful photograph that unfortunately surfaced too late to include in the book, and even more for sharing with me his unquenchable enthusiasm for all things Winnie.

For responding to inquiries and helping me track down additional information, documents, and images, I thank Mrs. I. Engel of the School of the Blessed Sacrament in New York City, William P. Gorman of the New York State Archives, Lee Grady of the Wisconsin Historical Society, Olive Hildreth of East Hampton, New York, Henry Jenkins of the University of Southern California, Thomas Lisanti of the New York Public Library, Abigail Nye of the University of Wisconsin-Milwaukee Libraries, Rich Saylor of the Pennsylvania State Archives, David Sean of University of Alberta Libraries, Ruth Van Stee of the Grand Rapids Public Library, Sylvia Wang and Mark Swartz of the Shubert Archives, and Laura Wittern–Keller of the University of Albany. I am grateful to all of them and also to the many archivists and librarians who gave me equally generous help but not their names.

I am grateful for the hard work and dedication of director Leila W. Salisbury, project editor Valerie Jones, editorial assistant Lisa McMurtray, art director John Langston, and the many other staff members at the University Press of Mississippi who helped bring this project to fruition. Special thanks are due copyeditor Lisa Paddock, whose numerous corrections were both welcome and humbling.

Finally, I want to acknowledge my indebtedness to the authors of the hundreds of memoirs, biographies, monographs, and articles that I consulted in my effort to understand the milieus in which Winnie Lightner worked and the people with whom she interacted. Only those secondary works of which I made specific use are cited in the notes, but I could not have written this book without immersing myself in the others as well. When I began my research, I knew next to nothing about the history of the motion picture industry, much less of earlier forms of entertainment like vaudeville and Broadway revues. Learning about them has afforded me much pleasure, and I hope I have conveyed to the reader of this book some of my own newfound fascination with the history of show business, as well as the special place within it that forever belongs to Winnie Lightner, the tomboy of the talkies.

STAGE CAREER AND FILMOGRAPHY

Keith-Orpheum, 1915–22, 1927, 1928
Loew's Capitol (New York City) and Fox Theater (Philadelphia), 1927
London (United Kingdom) variety theaters and nightclub, 1928
Warner Bros. eastern theaters, 1930, 1931

BROADWAY REVUES

George White's Scandals, fourth edition, 1922
George White's Scandals, fifth edition, 1923
George White's Scandals, sixth edition, 1924
Gay Paree, 1925
Gay Paree, second edition, 1926
Harry Delmar's Revels, 1927

FILMS

Winnie Lightner Singing Two Songs: Nagasaki Butterfly and Everybody Loves My Girl
Fox Case Corp., short subject, 1928
Role: herself
Director: Marcel Silver

Winnie Lightner, The Song a Minute Girl
Vitaphone Corp.-Warner Bros., short subject, 1928
Role: herself

Winnie Lightner, Broadway's Favorite
Vitaphone Corp.-Warner Bros., short subject, 1928
Role: herself

Gold Diggers of Broadway
Warner Bros., 1929
Role: Mabel
Cast: William Bakewell, Helen Foster, Albert Gran, Nick Lucas, Ann Pennington, Gertrude Short, Lilyan Tashman, Conway Tearle, Nancy Welford
Director: Roy Del Ruth

The Show of Shows
Warner Bros., 1929
Role: herself
Cast: Johnny Arthur, Mary Astor, William Bakewell, Irène Bardoni, John Barrymore, Richard Barthelmess, Noah Beery, Hobart Bosworth, Georges Carpentier, Dolores Costello, William Courtenay, Sally Eilers, Douglas Fairbanks Jr., Frank Fay, Albert Gran, Beatrice Lillie, Myrna Loy, Nick Lucas, Tully Marshall, Bull Montana, Chester Morris, Rin Tin Tin, Ann Sothern, Ben Turpin, H. B. Warner, Alice White, Loretta Young
Director: John G. Adolfi

She Couldn't Say No
Warner Bros., 1930
Role: Winnie Harper
Cast: Johnny Arthur, Sally Eilers, Tully Marshall, Chester Morris
Director: Lloyd Bacon

Hold Everything
Warner Bros., 1930
Role: Toots Breen
Cast: Joe E. Brown, Georges Carpentier, Sally O'Neil
Director: Roy Del Ruth

An Intimate Dinner in Celebration of Warner Bros. Silver Jubilee
Warner Bros., short subject, 1930
Role: herself
Cast: Joan Blondell, Joe E. Brown, Irene Delroy, Douglas Fairbanks Jr., Betty Jane Graham, Walter Huston, Charles Judels, Evalyn Knapp, Beryl

Mercer, Walter Pidgeon, Edward G. Robinson, Otis Skinner, Jack Whiting, Loretta Young
Director: John G. Adolfi

The Life of the Party
Warner Bros., 1930
Role: Flo
Cast: Charles Butterworth, Irene Delroy, Charles Judels, Jack Whiting
Director: Roy Del Ruth

Sit Tight
Warner Bros., 1931
Role: Dr. Winnie O'Neil
Cast: Joe E. Brown, Claudia Dell, Paul Gregory
Director: Lloyd Bacon

The Stolen Jools
Masquers Club of Hollywood-National Variety Artists, short subject, 1931
Role: herself
Cast: Wallace Beery, Charles Butterworth, Maurice Chevalier, Gary Cooper, Joan Crawford, Douglas Fairbanks Jr., Mitzi Green, Oliver Hardy, Buster Keaton, Stan Laurel, Edward G. Robinson, Norma Shearer, Barbara Stanwyck, Fay Wray, Loretta Young
Directors: William C. McGann et al.

Gold Dust Gertie
Warner Bros., 1931
Role: Gertie Dale
Cast: Claude Gillingwater, Chic Johnson, Ole Olsen
Director: Lloyd Bacon

Side Show
Warner Bros., 1931
Role: Pat
Cast: Charles Butterworth, Donald Cook, Guy Kibbee, Evalyn Knapp
Director: Roy Del Ruth

Manhattan Parade
Warner Bros., 1931
Role: Doris Roberts

Cast: Luis Alberni, Charles Butterworth, Charles Dale, Greta Granstedt,
Walter Miller, Joe Smith, Bobby Watson
Director: Lloyd Bacon

Play-Girl
Warner Bros., 1932
Role: Georgine Hicks
Cast: Norman Foster, Guy Kibbee, Loretta Young
Director: Ray Enright

She Had to Say Yes
First National Pictures, 1933
Role: Maizee
Cast: Lyle Talbot, Regis Toomey, Loretta Young
Directors: George Amy, Busby Berkeley

Dancing Lady
Metro-Goldwyn-Mayer, 1933
Role: Henrietta Rosette LaRue
Cast: Joan Crawford, Clark Gable, Franchot Tone
Director: Robert Z. Leonard

I'll Fix It
Columbia Pictures, 1934
Role: Elizabeth
Cast: Mona Barrie, Edward Brophy, Jimmy Butler, Jack Holt
Director: Roy William Neill

NOTES

Much of the factual information in this book derives from thousands of scattered references in newspapers and show-business periodicals. To keep the volume of notes manageable, those sources generally are cited only when their content either is especially significant or is quoted in the text. For the same reason, citations to secondary works generally are provided only when the text relies upon or quotes a specific source, as opposed to presenting information that is duplicated in a great many works.

INTRODUCTION

3   *From stage right.* "Pingo Pongo," by Al Dubin (lyrics), and Joe Burke (music), as performed by Winnie Lightner in *The Show of Shows* (Warner Bros., 1929).

3   *Born on the eve.* Sources are often ambiguous or contradictory on whether the word "theater" is part of the proper name of any particular venue. For convenience and consistency, throughout this book the word will be included and spelled conventionally. Here, for example, the name "Palace Theater" is used, even though most sources call it the "Palace Theatre" or just the "Palace."

CHAPTER 1: A TOMBOY IN PIGTAILS

6   *People screamed and scattered.* "Four Men Knocked Out, Clubbed Insensible and Carted Off to Jail," Brooklyn Eagle, 3 Dec. 1893, 2.

6   *These stirring events.* Chauncey Reeves obituary, Variety, 25 June 1947, 55.

7   *Less than a year after his encounter.* Chauncey Reeves was born 25 Dec. 1874. On 11 Oct. 1894 he married Winifred Touhey, born 1876 (possibly later). The Reeveses were Protestant, while the Touheys were Catholic, which may mean the marriage pleased neither family. Sons Joseph and Frederick were born 7 April 1895 and 7 Sept. 1897, respectively. Chauncey had remarried by the time of the 1910 census. (Chauncey Reeves <www.longislandsurnames.com>. Joseph W. Touhey <www.findagrave.com>. Frederick R. Lightner, ibid. Winifred Reeves obituary, Brooklyn Eagle, 20 Sept. 1899, 7. Detmold Reeves household, 1900 US census. Chauncey Reeves household, 1910 US census.)

7   *Winnie's foster parents.* Andrew Hansen household, 1900 US. census. G. W. Bromley & Co. *Atlas of the City of New York, Borough of Manhattan,* 1902 and 1911 eds. The

Hansens lived in or very near a five-story tenement at 132 West Sixty-Sixth Street, the sale of which was reported in New York Post, 5 Aug. 1909, 6.

8   *The tragic circumstances.* "Winnie Lightner Granted Divorce," Los Angeles Times, 24 Nov. 1932, 9 ("aided by her foster father"). In a 1930 interview Winnie said she was about eleven years old when she first learned that the Hansens were not her real parents, and that she was thirteen when her birth father first came to see her. Those assertions are somewhat suspect, however, as the purpose of the interview was to portray Winnie as unhappy in order to publicize the UK release of the film *She Couldn't Say No*, in which she played an unhappy entertainer. In the interview she dwelt on her three failed marriages, while not divulging that she had settled into a congenial relationship with Roy Del Ruth. (Winnie Lightner, as told to Helen Louise Walker, "Love Has Eluded Me," Film Weekly [London, UK], 30 Aug. 1930, 9.)

8   *The Hansen family.* Winnie Lightner, as told to Frieda Wynott, "More Tomboys, Less Parlor Petting and Greater Safety for Girlhood, Says Broadway Star," Abilene (TX) Reporter-News, 1 May 1927, 46.

9   *Winnie believed.* Ibid.

9   *Winnie's childhood world.* O. O. McIntyre, "New York Day By Day," Miami (FL) News, 13 Dec. 1936, 6, quotes what he says is a recent telegram from Winnie naming but not describing the Sixty-Sixth Street landmarks. Information about them has been acquired from sources too numerous to cite.

10   *Next door to Healy's.* Lightner as told to Wynott, "More Tomboys"("It is far healthier"). During her motion picture career, Winnie was among the movie stars who regularly attended Friday night boxing matches in Hollywood. (Hubbark Keavy, "Screen Life in Hollywood," Plattsburgh [NY] Sentinel, 9 Sept. 1930, 5. Motion Picture Classic, vol. 32 [Oct. 1930], 42.)

11   *Even more memorable.* In her 1936 message to O. O. McIntyre, Winnie said she had been a friend of Conway, but mistakenly gave his first name as Dan. (McIntyre, "New York Day By Day.") She said nothing else about Central Park, but it seems safe to assume that she and her playmates ventured beyond just the Sheep Meadow.

12   *While the streets of New York.* In the 1915 New York State census, the Hansens in Manhattan reported that Winnie was in school, while the Reeveses in Greenport reported that she was an actress. "Something About Miss Lightner," New York Times, 21 Nov. 1926, X4, says she is a graduate of Father Taylor's school. Unfortunately, the school no longer has records pertaining to the years she was there.

12   *Winnie remembered one more.* Edwin Schallert, "Name Should Be Lightning," Los Angeles Times, 13 Feb. 1921, sec. 3, p. 1 ("I told him I'd go"). Frank Cullen et al., *Vaudeville, Old and New: An Encyclopedia of Variety Performers in America* (2 vols., New York: Routledge, 2006), 694–98 (Marcus Loew). In October 1927 Winnie played Loew's Capitol Theater at Broadway and Fifty-First Street, but there is no evidence that she ever performed professionally at Loew's Lincoln Square.

CHAPTER 2: THE EXPOSITION FOUR

15   *When Winnie Lightner was born.* Pittsburgh Gazette-Times, 31 May 1914, sec. 6, p. 4. J. W. Alexander household, 1900 US census.

15   *The first conclusive evidence.* New York Clipper, 1 Feb. 1896, 761; 22 Feb. 1896, 809; 8 Aug. 1896, 360 ("show has been laboring"). Newton's year of birth is uncertain. His

obituaries and California death record say it was 1884, which would mean he was only twelve when he joined the Belford troupe. The 1900 US census says he was born in 1879, which seems more likely, although it is conceivable that he lied to the census taker so as to pass as a legal adult. (Variety, 20 April 1949, 55. Billboard, 30 April 1949, 51. California Death Index, 1940–97. US census 1900, Atlantic City, ward 4.)

16   *Soon after his stint.* "Russell Alexander," Band Wagon, May 1971, 30–32 <www.circushistory.org>.

16   *While Russell was overseas.* New York Clipper, 9 April 1898, 90 ("Old Glory"); 29 Aug. 1897, 90 ("In Old Maine"). Newton had joined the Sawtelle company by September 1897. (New York Dramatic Mirror, 11 Sept. 1897, 2.)

16   *After their respective engagements.* New York Clipper, 7 May 1898, 169.

17   *Success came quickly.* Ibid., 28 Jan. 1899, 820. Frank Dumont, "The Younger Generation in Minstrelsy and Reminiscences of the Past," ibid., 27 Mar. 1915, 6. The Field show reflected the transformation of minstrelsy that had begun soon after the Civil War. (Robert C. Toll, *Blacking Up: The Minstrel Show in Nineteenth-Century America* [New York: Oxford University Press, 1974], chap. 5.)

17   *The next step up.* Irving Zeidman, *The American Burlesque Show* (New York: Hawthorn Books, 1967), 36, notes the lack of any clear demarcation between burlesque and vaudeville. Andrew L. Erdman, *Blue Vaudeville: Sex, Morals and the Mass Marketing of Amusement, 1895–1915* (Jefferson, NC: McFarland & Company, 2004), demonstrates that the vaunted wholesomeness of vaudeville was more posturing than real difference. M. Alison Kibler, *Rank Ladies: Gender and Cultural Hierarchy in American Vaudeville* (Chapel Hill: University of North Carolina Press, 1999) explores the complexities of race, class, and especially gender as evidenced on the Keith circuit.

18   *If they had a choice.* Brooklyn Eagle, 28 Aug. 1900, 6 ("scene of the play" "musical wonders").

19   *The Four had returned to vaudeville.* New York Clipper, 22 Sept. 1900, 663. Brooklyn Eagle, 30 Sept. 1900, 24; 9 Oct. 1900, 5. New York Clipper, 20 Oct. 1900, 750.

Of the many books on vaudeville, Trav S. D. [pseud., Donald Travis Stewart], *No Applause, Just Throw Money, or, the Book that Made Vaudeville Famous: A High Class, Refined Entertainment* (New York: Faber and Faber, 2005) provides the best overview. Frank Cullen et al., *Vaudeville, Old and New: An Encyclopedia of Variety Performers in America* (2 vols., New York: Routledge, 2006) is a splendid reference work that covers not only performers but also entrepreneurs and all aspects of the business. Arthur Frank Wertheim, *Vaudeville Wars: How the Keith-Albee and Orpheum Circuits Controlled the Big-Time and Its Performers* (New York: Palgrave Macmillan, 2006) is good on the machinations of Edward Albee.

Other useful works include Douglas Gilbert, *American Vaudeville, Its Life and Times* (New York: McGraw Hill, 1940); Joe Laurie Jr., *Vaudeville: From the Honky-Tonks to the Palace* (New York: Henry Holt and Co., 1953); Albert F. McLean, *American Vaudeville as Ritual* (Lexington: University of Kentucky Press, 1965); John E. DiMeglio, *Vaudeville U.S.A.* (Bowling Green, OH: Bowling Green University Popular Press, 1973); Charles and Louise Samuels, *Once upon a Stage: The Merry World of Vaudeville* (New York: Dodd, Mead, 1974); Bill Smith, ed., *The Vaudevillians* (New York: Macmillan, 1976); Robert W. Snyder; *The Voice of the City: Vaudeville and Popular Culture in New York* (New York: Oxford University Press, 1989); and Anthony Slide, *The*

Encyclopedia of Vaudeville (Westport, CT: Greenwood, 1994, reprinted Jackson: University Press of Mississippi, 2012).

20   *After sharing the bill.* New-York Tribune, 21 Oct. 1900, 14.

21   *Long after the demise.* Cullen, *Vaudeville, Old and New,* has biographical entries for all of these individuals.

22   *It would be a while.* Brooklyn Eagle, 16 Dec. 1900, 12 ("Comedy Drama").

22   *Born in Cornwall.* Washington Times, 16 April 1901, 5 ("Look at me").

23   *Just where the Exposition Four fit.* Utica (NY) Herald-Dispatch, 11 Dec. 1900, 5 ("in its way inimitable"). Utica (NY) Observer, 11 Dec. 1900, 5 ("encores were numerous").

23   *When* The Honest Blacksmith *finished its season.* New York Clipper, 8 June 1901, 329. Brooklyn Eagle, 19 Aug. 1901, 5. On the Orpheum, see Smith, *The Vaudevillians,* 33, and Wertheim, *Vaudeville Wars,* 124.

24   *In the 1901–2 season.* Washington Times, 3 April 1902, 7.

24   *In the summer of 1902.* Boston Globe, 10 Aug. 1902, 22.

24   *Despite having made.* Syracuse (NY) Journal, 9 Feb. 1904, 5 ("Uncle Tom's Cabin"). It is assumed here that the Exposition Four members played the same roles in 1902–3 as they did the following year. Their roles in 1903–4 are specified in Rochester (NY) Democrat and Chronicle, 7 Feb. 1904, 10. A report toward the close of the 1902–3 season said that William Patton, James Brady, and Woodruff Alexander were among the seven Yellow Kids in the show, but presumably they could have played the other roles as well, or perhaps some of the named characters that they played *were* Yellow Kids. (New York Times, 8 Mar. 1903, 26.)

25   *It was the Exposition Four's bad luck.* M. Alison Kibler, "Pigs, Green Whiskers, and Drunken Widows: Irish Nationalists and the 'Practical Censorship' of *McFadden's Row of Flats* in 1902 and 1903," Journal of American Studies 42 (Dec. 2008): 489–514, quotation on 508. Kibler says the script called for Mrs. Murphy to make her first appearance in Kerrigan's wheelbarrow, but some contemporary reviews refer to her arriving in a donkey cart. Thus it is uncertain whether James Brady as Kerrigan wheeled her in.

25   *When* McFadden's Row of Flats *played Denver.* New York Times, 28 March 1903, 1 ("red-headed Irish policeman").

26   *Because the* McFadden's *company ended.* Variety, 20 Jan. 1906, 7 ("the girls"); 16 Dec. 1905, 14 ("rustic characters").

27   *When the Exposition Four then returned.* New-York Tribune, 24 Sept. 1907, 7. Having gradually expanded what was originally a modest display of a few plants and animals, the rooftop farm was fully developed by the time Farmer Wilke appeared in 1909. (New York Times, 30 May 1909, X8.) Laurie, *Vaudeville: From the Honkey-Tonks,* 388–89, mentions heating the lift.

27   *Between 1907 and 1915.* New York Clipper, 3 Aug. 1912, 8, 11. Variety, 1 Nov. 1912, 9.

27   *In 1910.* Variety, 31 Jan. 1913, 20 ("Why borrow trouble?"). On the legal case, see ibid., 11 Sept. 1909, 8; ibid., 27 Nov. 1909, 6; ibid., 26 Mar. 1910, 5; Billboard, 2 April 1910, 41; Variety, 8 April 1911, 10.

28   *In these their glory years.* A good description of the act appeared in Variety, 4 Aug. 1906, 8. Numerous brief reports mention some, although never all, of its features. Some examples are: New York Evening Telegram, 24 Nov. 1906, 13; Syracuse (NY) Post-Standard, 22 Jan. 1907, 4; Variety, 20 June 1908, 16; ibid., 19 Dec. 1908, 18; Lowell (MA) Sun, 23 Feb. 1909, 5; Utica (NY) Daily Press, 21 Dec. 1910, 4;

New York Clipper, 29 April 1911, 14; Billboard, 14 Dec. 1912, 58; (Portland, OR) Oregonian, 8 July 1913, 9; Middletown (NY) Daily Times-Press, 21 April 1914, 6; Syracuse (NY) Journal, 12 Mar. 1915, 8.

28   *Often the act included.* Variety, 20 Jan. 1906, 7 ("they do not want choir boys").

29   *Another feature was supplied.* Billboard, 23 April 1910, 44 ("not overdone"). James V. Hatch et al., *Inside the Minstrel Mask: Readings in Nineteenth-Century Blackface Minstrelsy* (Hanover, NH: Wesleyan University Press, 1996) probes the complex meanings of blackface, while its legacy is discussed in Michael Rogin, *Blackface, White Noise* (Berkeley: University of California Press, 1996); W. T. Lhamon Jr., *Raising Cain: Blackface Performance from Jim Crow to Hip Hop* (Cambridge: Harvard University Press, 2000); John Strausbaugh, *Black Like You: Blackface, Whiteface, Insult & Imitation in American Popular Culture* (New York: Jeremy P. Archer/Penguin, 2007); Yuval Taylor and Jake Austen, *Darkest America: Black Minstrelsy from Slavery to Hip Hop* (New York: W. W. Norton, 2012); and Stephen Burge Johnson, ed., *Burnt Cork: Traditions and Legacies of Blackface Minstrelsy* (Amherst: University of Massachusetts Press, 2012).

29   *Beginning about 1906.* Fort Wayne (IN) Journal-Gazette, 2 April 1913, 8; 1 April 1913, 8. As early as August 1906 the act included "an extraordinarily quick change" from Rough Rider uniforms to evening dress, as well as "another quick change into minstrel garb for an encore." (Variety, 4 Aug. 1906, 8.) Two years later there were five quick changes. (New York Dramatic Mirror, 31 Oct. 1908, 19.)

30   *On 26 April 1915.* "Victoria Theater Playbills and Reviews, 26 April 1915," *The Papers of Will Rogers,* ed. Arthur Frank Wertheim and Barbara Bair, vol. 3: *From Vaudeville to Broadway, September 1908–August 1915* (Norman: University of Oklahoma Press, 2001), 373–77.

30   *Indeed they had made good.* Joe E. Laurie Jr., "Vaudeville Memories," Variety, 5 Jan 1938, 177 ("I can name many"). Imhof no longer recalled accurately all of the things that had made the Exposition Four so versatile. He had forgotten about their blackface comedy and quick changes and instead said they were "roller skaters" and "trick cyclists."

31   *Sadly, that final show.* Variety, 3 June 1911, 8 ("gone to the Adirondack Mountains"). San Francisco Call, 24 July 1913 ("Willing and Cooper"). That Frank Willing and William H. Cooper had performed in the Exposition Four act is mentioned in Willing's obituary (Variety, 11 May 1938, 54) and in a report on Cooper's marriage (ibid., 9 July 1915, 9). While performing as a blackface single at Jamestown, NY, following the disbandment of the Exposition Four, Woodruff Alexander stayed with Cooper and his wife. (Jamestown Evening Journal, 31 Dec. 1915, 7.)

31   *Russell Alexander died.* Newton Alexander to C. L. Barnhouse, 21 Oct. 1915, in C. L. Barnhouse Company archive, courtesy Andrew Glover. Woodruff performed in small-time under the name Wood Alexander at least as late as January 1916. After his death his widow published a memorial advertisement. (Variety, 7 Jan. 1916, 20; 10 May 1918, 20.)

Even before the demise of the Exposition Four, the act's name was being used by another quartet. As early as January 1915 four African American musicians calling themselves the Exposition Four were touring in the far West on the Pantages circuit, and by the following spring they were playing small-time UBO houses in the East. In February 1916 *Variety* reported that Fred H. Brown had purchased "Wood Alexander's interests in the Exposition Four Act." Brown then tried to stop the black Exposition Four from using the name, but apparently without success. The personnel of the black Exposition Four changed over time, but the quartet remained active throughout the 1920s. (Variety, 25 Feb. 1916, 32; 26 May 1916, 44. New York Clipper, 24 June 1916, 6.)

CHAPTER 3: NEWTON AND THEO

32 *The Exposition Four.* In vaudeville jargon, the word "time" referred to a period of employment on any particular circuit. For example, an act touring the Orpheum chain was said to be "doing Orpheum time."

32 *Giving three or more shows.* Fort Wayne (IN) Journal-Gazette, 3 April 1913, 8.

33 *The 1900 federal census.* Information on Theo's personal background is from the federal census, 1900 and 1910. Her early vaudeville appearances were reported in New York Dramatic Mirror, 30 Oct. 1909, 26, and Variety, 30 Oct. 1909, 12 ("If Theo. is a beginner").

34 *In 1911 Theo teamed up.* New York Clipper, 22 July 1911, 21 (Bates and Lightner act formed). New York Times, 12 Mar. 1905, X5 ("Her Last Rehearsal"). Worcester (MA) Telegram, 6 May 1912, 1 (*Titanic* benefit).

35 *Later that year.* Variety, 13 Sept. 1912, 36 (Lightner and Jordan act). New York Clipper, 15 June 1901, 344 (Jordan in burlesque). Variety, 20 Dec. 1913, 200 ("two classy girls"). Cedar Rapids (IA) Gazette, 6 Nov. 1913, 10 ("talk of appreciation").

35 *Their reputation grew.* New York Clipper, 7 March 1914, 4 ("sang and danced acceptably").

35 *They fared even better.* Ibid., 28 March 1914, 17. Billboard, 28 Mar. 1914, 10. Variety, 27 Mar. 1914, 14.

36 *What might have been.* Variety, 7 Aug. 1914, 19.

36 *On their way up.* Ibid., 16 Jan. 1915, 19 ("usual style"); 30 Jan. 1915, 13 ("idea of using a piano bench lengthwise"); 5 Feb. 1915, 8 ("I met you on Broadway").

37 *It is, then, no great surprise.* The Willing and Jordan act performed regularly from 1915 through at least 1927. Except for an Orpheum tour in 1917, they played Loew's and other small-time. A few of the hundreds of reports on them are: Variety, 17 Sept. 1915, 18 (in Chicago); 12 Jan. 1917, 41 ("went big" at Orpheum, San Francisco); 2 Nov. 1917, 17, 23 (at Fifth Avenue Theater, NYC); 13 May 1921, 10 (at Loew's Casino, San Francisco); 2 Mar. 1927, 50 ("are nice for the family houses").

38 *The Lightner and Jordan partnership.* New York Dramatic Mirror, 21 July 1915, 18, reported belatedly that agent "Edward S. Keller is booking Theo Lightner, late of Lightner and Jordan, and Newton Alexander, in a new two-act."

38 *In 1930 Winnie told an interviewer.* Russsel Crouse, "Lightner vs. Crouse," New Movie Magazine, May 1930, 38–39, 130.

39 *A summary of Winnie's career.* Manuel Weltman, "Winnie Lightner, Broadway's Favorite," Classic Film Collector, no. 19 (fall 1967), 9. A variant of the story about the hotel room interview was recounted by a resident of Marysville, PA, where Winnie and her partners had spent vacation time. In that version, a clerk at the hotel (a friend, not an uncle) recommended Winnie. ("All About Winnie Lightner!," Harrisburg [PA] Telegraph, 14 Jan. 1930, 9.) Both accounts agree that the hotel was the Gerard, which was located at 123 West Forty-Fourth Street and popular among actors.

41   *Jack Haley, an actor.* Jack Haley, *Heart of the Tin Man: The Collected Writings of Jack Haley*, ed. Mitchell Cohen (Beverly Hills, CA: Tinman Publishing, 2000), 81–82. Billy Glason in Bill Smith, ed., *The Vaudevillians* (New York: Macmillan, 1976), 30.

CHAPTER 4: A JOLLY TRIO

43   *In July 1915.* Buffalo (NY) Express, 4 July 1915, 38, specifies the bill. Ibid., 5 July 1915, 5, says evening prices will prevail at the "special holiday matinee."
   According to a route card sent by Newton Alexander to the C. L. Barnhouse Company, the Lightner Sisters and Alexander first performed in Syracuse beginning 1 July. Probably that was an incognito try-out lasting three or four days. The only vaudeville theater in Syracuse was the Temple, a small-time house that advertised two six-act bills a week without naming who was on them, at admission prices from five to fifteen cents.

45   *A closer look.* Because few details about the acts at Shea's were recorded at the time, most of the following particulars are drawn from descriptions published when those same acts performed elsewhere. Thus the actual performances at Shea's were similar but not necessarily identical to those described.

45   *American audiences.* New York Clipper, 10 Mar. 1920, 9, has the most thorough description of the act. An appearance by Jimmy was advertised in the (Madison) Wisconsin State Journal, 15 Sept. 1938. He had retired by 1944, but his daughter carried on family tradition by performing as a juggling unicyclist into the 1950s. (Billboard, 17 June 1944, 24; 24 Nov. 1951, 77.)

45   *Performers hated being placed.* See the entry on Mike Shea in Frank Cullen, *Vaudeville, Old and New: An Encyclopedia of Variety Performers in America* (2 vols., New York: Routledge. 2006), 1011–12. Joe Laurie Jr., *Vaudeville: From the Honky-Tonks to the Palace* (New York: Henry Holt and Co., 1953), 412, says Shea was "the most colorful and nicest guy of all the owner-managers."

46   *Exactly what the Jolly Trio did.* Buffalo (NY) Express, 4 July 1915, 38; 7 Nov. 1915, 47.

46   *Edward Blondell.* Matthew Kennedy, *Joan Blondell: A Life Between Takes* (Jackson: University Press of Mississippi, 2007), 11–13.

47   *The last act before intermission.* New York Dramatic Mirror, 12 May 1906, 22. New York Age, 17 June 1909, 6.

48   *Out in the wider society.* Errol G. Hill and James V. Hatch, *A History of African American Theatre* (New York: Cambridge University Press), 204. Lester A. Walton, "Social Equality," New York Age, 17 Dec. 1914, 6.

48   *Following intermission.* Buffalo (NY) Express, 4 July 1915, 38. New York Clipper, 2 May 1917, 25. According to Joe Laurie, "Ed Vinton & Buster were good; the dog imitated everything the trainer did." Laurie denied that vaudeville animals were mistreated, but then contradicted himself by joking that a trainer should "see that the dogs don't bark loudly when you whip them off stage, as the audience may think you are cruel." (Laurie, *Vaudeville: From the Honky-Tonks*, 161 ["Vinton & Buster were good"], 162 [not mistreated], 478 ["whip them off stage"].)

49   *The sixth act on the bill.* Cullen, *Vaudeville, Old and New*, 457–58 (Mitzi Green). New York Dramatic Mirror, 3 July 1909, 21 (Burns and Fulton). Moving Picture World, 25 Dec. 1915, 2444 (*Sammy's Scandalous Scheme*).

49   *The next-to-closing slot.* Cullen, *Vaudeville, Old and New*, 315–16.

50 *The final live act.* Ibid., 656.

50 *The program at Shea's ended.* Charles Musser and Robert Allen, "The 'Chaser Theory,'" Studies in Visual Communication, 10 (fall 1984): 24–52. Michael Slowik, "Film Exhibition in Vaudeville: What We Learn from Keith-Albee Managers' Reports," Nineteenth Century Theatre and Film, 39 (winter 2012): 73–92.

50 *How the audience responded.* Schenectady (NY) Gazette, 20 July 1915, 8.

51 *Still, it is evident.* Variety, 15 Oct. 1915, 35 ("Booked Solid"). Jack Haley, *Heart of the Tin Man: The Collected Writings of Jack Haley,* ed. Mitchell Cohen (Beverly Hills, CA: Tinman Publishing, 2000), 85. Haley was describing here his more personally significant appearance at the Palace in 1924 as half of the (Charles) Crafts and Haley act, rather than his 1921 debut as a juvenile in Winnie's mini-revue.

Estimates of the number of vaudeville theaters vary, but Haley's figure of fifteen thousand is over the top. Frank Cullen says that in the late 1910s there were about two thousand theaters, along with perhaps an equal number of other venues such as storefronts, saloons, showboats, and seaside piers that also staged vaudeville. Trav S. D. follows Joe Laurie Jr. in putting the total at five thousand. (Cullen, *Vaudeville, Old and New,* xxxiii. Trav S. D. [pseud., Donald Travis Stewart], *No Applause, Just Throw Money, or, the Book that Made Vaudeville Famous: A High Class, Refined Entertainment* [New York: Faber and Faber, 2005], 155. Laurie, *Vaudeville: From the Honky-Tonks,* 246.)

51 *At the Palace.* Billboard, 9 Oct. 1915, 7. Variety, 8 Oct. 1915, 13. New York Dramatic Mirror, 16 Oct. 1915, 18.

52 *While the Jolly Trio was only moderately successful.* Winnie evidently took to the stage like the proverbial duck to water. In a revealing comment made a decade into her career, she said she had never known the meaning of stage fright. "I have been on the stage now nearly ten years," she added, "and I have never had any qualms about facing any audience. Perhaps that will account for the reason my acts get over." ("Winnie Won't Worry Over Stage Fright," Philadelphia Inquirer, 13 Sept. 1926, 20.)

52 *The week following their Palace debut.* Brooklyn Eagle, 12 Oct. 1915, 6 ("undeviating measure of merit").

54 *Vaudeville reflected.* Schenectady (NY) Gazette, 20 July 1915, 8. As late as September 1916 the trio shared a bill with a dramatic sketch said to portray "in a gripping manner the attitude of a man, who believes his first duty is to his wife and children instead of his king, who is shown often to wage an unjust war for oppression or personal aggrandizement." (San Antonio Light, 24 Sept. 1916, 7.)

54 *The week America entered the conflict.* Brooklyn Eagle, 4 Sept. 1917, 10.

55 *Winnie and her partners.* Ibid., 4 Dec. 1917, 13 (Red Cross). Albany (NY) Journal, 19 July 1918, 10 ("gorgeous patriotic spectacle"). New-York Tribune, 30 July 1918, 9 ("pelt the Kaiser").

55 *In 1916.* Insight into what it was like to tour the West may be gleaned from Herbert Lloyd, *Vaudeville Trails thru the West, Chicago to the Coast to the Gulf, by "One Who Knows"* (Philadelphia: Herbert Lloyd, 1919), a guidebook for vaudevillians. It advises, for example, that if playing Denver, "Nurse your voice in this altitude. Don't cut your act, but take it easy and don't strain." When your train passes an isolated ranch or farmhouse, throw any unneeded newspapers and magazines out the window, as they will be "greatly appreciated" by the inhabitants. "To please San

Francisco people, never say 'Frisco' and always speak of the earthquake as the 'big fire.' (They are sensitive on both of these points)." (Ibid., 5, 76, 173.)

55 *During the Orpheum tour out west.* Review dated 27 Dec. 1915 in New York Clipper, 1 Jan. 1916, 9 ("comedy vein"). Pittsburgh Press, 3 April 1917, 9 ("comedy cut-up"). Utica (NY) Herald-Dispatch, 8 May 1917, 3 ("funniest young person").

56 *For a long time.* New York Clipper, 22 May 1918, 8 ("younger"). Ibid., 19 June 1918, 8 ("slighter"). Variety, 2 Mar. 1917, 40 ("sprightly"). Brooklyn Eagle, 4 Dec. 1917, 13 ("snappier"). Fort Wayne (IN) Sentinel, 7 April 1917, 3 (Farber). Brooklyn Eagle, 4 Sept. 1917, 10 (White). Ibid., 22 July 1919, 42 (Baker). New York Clipper, 23 May 1917, 7 (Foy, Fay). Philadelphia Public Ledger, 29 July 1919, 11 (Moore).

56 *The* Variety *critic.* Variety, 30 Nov. 1917, 20 ("Elfie Fay facial twist"); 5 July 1918, 33 ("good chooser"). New York Clipper, 3 July 1918, 10 ("scored the big hit").

57 *By the summer of 1917.* Hog purchases by Thea Lightner, 27 April 1914, in American Berkshire Record, 46 (1915), p. 46,195 entries 192,321 and 192,323, and p. 46,196 entry 192,328. Harrisburg (PA) Telegraph, 22 May 1915, 11. Russell Alexander royalty ledger, C. L. Barnhouse Company archives.

57 *In June 1917.* Harrisburg (PA) Telegraph, 30 June 1917, 8; 16 Aug. 1917, 2.

58 *Following their summer holiday.* New York Clipper, 17 Oct. 1917, 7. Variety, 19 Oct. 1917, 24. Billboard, 20 Oct. 1917, 7.

58 *Only six weeks after.* Billboard, 25 May 1918, 17. Variety, 2 May 1919, 24; 11 July 1919, 24. Billboard, 12 July 1919, 7.

58 *Usually the Trio's Palace engagements.* "Van and Schenck Quit Colonial in a Huff," New York Dramatic Mirror, 13 May 1919, 730.

59 *Between their visits.* Marian Spitzer, *The Palace* (New York: Atheneum, 1969), 95–97.

59 *Winnie had emerged by then.* New York Clipper, 30 April 1919, 9 ("clever comedienne"). New York Times, 11 May 1919, 4 ("star of the act"). New York Dramatic Mirror, 20 May 1919, 805 ("the winner").

60 *Winnie agreed to appear.* New-York Tribune, 13 May 1919, 13, reports the signing. Later reviews of the show describe its content.

60 *Unfortunately, the tryout.* New York Clipper, 4 June 1919, 6.

60 *Despite that setback.* "A Pair of Farmerettes," Washington Post, 8 June 1919, A3.

61 *In its second tryout.* Washington Times, 9 June 1919, 8. Washington Star, 9 June 1919, 21.

61 *It soon became clear.* Washington Herald, 9 June 1919, 3.

61 *Winnie and her partners.* Brooklyn Eagle, 29 June 1919, 6 ("prettiness, cleverness"). New York Dramatic Mirror, 6 May 1919, 672 ("facial contortions").

62 *In July the Trio.* New York Clipper, 9 July 1919, 9 ("clowned and mugged"). Ibid., 14 Jan. 1920, 21 (cancellation). Ibid., 21 July 1920, 9 ("wonderful personality").

63 *"Little Miss Vamp" opened.* Variety, 15 Oct. 1920, 19. Variety commented that the toy airplane joke was similar to "a stunt used for a finish in a well-known comedy turn of several years ago, but, perhaps, its service here will bring no objection." The previous stunt was by Ed Gallagher and Joe Barrett in their skit "Battle of Too Soon," introduced in 1907. (Variety, 9 Dec. 1921, 23. New York Dramatic Mirror, 8 June 1907, 16.)

63 *After an unadvertised three-day break-in.* New York Dramatic Mirror, 16 Oct. 1920, 685 ("And what a hit"), 686 ("bright shining star"). The reviewer seems to have misheard the opening line—"Old Man Jazz has just arrived in town"—of the song

"Old Man Jazz," causing him to misidentify the song as "Since That Jazz Has Gone to China Town," a title that does not appear to exist.

64   *For Winnie "Little Miss Vamp" was both.* New York Clipper, 22 Sept. 1920, 18.

64   *With a year's worth.* New York Clipper, 13 Oct. 1920 (route lasting nearly a year), 8. Ibid., 26 Jan. 1921, 8 (golf). Edwin Schallert, "Name Should Be Lightning," Los Angeles Times, 13 Feb. 1921, sec. 3, p. 1 (Winnie at pool).

65   *While headlining.* Schallert, "Name Should Be Lightning."

65   *For now Winnie was happy.* Ibid.

66   *Despite her openness.* Ibid. "Winnie Lightner Sues for Divorce," Los Angeles Times, 25 Mar. 1921, sec. 3, p. 4.

66   *Just a few years older.* Physical description of Pyle based on his World War I and World War II draft registration cards and a photograph published in Los Angeles Times, 29 Mar. 1929, sec. 3, p. 4. His career traced through numerous press reports. Divorce decree reported in Variety, 15 April 1921, 4.

66   *One wonders.* It appears Pyle's career faltered in the transition from silents to talkies. What seems to have been his last film credit (as John Patrick) was a Vitaphone short, "Last But Not Leased." (Film Daily, 12 Oct. 1930, 5.)

67   *Winnie's second marriage.* Variety, 29 April 1921, 39 ("somehow missed"). Chicago Tribune, 29 Mar. 1923, 5, says Winnie married Harold 27 April 1921, separated from him after a few days, and divorced him 28 March 1923.

67   *If Harold really was the orchestra conductor.* In a 1930 interview Winnie referred to Harold as "a Chicago boy." (Winnie Lightner, as told to Helen Louise Walkier, "Love Has Eluded Me," Film Weekly [London, UK], 30 Aug. 1930, 9.)

67   *Now unburdened.* Variety, 25 Feb. 1921, 4. Vaudeville News, 18 Mar. 1921, 5. New York Dramatic Mirror, 23 April 1921, 695. Brooklyn Eagle, 27 Mar. 1932, E2. Ibid., 8 Jan. 1922, C9.

68   *The new act found its legs.* New-York Tribune, 27 Sept. 1921, 10 ("less of Winnie"). New York Dramatic Mirror, 1 Oct. 1921, 488. Variety, 30 Sept. 1921, 18.

69   *Over the next few months.* New York Dramatic Mirror, 29 Oct. 1921, 634 ("a snappy miss"). Philadelphia Public Ledger, 14 Nov. 1921, 9 ("one of the most decided"). Variety, 16 Dec. 1921, 31. Vaudeville News, 17 Mar. 1922, 8.

70   *As a well-known standard act.* Brooklyn Eagle, 30 April 1922, C10 ("one of the few survivors").

CHAPTER 5: SCANDALS AND REVELS

71   *In the early 1920s.* Another difference was that in a vaudeville show a performer normally appeared only once, whereas in a revue a principal cast member would turn up in several scenes, thus providing a touch of continuity.

While the literature on American musical theater is immense, surprisingly few books focus specifically on the great revues: Robert Baral, *Revue: A Nostalgic Reprise of the Great Broadway Period* (New York: Fleet Publishing, Corp., 1962); Gerald Martin Bordman, *American Musical Revue: From The Passing Show to Sugar Babies* (New York: Oxford University Press, 1985); Lee Allyn Davis, *Scandals and Follies: The Rise and Fall of the Great Broadway Revue* (New York: Limelight Editions, 2000).

72   *Winnie Lightner made her Broadway debut.* New York Times, 19 Dec. 1926, X4 ("curious resemblance").

72 *Along with Winnie.* The cuts made after the opening were reported in New York Clipper, 6 Sept. 1922, 20, and Variety, 8 Sept. 1922, 16. On "Blue Monday," see also Howard Pollack, *George Gershwin: His Life and Work* (Berkeley: University of California Press, 2006), 268, 269–75.

72 *Winnie appeared in eight.* Descriptions of this and the other revues in which Winnie appeared have been compiled from printed programs and from advertisements, reviews, and illustrations published in newspapers and the show-business press. Because the dating of those sources varies widely, and because a revue could change over time, the descriptions given here are composites that provide an overall sense of what a given production was like but are not strictly applicable to any particular performance.

73 *Three skits paired Winnie.* Winnie's swallowing the canary is a good example of the uncertainty about exactly what was in the show at any given time. Reviewers of the Broadway opening did not mention the stunt, but during the post-Broadway engagement in Chicago a local newspaper published a photograph of Winnie with a caption saying she "daily convinces her audiences that she eats a live canary." Many years later, a New York City columnist writing about W. C. Fields said, "It is not hard to recall that he and Winnie Lightner, getting her first big break, played numerous skits together. One most readily remembered is that one in which Winnie escaped the tirade Fields was delivering to her in order to seize and swallow a chirping canary." (Chicago Tribune, 29 Mar. 1923, 5. George Tucker, "Man About Manhattan" column, Big Spring [TX] Daily Herald, 3 April 1936, 8.)

74 *A reviewer of the opening night.* New-York Tribune, 29 Aug. 1922, 6. Another reviewer said that even at the opening performance, when "the skirts of the girls commenced to drop off," there was "an exclamation from the women in front, who thought it was accidental." Perhaps the women's reaction gave George White the inspiration to make a more elaborate version of the "accident" a regular feature. (Variety, 1 Sept. 1922, 17.)

74 *Because of the time.* Chicago Tribune, 29 March 1923, 5; 25 March 1923, D13 ("ebullient young person"). Brooklyn Eagle, 29 Aug. 1922, 4 ("Mr. Fields might have").

75 *But if Winnie had not dazzled the critics.* New York Clipper, 27 June 1923, 5.

75 *The 1923* Scandals *ran on Broadway.* New York Times, 19 June 1923, 22 ("regardless of this inconvenience").

75 *Winnie was not quite so ubiquitous.* "The Stylish Side by Pam," Variety, 28 June 1927, 27 ("suited her unusually"). "The Reviewing Stand . . . by New York Herald, New York, June 23," in Philadelphia Inquirer, 24 June 1923, 31 ("best assets"). Walter J. Kingsley, "Vaudeville and Review," New York Times, 8 July 1923, sec. 6, p. 1 ("pets and prides").

76 *Another big scene.* S. Jay Kaufman, "Round the Town," New York Evening Telegram, 30 July 1923, 8.

76 *Just as important.* Brooklyn Eagle, 19 June 1923, 5. New York Times, 19 June 1923, 22. Robert Benchley in Life, 12 July 1923, 20. Kaufman, "Round the Town."

77 *Less than two months.* Sioux City (IA) Journal, 30 Dec. 1923, 18 ("only recently"). Variety, 8 Nov. 1923, 18.

77 *Knowing she would be spending another lucrative season.* Chicago Tribune, 17 June 1932, 10, reports their divorce and also gives their marriage date. At the time of the divorce, Holtrey was widely but wrongly reported to be a wealthy stockbroker. More

accurate reports about his work include: Playbill Vault <playbillvault.com> (on technical staff of play *Mendel, Inc.*, which ran 25 Nov. 1929 to 31 May 1930); Alma Whitaker, "Who's Married to Whom Listed," Los Angeles Times, 17 Aug. 1930, B22 (New York stage manager); Walter Winchell, "On Broadway," (Madison) Wisconsin State Journal, 27 June 1932, 3 (stagehand); US census 1940 (stage electrician); Holtrey's World War II draft registration card (employed by Shubert, New York).

Just when Winnie and Holtrey moved into the Osborne Apartments is uncertain, but they were resident there by the time of the 1925 New York State census.

Holtrey had two sons by a previous marriage. In March 1930 Winnie reportedly visited the two boys, who lived with Holtrey's mother in Fort Wayne, Indiana. (Greencastle [IN] Herald, 7 Mar. 1930, 4.)

78   *The most elaborate production number.* Burns Mantle, "Mr. White Goes in for Changing Lights," Chicago Tribune, 6 July 1924, D1 ("chaste and white").

80   *The 1924* Scandals *was so successful.* A flyer advertising an engagement at the Maryland Theater, Cumberland, MD, 4–5 Sept. 1925, boasts that the show is coming "intact in 3 special baggage cars." A report on preparations for the 1926 renewed road show says that seventy-five cast members have already been registered, with more to come, and that "Freddie Lightner will again head the cast." (Variety, 28 July 1926, 42.) When augmented by the additional cast members as well as the many employees working in other capacities, the entourage likely did approach the advertised total of one hundred people.

80   *Although Winnie had departed.* Information on Fred Lightner has been compiled from several hundred reports in newspapers and the show-business press. The injury that ended his baseball career was reported in Harrisburg (PA) Telegraph, 16 June 1919, 13, and Billboard, 28 June 1919, 12.

81   *It was a big break for Fred.* The visit to Mingo Junction was reported in Steubenville (OH) Herald Star, 12 June 1926, 12.

82   *On Saturday 1 August 1925.* "Geo. White and Le Maire Fight," Variety, 5 Aug. 1925, 5.

82   *Despite those nasty preliminaries.* Brooklyn Eagle, 22 Sept. 1925, M7, reports the tea-shop ownership.

82   Gay Paree*'s thirty-four scenes.* Brooklyn Daily Star, 21 Sept. 1925, 14, describes the measures taken to add dressing rooms and accommodate props and scenery.

83   *The closing scene of the show.* Jack Haley, *Heart of the Tin Man: The Collected Writings of Jack Haley*, ed. Mitchell Cohen (Beverly Hills, CA: Tinman Publishing, 2000), 83.

83   *Critical reaction to* Gay Paree. Variety, 26 Aug. 1925, 17.

84   *The* New York Times *said.* New York Times, 19 Aug. 1925, 14. Brooklyn Eagle, 19 Aug. 1925, 7. Brett Page, Lincoln (NE) Star, 13 Sept. 1925, 22.

84   *While one might think.* Alvin J. Kayton, "In the Theatres on Broadway," Brooklyn Daily Star, 1 Sept. 1925, 12, credits the block party idea to Winnie and says she was "given full authority to make all arrangements." Variety, 2 Sept. 1925, 10, says "Winnie Lightner is blamed by the press agent for the scheme," but then in a later report (16 Sept. 1925, 11) credits the concept to Shubert press agent Henry Myers and says he made the arrangements with assistance from Rufus Le Maire and Irving Sherman.

85   *After* Gay Paree *ended.* "Winnie Lightner Hit a Cop in Boston," Variety, 10 Feb. 1926, 5.

85   *The show continued touring.* Barbara Barondess, who began her stage career with a minor role in the second *Gay Paree*, was Winnie's understudy. "Winnie Lightner

took me under her wing," Barondess later recalled. "I tagged along with her to song publishing firms in Tin Pan Alley and she taught me how to put over a song." It wasn't like Winnie to miss a performance, however, so Barondess never got to go on in her place. (Barbara Barondess MacLean, *One Life Is Not Enough: My Life in Russia and the Broadway and Hollywood Years* [New York: Hippocrene Books, 1986], 100.)

86   *The most memorable song.* Alvin J. Kayton, "In the Theatres on Broadway," Brooklyn Daily Star, 27 Dec. 1926, 12 (Gaby's kick).

86   *A happier role.* Winnie Lightner, as told to Frieda Wynott, "More Tomboys, Less Parlor Petting and Greater Safety for Girlhood, Says Broadway Star," Abilene (TX) Reporter-News, 1 May 1927, 46 ("I am called 'America's Tomboy'"). A photograph of Winnie wearing a suit and boater for her burlesque of Chevalier was published in Manuel Weltman, "Winnie Lightner, Broadway Favorite," Classic Film Collector, no. 19 (fall 1967), 9. A caricature of her wearing a tuxedo and top hat appeared in Brooklyn Eagle, 5 Dec. 1926, 48, but perhaps she did that in some other scene of the show.

87   *By the spring of 1927.* Confusingly, the second Gay Paree was at first called the 1926 edition, but beginning 16 Nov. 1926 the producers advertised it as the 1927 edition. Then after the show was revamped on 21 Mar. 1927, it was called the spring 1927 edition.

87   *By coincidence.* Marshall Van Winkle, *Sixty Famous Cases* (10 vols., Long Branch, NJ: Warren S. Ayres, 1956), 7: 279–329. Ken Murray, *The Body Merchant: The Story of Earl Carroll* (Pasadena, CA: Ward Ritchie Press, 1976), chaps. 6–11.

87   *In her lawsuit.* "Bath Picture Brings Suit," New York Times, 22 March 1927, 10.

88   *Besides her lawsuit.* Lewis Yablonsky, *George Raft* (New York: McGraw-Hill, 1974), 47. Mark A. Knowles, *The Wicked Waltz and Other Scandalous Dances: Outrage at Couples Dancing in the 19th and Early 20th Centuries* (Jefferson, NC: McFarland & Company, 2009), 230, discounts Raft's story on the grounds that he was not in the cast of *Gay Paree.* Knowles was mistaken because although Raft was not in the original cast, he did join it later. ("'Gay Paree' Anew at Winter Garden," New York Times, 22 Mar. 1927, 31. Armond Fields, *Sophie Tucker: First Lady of Show Business* [Jefferson, NC: McFarland & Company, 2003], 127–34.)

88   *Winnie returned to vaudeville.* "Winnie Lightner Back," Variety, 13 April 1927, 30. "14 Big Timers Left in U.S.," ibid., 25 May 1927, 25, says that of the current sixteen two-a-day theaters, one will switch to a "grind" (multi-show) policy, and another will close over the summer.

88   *When Winnie played Chicago.* Hazel Canning, "Winnie Lightner in Maid's Role Enjoys Fun Until Waiter Proposes," Hamilton (OH) Daily News, 21 May 1927, magazine sec., 3. The accompanying photograph of Winnie wearing a maid's uniform and holding her dog raises suspicion that the story is embellished if not false. Canning says vaguely that these events happened "the other day" in "a big Midwestern city." Canning says also, "Miss Lightner is leading comedienne in a Broadway show," but perhaps intended to say "was." The most likely location for these incidents is Chicago, where Winnie headlined at the Orpheum circuit's Palace Theater the week of 13 May 1927, and then was held over for a second week. (Chicago Tribune, 15 May 1927, H3. Variety, 25 May 1927, 50.)

89   *In June Winnie worked the subway circuit.* Brooklyn Eagle, 10 June 1927, 12A ("extremely pretty"). "When she appeared at the New York Palace, something like five

years ago in a trio, she hoped some day to have the star dressing room. Last week her dream came true . . . and the joy of having the coveted quarters all to herself may be better imagined than described." (Vaudeville News, 25 June 1927, 20.)

89   *Her opening performance.* Variety, 15 June 1927, 26. Brooklyn Eagle, 21 June 1927, 12A.

90   *In July Winnie returned to Chicago.* Variety, 24 Aug. 1927, 52 ("don't point him").

91   *Le Maire's Affairs premiered.* Chicago Tribune, 16 Aug. 1927, sec. 3, p. 27.

91   *Considering the show's strong points.* Ibid., 10 June 1927, sec. 3, p. 31 ("Lemaire's dislike").

92   *Supporting the acts.* Variety, 26 Oct. 1927, 27 ("did nine minutes"). Ibid., 26 ("staggering layout"). Ibid., 29, compares admission prices and revenues at Capitol and Palace.

92   *Meanwhile, four blocks down Broadway.* Ibid., 26 ("figure hard").

92   *Winnie next performed.* Philadelphia Inquirer, 6 Nov. 1927, 10 (at Fox). "The Producer Nobody Knows," New York Evening Post, 10 Dec. 1927, 9 (fire, flood). Brooklyn Eagle, 20 Nov. 1927, A13 (replaces Seeley). Brooklyn Standard Union, 22 Nov. 1927, 4 (successful tryout).

93   *"Revels" featured.* New York Times, 29 Nov. 1927, 30 ("impersonations of jelly fish").

94   *Reviewers noted.* Brooklyn Eagle, 22 Nov. 1927, 14A. Life, 22 Dec. 1927, 19. New Yorker, 10 Dec. 1927, 35. The reviewers did not describe the "pony ballet." It is possible that it was just a conventional dance number, because in show-business slang chorus girls were called "ponies," although it seems doubtful that the public program for a show would use that rather derogatory term.

94   *Although it pleased the critics.* John Lahr, *Notes on a Cowardly Lion: The Biography of Bert Lahr* (New York: Knopf, 1980; reprint Berkeley: University of California Press, 2000), 91. Variety, 11 Jan. 1928, 36 (Winnie replaced by Roth).

95   *As it happened.* UK Incoming Passenger Lists, 1878–1960, National Archives, London <archives.com>. Theo seems to have come along, as the passenger list includes also the name "Thea L. Alexander," but she stayed at a different hotel.

95   *Many American vaudeville stars.* Variety, 25 Jan. 1928, 3 ("opened indifferently"). Chicago Tribune, 23 Mar. 1928, 35 ("didn't get her").

95   *Winnie had to cancel.* Times (London), 14 Feb. 1928, 12 ("a feat which she achieves").

96   *On the evening of 24 January.* Daily Mail (London), 26 Jan. 1928, 8.

96   *There was a final surprise.* Variety, 28 Mar. 1928, 6 (Pittsburgh cancellation). Oakland (CA) Tribune, 12 May 1928, 5 ("singing, capering"). Los Angeles Times, 20 May 1928, C30 ("lend effervescence" "full-fledged star"). It is uncertain whether Winnie had a professional engagement in Paris or just went there on holiday.

97   *After Winnie performed.* Variety, 11 July 1928, 31 (illness). Brooklyn Eagle, 14 Aug. 1928, 5 ("sparkling material"). New York Times, 11 Sept. 1928, 30 ("abundance of gusto"). Brooklyn Eagle, 23 Sept. 1928, F3 ("line up the stage vote").

97   *Following six weeks on the subway circuit.* Variety, 25 Aug. 1928, 43; 31 Oct. 1928, 42.

97   *Winnie was part.* Brooklyn Eagle, 10 Sept. 1928, 14A, has a photograph captioned, "At the Palace: Winnie Lightner, featured this week at the Manhattan vaudeville house." Next to the photo is an advertisement for the Gaiety Theater featuring the film *The Air Circus* (a silent but "with Music and Sound Effects") as well as several Fox Movietone talking shorts, including Winnie's.

CHAPTER 6: MOVIES THAT TALK AND SING

99 *In late December 1927.* Film Daily, 29 Dec. 1927, 1, 6–7, 10. While Winnie's Movietone reel was her first talking appearance on screen, she apparently established a cinema presence of a sort even earlier when Pathé released two short subjects under the title *Words and Music By*—. Although silent, the shorts included "a special music cue synchronizing perfectly with the picture." A list of twenty-six names in the "distinguished cast" consisted largely of Tin Pan Alley composers and lyricists, but also included several performers, including Winnie. Possibly a still image of her was projected while someone played (and possibly also sang) on cue one of her popular numbers. (Motion Picture News, 23 Sept. 1927, 21 ["music cue" "distinguished cast"]. Vaudeville News, 1 Oct. 1927, 10.) Film Daily, 9 Sept. 1928, 9 ("in her characteristic manner").

99 *When Winnie made her film debut.* Among the more important works discussing the Warner brothers and the technological innovations that gave birth to Vitaphone and Movietone are: Harry M. Geduld, *The Birth of the Talkies: From Edison to Jolson* (Bloomington: Indiana University Press, 1975); Charles Higham, *Warner Brothers* (New York: Scribner's, 1975); Alexander Walker, *The Shattered Silents: How the Talkies Came to Stay* (London, UK: Elm Tree Books, 1978); Cass Warner Sperling and Cork Millner, *Hollywood Be Thy Name: The Warner Brothers Story* (Lexington: University Press of Kentucky, 1994); Scott Eyman, *The Speed of Sound: Hollywood and the Talkie Revolution, 1926–1930* (Baltimore: Johns Hopkins University Press, 1999); Donald Crafton, *The Talkies: American Cinema's Transition to Sound, 1926–1931* (Berkeley: University of California Press, 1999); and Douglas Gomery, *The Coming of Sound: A History* (New York: Routledge, 2005).

100 *Warner Bros. called its sound technology Vitaphone.* "The Amazing Story of the Talkies," Popular Mechanics Magazine, December 1928, 938–45, is a fascinating discussion of Vitaphone and Movietone published at a time when the future of sound was far from clear. The article quotes a British critic who believes that in adopting sound the American movie industry is committing suicide. The critic points out that most of the world's peoples do not speak English, and even those that do may not tolerate American accents and idioms.

101 *The top Hollywood studios.* Uniontown (PA) Morning Herald, 2 Mar. 1928, 14. Augusta (GA) Chronicle, 22 Mar. 1928, excerpt at <scmovietheatres.com>. Variety, 11 April 1928, 34.

101 *The future of sound.* Waterloo (IA) Evening Courier, 21 July 1928, 13 ("new policy contemplates no present change"). New York Times, 3 Sept. 1928, 17 ("I, too, have lost").

102 *In late August.* Variety, 29 Aug. 1928, 43 ("half real-half reel"). The stationary microphones and other primitive aspects of *Lights of New York* are described in Geduld, *Birth of the Talkies*, 206, and Eyman, *Speed of Sound*, 176. Who first used a boom microphone is disputed, but in describing the advances that Vitaphone made during the year 1928, Harry Warner said that *The Singing Fool* "illustrates how perfectly we have mastered the moving camera and the moving microphone." ("Vitaphone— Past and Future," Exhibitors Daily Review, 29 Dec. 1928, 10.)

102 *By then Winnie's Movietone reel.* Variety, 2 May 1928, 38; 12 Sept. 1928, 12 ("characteristic nut manner"). Winnie later prided herself on the fact that she had concealed her

pregnancy so successfully. "And no one ever knew," she said. "Smart, wasn't I?" (Alma Whitaker, "Winnie Just a Home Body," Los Angeles Times, 6 October 1929, 31.)

Later on during her feature film career Winnie would make brief appearances in two more short subjects: *An Intimate Dinner in Celebration of Warner Bros. Silver Jubilee* (1930) and *The Stolen Jools* (1931).

103 *The first of Winnie's Vitaphone releases.* Variety, 12 Sept. 1928, 12 ("hot number" "mob pleaser"). Ibid., 15 Aug. 1928, 17 ("show stopper" "strong for Winnie"). Curiously, Variety reviewed the second release first. Film Daily, 22 July 1928, 31, was unimpressed by Winnie's voice and songs but admitted she "certainly has a way about her, and there is no question that she is a comedienne who knows how to get her audience."

104 *Of the tunes.* Variety, 12 Sept. 1928, 12 ("double entendre lyrics"); 22 Aug. 1928, 44 ("pretty blue" "talking short people"). Winnie's Movietone short is believed lost, as is the picture element of her Vitaphone shorts.

104 *Actually, the talking short people.* Jack Warner to Will H. Hays, Hollywood, 30 June 1928, Record 424, MPPDA Digital Archive, Flinders University, Adelaide, South Australia <mppda.flinders.edu.au>. Technically Winnie was censored for words that were sung rather than spoken, but the censors made no distinction between the two.

104 *Censorship itself.* Stephen Tropiano, *Obscene, Indecent, Immoral, and Offensive: 100+ Years of Censored, Banned, and Controversial Films* (New York: Limelight Editions, 2009), 4–5, 9. Laura Wittern-Keller, *Freedom of the Screen: Legal Challenges to State Film Censorship, 1915–1981* (Lexington: University Press of Kentucky, 2008), 22–28.

James N. Rosenberg, "Address Delivered at the Association of the Bar of the City of New York," 15 March 1928, Record #403, MPPDA Digital Archive, says the states of Illinois, Kansas, Maryland, New York, Ohio, Pennsylvania, and Virginia have film censorship laws, and there are over thirty cities where "erudite chiefs of police protect morals and act as arbiters of taste."

105 *In June 1928.* Variety, 27 June 1928, 3; 3 Oct. 1928, 16. Walker, *Shattered Silents*, 48, gives the impression that a talking sequence in *Tenderloin* was censored shortly after that film premiered on 14 Mar. 1928. If true, that might mean the censoring of *Tenderloin* preceded that of Winnie's shorts. Contemporary sources demonstrate, however, that the *Tenderloin* scene was not removed by censors; rather, Warner Bros. decided to delete it because the first-night audience had laughed at its over-the-top melodramatic dialogue.

That it was Warners's own decision to cut the sequence in *Tenderloin* is made especially explicit in "'Movie Surgery': The Warners Perform an Operation on 'Tenderloin' in a Flatbush Clinic," Brooklyn Eagle, 25 Mar. 1928, E3. Later on in his book, Walker says that New York State began censoring talkies at the end of July 1928. (Walker, *Shattered Silence*, 77.)

105 *Both Fox and Warners.* Wittern-Keller, *Freedom of the Screen*, 65. Supreme Court of Pennsylvania, Appeal of Vitagraph, Inc., 4 February 1929, document 527, MPPDA Digital Archive.

106 *Even people who enjoyed.* Gomery, *The Coming of Sound*, chap. 5, conclusively demonstrates the importance of *The Singing Fool*, but unfairly attacks Donald Crafton for having made *The Jazz Singer* the centerpiece of Crafton's earlier book. Crafton had indeed done so, but he also said explicitly that it was not *The Jazz Singer*, but rather "the one-two punch" of *Lights of New York* and *The Singing Fool* that "proved beyond

doubt to producers and exhibitors that a feature sound film with a big star had the potential to make millions." (Crafton, *The Talkies*, 275.)

The myth that Jolson shocked the audience when he uttered the words "You ain't heard nothin' yet" in *The Jazz Singer* probably arose from people confusing their memories of that film with their memories of Jolson's earlier Vitaphone short, *A Plantation Act*, which was released 7 October 1926. That Jolson had used the same phrase in the short was not widely known until 13 April 1995 when *A Plantation Act*, having been found and restored largely through the indefatigable efforts of the Vitaphone Project, was exhibited for the first time in more than sixty years.

106 *In 1929 the talkies reached the tipping point.* Crafton, The Talkies, 253.

CHAPTER 7: GOLD DIGGERS OF BROADWAY

108 *The first of the great.* "Warners Wins Verdict on Rights to 'Desert Song,'" Film Daily, 7 Nov. 1928, 6. Exhibitors Forum, 5 Dec. 1928, 4 ("'Desert Song' has been completed"). Richard Barrios, *A Song in the Dark: The Birth of the Musical Film* (2nd ed., New York: Oxford University Press, 2010), 80–81.

109 *Warner Bros. scurried.* H[erbert] T. Kalmus, "Technicolor Adventures in Cinemaland," Journal of the Society of Motion Picture Engineers, 31 (Dec. 1938): 564–85. Richard W. Haines, *Technicolor Movies: The History of Dye Transfer Printing* (Jefferson, NC: McFarland & Co., 1993), chap. 1. James Layton and David Pierce, *The Dawn of Technicolor, 1915–1935* (Rochester, NY: George Eastman House, 2015) provides an exhaustive history of the Technicolor company and its technological developments.

110 Gold Diggers of Broadway, *a backstage musical.* New York Times, 31 Aug. 1929, 13.

110 *The improved sound and color.* The soundproof box is described in Donald Crafton, *The Talkies: American Cinema's Transition to Sound, 1926–1931* (Berkeley: University of California Press, 1999), 230–32; Douglas Gomery, *The Coming of Sound: A History* (New York: Routledge, 2005), 42–43; and Barrios, *Song in the Dark*, 19. A newspaper report describing the intense lighting said, "There have been cases of clothes bursting into flame or scorching." (Mordaunt Hall, "On the West Coast," New York Times, 14 July 1929, X3.) Charles Higham, who lists Winnie among the informants who shared their memories with him, says filming lasted up to eighteen hours a day, and the actors' hair smoked from the heat. (Charles Higham, *Warner Brothers* [New York: Scribner's, 1975], vii–viii, 83.) The sound stage measured 175 by 200 feet and had a ninety-foot ceiling. Two decades later it was still the largest in Hollywood. (Long Beach [CA] Independent, 16 Oct. 1949, 24C.)

111 *Del Ruth also hit upon.* "Talkies Use Megaphone, But Just at Rehearsal," Philadelphia Inquirer, 22 Sep. 1929, 7.

111 *Although it looked and sounded.* Throughout this book, film characters generally are referred to by the names of the actors who played them, simply because doing so makes it easier to keep straight who people are when plots are summarized.

111 *What was intrinsically.* It took the Hollywood studios a long time to work out how to incorporate dialogue while maintaining the visual pace of movies. Roy Del Ruth seems to have been one of the first directors to master the art. Lea Jacobs, *Film Rhythm after Sound: Technology, Music, and Performance* (Oakland: University of California Press, 2015), 6, points out that *Variety* praised Del Ruth for the excellent pacing of Winnie's next musical comedy, *Hold Everything* (1930), but the tempo of *Gold*

Diggers of Broadway may have been just as good. It is not possible to be sure, because the visuals of both films are now mostly lost.

112 *Despite his continued protests.* Winnie's plunge from the tabletop onto Gran was so impressive that both the *New Yorker* and *Punch* published drawings of it. That is a happy accident itself, because the visuals of that episode in the film are lost. (New Yorker, 28 Sept. 1929, 34. Punch, 8 Jan. 1930, 48.) When *Gold Diggers of Broadway* was showing in Australia, a rumor spread that Winnie Lightner was dead. Three conflicting explanations for her demise were circulated: "One was that she had been killed in a motor accident, and another that she had died through excessive drug-taking. But the third was the best of all: that she had fatally injured herself when, in a scene in the 'Gold Diggers,' she had to jump off a table on to the fat solicitor!" ("Exaggerated! Winnie Lightner Rumor," Perth Daily News, 13 June 1930, 9.)

113 *Winnie's performance.* Variety, 4 Sept. 1929, 75. Movie Age, 26 Oct. 1929, 16. Film Daily, 3 Sept. 1929, 1. New Movie Magazine, Jan. 1930, 120. Picture Play, Dec. 1929, 64.

114 *Reviewers in the popular press.* Life, 27 Sept. 1929, 23. Brooklyn Standard Union, 31 Aug. 1929, 6. Albany (NY) Evening News, 28 Sept. 1929. Chicago Tribune, 9 Nov. 1929, 15. Los Angeles Times, 28 Sept. 1929, A9. Montreal Gazette, 25 Nov. 1929, 6. (Perth, AUS) Western Mail, 30 Jan. 1930, 4 ("marvellously glittering"). "What's On in London," Times of India, 29 Nov. 1929, 16 ("greatest comedienne"). Daily Mail (London), 2 Jan. 1930, 13. Adelaide Advertiser, 23 June, 1930, 11.

Amidst the euphoria, there were at least two dissents. *Time* magazine called the film a failure because its storyline was "smothered by the constant singing," "ballets in bright, blurry costumes," and "Winnie Lightner's noisy wisecracks." The reviewer for *Punch* objected to the movie's frequent cuts from close to distant views, and to its overall "restlessness and jumpiness." He added that Winnie exhibited "a broad comic style with a negroid flavour," and that her performance was "excellent without being attractive or suggesting any Sex Appeal." At bottom these two reviews simply did not accept the musical comedy film as a new model of entertainment. The *Time* critic was unhappy that the picture was nothing like the stage play from which it derived, and the *Punch* reviewer was distressed that the movie's visual style departed radically from the conventions of silent film. (Time, 16 Sept. 1929, 20. Owen Seaman, "At the Pictures: 'Gold Diggers of Broadway,'" Punch, 8 Jan. 1930, 48–49.)

115 *Winnie had so successfully.* Florabel Muir, "New Faces for Old: What the Talkies Have Done to Hollywood," Liberty, 17 May 1930, 60–62.

A key factor in Winnie's success was her speaking voice, which was always clearly audible yet sounded natural, unlike, for example, that of Nancy Welford, who spoke as though she were delivering her lines on a stage. "And that," a syndicated columnist pointed out, "in these days of sound-recording devices, is considerably more important than the ability to photograph well." (Dan Thomas, Niagara Falls Gazette, 19 Oct. 1929, 8.)

115 Gold Diggers of Broadway *did indeed make a gratifying profit.* Motion Picture News, 9 Nov. 1929, 41 ("shame to have the run cut"). North Adams (MA) Transcript, 28 Sept. 1929, 7 ("relieve the congestion"). Altoona (PA) Mirror, 27 Sept. 1929, 26 ("attend matinees"). (Weedsport, NY) Cayuga Chief, 11 July 1930, 4 ("have had requests").

116 Gold Diggers of Broadway *was in wide release.* The best available data on MGM and Warner Bros. revenues are in H. Mark Glancy, "MGM Film Grosses, 1924–1948: The Eddie Mannix Ledger," Historical Journal of Film, Radio, and Television, 12 (June 1992) 127–44 and microfiche supplement; and H. Mark Glancy, "Warner Bros. Film Grosses, 1921–51: The William Schaefer Ledger," ibid., 15 (Mar. 1995) 55–73 and microfiche supplement. Because each studio had its own accounting system, the figures from one are only roughly comparable with those from the other.

117 *In the popular imagination.* "Winnie Lightner on Gold Digging," Brooklyn Standard Union, 7 Dec. 1929, 6.

117 *But as the already straitened circumstances.* "Director Sued for Money 'Spent on Actress,'" Victoria (TX) Advocate, 20 Jan. 1952, 3A. "The Screen and Its Stars," Carnavon (AUS) Northern Times, 18 June 1931, 5 ("I was a playgirl"). Malcolm H. Oettinger, "One Vote for Hollywood," Picture Play, March 1930, 34 ("crowd started Sunday-dropping-in"). Winnie said in another interview that she gave up partying after her foster mother died. (Helen Louise Walker, "Winnie Lightner . . . says 'Love Has Eluded Me,'" Film Weekly [London, UK)], 30 Aug. 1930, 9.)

118 *Roy and Winnie kept quiet.* Jimmy Starr, *Barefoot on Barbed Wire: An Autobiography of a Forty-Year Hollywood Balancing Act* (Lanham, MD: Scarecrow Press, 2001), chap. 12, "The Spoiled Brat," 203 ("strange, talented man" "spoiled-brat wives"), 204 ("didn't like each other" "Why not?").

Using the stage name Olive Dale, Olive appeared in five Fox comedy short subjects in 1920–21, three of them directed by Roy. She also was in the Universal comedy short *On Account,* according to a review in Exhibitors Herald, 18 June 1921, 67. She married Roy on 14 March 1921 (Moving Picture World, 2 April 1921, 477).

119 *It may seem strange.* Russel Crouse, "Lightner vs. Crouse," New Movie Magazine, May 1930, 130.

119 *When not playing to an audience.* H. J. M. [Herman J. Mankiewicz], "News and Gossip of the Two Wideapart Rialtos," New York Times, 14 April 1929, 121.

120 *Along with her little boy.* Alma Whitaker, "Winnie Just a Home Body," Los Angeles Times, 6 Oct. 1929, 31 ("Watch me"). Eugene Earle, "Winnie Wows 'Em!" Photoplay, Mar. 1930, 150 ("wanted a big dog").

120 *Winnie confessed.* Earle, "Winnie Wows 'Em!" 151 ("It isn't like it used to be"). Network radio also lured talent away from vaudeville. It is curious that Winnie singled out the Duncans, Surratt, and Barnes—especially the latter two—as she had appeared on bills with many vaudeville stars who were far more famous.

121 *Winnie was paying.* Whitaker, "Winnie Just a Home Body."

CHAPTER 8: SHE COULDN'T SAY NO

122 *Confident that Winnie's bravura performance.* H. Mark Glancy, "MGM Film Grosses, 1924–1948: The Eddie Mannix Ledger," Historical Journal of Film, Radio, and Television, 12 (June 1992): 127–44 and microfiche supplement.

122 *Jack Warner figured.* New York Times, 17 Nov. 1929, X7 ("1,000 Hollywood beauties"). H. Mark Glancy, "Warner Bros. Film Grosses, 1921–51: The William Schaefer Ledger," Historical Journal of Film, Radio, and Television, 15 (Mar. 1995): 55–73 and microfiche supplement.

122 *Well for starters.* Richard Barrios, *A Song in the Dark: The Birth of the Musical Film* (2nd ed., New York: Oxford University Press, 2010), 164–69; see especially 165n10 on the shortage of Technicolor cameras. Herbert T. Kalmus, head of the Technicolor company, said in late September 1929 that there were just twenty-five such cameras, "working night and day," but a new one was being added each week. (New York Times, 29 Sept. 1929, X6.)

123 *Fortunately, most of these deficiencies.* Because most of *The Show of Shows* survives only in black and white, it is uncertain whether Winnie's scenes were originally in Technicolor.

124 *Funny as it was.* Barrios, *Song in the Dark*, 166n12, says studio correspondence confirms that Mayer contemplated suing.

125 *In* The Show of Shows *Winnie appears to enjoy herself.* Malcolm H. Oettinger, "One Vote for Hollywood," Picture Play, Mar. 1930, 92 ("odd jobs").

125 *She is a nightclub singer.* Although neither the sound disks nor the visuals of *She Couldn't Say No* are known to survive, a transcript of the spoken dialogue was submitted to the New York State censors and is now in the New York State Archives, Albany. The dialogue quoted here is from that transcript. Correspondence filed with the transcript indicates that following a complaint from the Polish Consul, Warner Bros. instructed exhibitors in New York State to delete the ethnic slur "Pollack mug;" however, it slipped through at some theaters. (Apparently the relevant sound disk was not altered; instead, exhibitors were merely told to cut off their speakers when the offending phrase occurred.) See also "'Dirty Pollack' Polish Insult," Variety, 12 Mar. 1930, 4.

A fictionalized version published in Talking Screen (May 1930), 36–38, 74–75, 91, is helpful in visualizing the context of the dialogue in *She Couldn't Say No.*

128 *The unfolding of this inconsequential but amusing story.* New York Clipper, 22 Sept. 1920, 18 ("richness of voice").

129 *Joe E. Brown recalled.* Joe E. Brown as told to Ralph Hancock, *Laughter Is a Wonderful Thing* (New York: A. S. Barnes and Co., 1956), 203 ("minds more on how they look"), 207 ("no one on the lot").

129 *After the completion.* Ibid., 196.

129 *With* Hold Everything *wrapped up.* Brooklyn Eagle, 7 Nov. 1929, 23. Film Daily, 8 Nov. 1929, 10.

130 *But Winnie soon had other preoccupations.* Walter Winchell, "On Broadway," (Glen Falls, NY) Post-Star, 30 Dec. 1929, 4.

130 *Instead of playing the Palace.* Gilbert Swan, "Keeping Fit at the Pace That Kills," Bismarck (ND) Tribune, 2 Aug. 1930, 6. Philadelphia Jack O'Brien, "How to Have a Hollywood Figure," Screenland, Aug. 1930, 18–19, 110–12. Helen Klumph, "His Way with Women," Picture Play, Sept. 1930, 63, 105. Film Daily, 23 Oct. 1930, 3.

131 *Months later.* Gene Mac, (St. Petersburg, FL) Independent, 17 April 1930, 21 ("Pennsylvania barn"). Harry Evans, Life, 14 Mar. 1930, 20 ("too fat to be cute").

131 *Although Winnie refused.* New York Times, 21 Nov. 1929, 31; 22 Nov. 1929, 31 (Warners advertisement quoting reviews).

131 *Winnie's fame had been growing.* Glancy, "Warner Bros. Film Grosses."

132 *"Singin' in the Bathtub."* The financial incentive for artists to make records was lessened because copyright law protected only composers and not performers. (Alex S.

Cummings, "From Monopoly to Intellectual Property: Music Piracy and the Remaking of American Copyright, 1909–1971," Journal of American History, 97 [Dec. 2010]: 659–81.)

On 18 June 1929, Winnie made a test recording of two popular songs, "Mean to Me" and "I'll Never Ask for More," by Fred E. Ahlert and Roy Turk, for the Victor Talking Machine Company, but it was never released. (Matrix BVE-Test-651, Encyclopedic Discography of Victor Recordings, University of California at Santa Barbara Library <victor.library.ucsb.ca>.)

132 *While not persuading Winnie.* Agreement between Warner Bros. Pictures, Inc., and Winnie Lightner, New York, 22 Nov. 1929, United Artists Corporation Records, Series 1.7: Warner Bros. Contracts and Legal Files, call no. U.S. Mss. 99 AN/1.7, Wisconsin Historical Society, Madison.

132 *The Warner Bros. publicity department.* Los Angeles Times, 9 Nov. 1930, B10 ("cornet and singing act").

133 *One story about.* Pittsburgh Press, 7 Dec. 1930, 68 ("rowdy tomboy"). Possibly the earliest appearance of the ubiquitous muddy-shoes story was in the Syracuse (NY) Herald, 20 Oct. 1929. Others include: Bakersfield (CA) Californian, 9 Nov. 1929, 6; Los Angeles Times, 26 Jan. 1930, B11; Galveston (TX) Daily News, 9 Feb. 1930, 19; Los Angeles Times, 2 Mar. 1930, B13; Lewiston (ME) Daily Sun, 18 June 1930, 4; Oakland (CA) Tribune, 8 Mar. 1931, 10; Woodland (CA) Daily Democrat, 19 Mar. 1931, 4; Schenectady (NY) Gazette, 22 June 1931, 14; Utica (NY) Observer-Dispatch, 1 Sept. 1931, 10; St. Lawrence (Canton, NY) Plaindealer, 25 Aug. 1931, 4; Syracuse (NY) Herald, 3 Jan. 1932, sec. 3, p. 10; Corning (NY) Leader, 14 Jan. 1933.

133 *It was claimed.* "Winnie Lightner Has No Luck in Pictures," Charleston (WV) Daily Mail, 29 Mar. 1931, 6 ("I'm not the type"). Rosalind Shepard, "The Tomboy of the Talkies," Photoplay, Feb. 1931, 57, 130–31.

Winnie's supposed deep unhappiness is elaborated also in J. M. S. Davies, "No Love for Winnie," (Adelaide, AUS) Register News-Pictorial, 22 Nov. 1930, 12, which quotes her as saying: "I have never had anything that I wanted. Life seems to elude me; love seems to evade me. I know that I shall never be happy. I hope I may learn to be content."

134 *As Warner Bros. began gearing up.* John Skinner, "It Works Both Ways," Brooklyn Daily Eagle, 3 Feb. 1930, 25.

134 She Couldn't Say No *premiered.* Variety, 2 April, 1930, 8 ("Male customers").

135 *Critical response to the film.* Columbia (University, NYC) Daily Spectator, 20 Feb. 1930, 2.

135 *Where the critics differed most.* Tom Lewis, Hollywood Filmograph, 1 Mar. 1930, 21 ("millions of new fans"). Mae Tinée, "Song Shouter Wins Applause," Chicago Tribune, 5 Mar. 1930, 29 ("heartsome and convincing"). Char [pseud.], Variety, 19 Feb. 1930, 33. New York Times, 15 Nov. 1930, 15.

135 *Some thought Winnie.* Life, 14 Mar. 1930, 20.

136 *Winnie did not attend.* Philadelphia Inquirer, 8 Mar. 1930, 28. Variety, 26 Feb. 1930, 11.

136 *Meanwhile, two thousand miles away.* Los Angeles Times, 22 Mar. 1930, A7. Hollywood Filmograph, 29 Mar. 1930, 28. Variety, 26 Mar. 1930, 25 ("best comedy picture"), 37 ("wouldn't be surprised").

137 *On 18 April.* Film Daily, 23 April 1930, 1 ("as distinguished an audience").

137 Hold Everything *received.* New York Times, 23 April 1930, 21. Brooklyn Standard Union, 23 April 1930, 7. Wall Street Journal, 25 April 1930, 4.

138 *Of the eighty-two films.* Glancy, "Warner Bros. Film Grosses."

CHAPTER 9: A SINGER SILENCED

139 *On the afternoon.* Uniontown (PA) Daily News Standard, 5 May 1930, 8 ("I'll miss New York"). Hollywood Filmograph, 5 April 1930, 21 ("more like Broadway").

139 *The talkies had indeed.* Dan Thomas, "No Such Thing as Key to Motion Picture Success," San Jose (CA) News, 19 Mar. 1931, 10. See also "Star Changes Up to Now," Variety, 18 Feb. 1931, 3, 28.

Winnie, along with most of the other early talkies stars at Warner Bros., appeared in *An Intimate Dinner in Celebration of Warner Bros. Silver Jubilee,* a promotional short subject released in August 1930.

142 *Thanks to Roy Del Ruth's superb direction.* The term "pre-code" is used here as convenient shorthand for any film made prior to the strict enforcement of the Motion Picture Code that began in 1934. Technically this usage is inaccurate, as a code was in effect (although not rigidly enforced) beginning in 1930.

142 The Life of the Party *was filmed in Technicolor.* Variety, 26 Feb. 1930, 11 (widescreen planned). Ibid., 17 Dec. 1930, 5 (experiments halted). Warner Bros. did exhibit one feature film, *Kismet* (1930), in widescreen format. (David Coles, "Magnified Grandeur: The Big Screen, 1926–31," 70mm Newsletter, issue 63 [Mar. 2001], <in70mm.com>.)

143 *While it narrowly missed.* Variety, 25 June 1930, 10 (Vitaphone improvements). Ibid., 14 ("by far the best method"). (Penrith, New South Wales, AUS) Nepean Times, 25 July 1931, 8 ("no flies on me"). On Vitaphone editing, see also Lea Jacobs, "The Innovation of Re-Recording in the Hollywood Studios," Film History: An International Journal, vol. 24 no.1 (2012), 11.

143 *Although moviemakers always try.* "Had Real Song Revival During Lull in Filming," Philadelphia Inquirer, 9 Nov. 1930, 9.

145 *While Winnie was making* The Life of the Party. Motion Picture Classic, Nov. 1930, 89 ("a favorite subject"). Myrtle Gebhart, "Appetites Go Haywire," Picture Play, May 1933, 19 ("interwoven in Hollywood's History"). Jimmie Fidler, "Hollywood Shots," Reading (PA) Eagle, 10 April 1939, 6 ("frenzied reducing vogue").

145 *Whether Winnie ever followed.* Carolyn Van Wyck, "Nothing Left on the Plates," Photoplay (Sept. 1930), 81, gives Winnie's recipe for her Italian salad dressing, as well as another one involving kidney beans, onion, celery, pickles, hardboiled eggs, pimentos, and mayonnaise.

145 *It appears certain.* Patricia Dillon, "In Hollywood," Brooklyn Standard Union, 1 July 1930, 7 ("I never did diet"). Perth (AUS) Sunday Times, 2 Nov. 1930, 11 ("storm centre"). Robbin Coons column, Niagara Falls Gazette, 24 Aug. 1931 (Nate Slott). Reading (PA) Eagle, 22 July 1932, 14 ("Each morning"). Perth (AUS) Mirror, 28 Feb. 1931, 7 ("One of my ambitions").

146 *Another preoccupation of Winnie's.* Dorothy Herzog, "Behind the Scenes in Hollywood," Logansport (IN) Pharos-Tribune, 27 May 1930, 3 (mother's death). Hubbard Keavy, "Screen Life in Hollywood," Sandusky (OH) Register, 1 Feb. 1933, 9 ("doesn't think so much"). Gregory Paul Williams, *The Story of Hollywood: An Illustrated History* (Malden, UK: Blackwell, 2005), 195 (mystics skirt law).

147 *Related to Winnie's alleged faith.* Herzog, "Behind the Scenes" (sleepless night). "True Ghost Stories by Famous People. . . . By Winnie Lightner, Actress," Batavia (NY) Times, 24 Jan. 1935, 7 ("gusts of wind"). A less elaborate version of the Sloe

story was published years earlier in Reno (NV) Gazette, 13 Feb. 1932, 8, and other newspapers.

147 *Between October 1930 and January 1931.* Exhibitors Herald-World, 27 Sept. 1930, 43. Film Daily, 30 Oct. 1930, 11. *Official Guide of the Railways*, Jan. 1930, xxvii, 306, 1010.

148 *When Winnie reached Manhattan.* Exhibitors Herald-World, 22 Nov. 1930, 32.

148 The Life of the Party *won high praise.* Film Daily, 9 Nov. 1930, 11. Picture Play, Feb. 1931, 66. Los Angeles Times, 3 Nov. 1930, A7. New York Times, 10 Nov. 1930, 16. Variety, 12 Nov. 1930, 21. Life, 19 Dec. 1930, 20.

149 *The general public.* Brooklyn Standard Union, 13 Dec. 1930, 7.

149 *Neither the critics.* Christopher Stone, "Film Notes," Gramophone, Jan. 1931, 36. Months earlier an American critic had expressed similar sentiments: "The talking films have now so over-worked the musical comedy's formulas that they seem pretty poisonous, even on the stage. I, for one, am so weary of seeing chorus girls in squads and regiments marching back and forth waving ostrich plumes that even the sight of policemen or boy scouts drilling is sufficient to bring on the jitters, along with that dizzy sensation and those spots before the eyes." (Creighton Peet, "The Movies," Outlook and Independent, 7 May 1930, 32.)

Many reference works and Internet sources say incorrectly that *The Life of the Party* originally contained the songs "Can It Be Possible?," "One Robin Doesn't Make a Spring," and "Somehow." The mistake arises from confusing Winnie's film with a stage musical with a similar name (identical except omitting the article), *Life of the Party*, which ran in Detroit 8 Oct. through 6 Dec. 1942 but never made it to Broadway. (Billboard, 24 Oct. 1942, 9. Dan Dietz, *The Complete Book of 1940s Broadway Musicals* [Lanham, MD: Rowman & Littlefield, 2015], 165–66.)

150 *Probably the picture.* Sheboygan (WI) Press, 8 Nov. 1930, 17 ("sings several" "You Ought to See the Horse"). Circleville (OH) Herald, 18 April 1931, 5.

150 *Even greater uncertainty.* Daily Mail, 11 May 1931, 4 ("theme song").

151 *The notion that.* (Leismore, New South Wales, AUS) Northern Star, 29 Aug. 1931, 3 ("sings several").

151 *At present.* "$2,980 Was Price Paid for Gown Worn in Film," Philadelphia Inquirer, 2 Nov. 1930, 9. To present day viewers the most striking aspect of the fashion show scene may be that all of the models are healthy looking, full-bodied women rather than anorexic waifs.

151 *While* The Life of the Party *was drawing crowds.* Picture Play, Feb. 1931, 33 (Richard's tonsils). "Theater Gossip," St. Petersburg (FL) Independent, 13 Dec. 1930, 9 (riding el).

152 *Another columnist.* Variety, 19 Nov. 1930, 43.

152 *Perhaps Winnie would not.* O. O. McIntyre, "Everyday New York," Newton (NY) Register, 7 Feb. 1931, 7.

153 *After a month at leisure.* Pittsburgh Press, 6 Dec. 1930, 13. Variety, 17 Dec. 1930, 9.

153 *During her week in Pittsburgh.* Pittsburgh Press, 8 Dec. 1930, 1.

153 *After the Stanley.* Variety, 17 Dec. 1930, 8 ("place isn't big enough"). Motion Picture News, 27 Dec. 1930, 21 ("new box office record"). Film Daily, 13 Jan. 1931, 1 (Indianapolis).

154 *With her usual knack.* New York Times, 19 Feb. 1931, 27. Brooklyn Standard Union, 14 Mar. 1931, 9. Variety, 25 Feb. 1931, 12. Los Angeles Times, 16 Mar. 1931, A9.

154 Sit Tight, *like* The Life of the Party. Wall Street Journal, 20 Feb. 1931, 4.

155 Sit Tight *was the sixth best moneymaker*. Mark H. Glancy, "Warner Bros. Film Gross-es, 1921–51: The William Schaefer Ledger," Historical Journal of Film, Radio, and Television 15 (Mar. 1995): 5–73 and microfiche supplement. Cass Warner Sperling and Cork Millner, *Hollywood Be Thy Name* (Lexington: University of Kentucky Press, 1998), 152, 160. Variety, 29 Mar. 1932, 17, reported that 2,721 American cinemas had closed since the Depression began.

156 *In February 1931*. Los Angeles Times, 20 June 1930, A8. Film Daily, 14 July 1930, 2. Los Angeles Times, 14 Jan. 1931, A9. Film Daily, 1 Feb. 1931, 4.

157 *Unfortunately, the finished picture*. A publicity release for *Gold Dust Gertie* quoted Lloyd Bacon as saying Winnie was "the greatest scene-saver in the picture business." The release explained, "Winnie plugs everything, holes in dialogue, awkward scenes in action, forgotten cues. When she works in a picture she sees to it that the production is water tight, air tight and laugh tight. She fills all empty spaces with her own personality." (Bakersfield Californian, 1 Aug. 1931.) No doubt Winnie did her best, but she could not overcome the picture's deficiencies.

158 Gold Dust Gertie *premiered*. New York Times, 30 May 1931, 17. Syracuse (NY) Herald, 31 May 1931, 10 ("Laughs in this farce"). Film Daily, 31 May 1931, 10 ("a rather weak story"). Edwin Schallert, "'Gold Dust Gertie' Hits Wild Pace," Los Angeles Times, 15 June 1931, A7. Daily Mail, 30 Nov. 1931, 4.

At around this same time Winnie was among the numerous film stars who could be seen in *The Stolen Jools*, a short subject distributed to raise funds for the support of the tuberculosis sanitarium sponsored by the National Variety Artists.

159 *It is sometimes rumored*. Los Angeles Times, 20 June 1930, A8 ("some musical features").

160 *Winnie's natural gifts*. On feminism and sex roles in the 1930s, see Lois Scharf, *To Work and to Wed: Female Employment, Feminism, and the Great Depression* (Westport, CT: Greenwood Press, 1960), and Winifred Wandersee, *Women's Work and Family Values, 1920–1940* (Cambridge, MA: Harvard University Press, 1981), chap. 6.

161 *Husbands and wives*. "100 Years of Marriage and Divorce Statistics: United States, 1867–1967," (Rockville, MD: US Department of Health, Education, and Welfare, 1973), 22 <cdc.gov/nchs>. Matthew J. Hill, "Love in the Time of Depression: The Effect of Economic Conditions on Marriage in the Great Depression," Journal of Economic History, 75 (Mar. 2015): 163–89.

CHAPTER 10: FEMINISM RESTRAINED

162 *Following the stock market crash*. Cass Warner Sperling and Cork Millner, *Hollywood Be Thy Name: The Warner Brothers Story* (Lexington: University Press of Kentucky, 1998), chap. 14 and pp. 160, 209, 211.

162 *In the spring of 1931*. Picture Play, April 1931, 27.

163 *The studio publicity department*. Brooklyn Daily Star, 6 Aug. 1931, 10 ("silken pajamas"). New Castle (PA) News, 18 Aug. 1931, 7 ("black lace").

163 *The most egregious example*. Police Gazette, 25 April 1931.

163 *Of course the attempted alteration*. Desmond Fitzpatrick, "Is It Men or Women Who Get the Most Fun Out of Life?" Syracuse (NY) Herald, 16 Aug. 1931, magazine sec., 8. Costello had appeared along with Winnie in the 1922 and 1924 editions of *George White's Scandals*.

164 *Winnie had a less roseate view.* Frederick James Smith, "Dead Pan Butterworth," Liberty, 31 Oct. 1936, 53 ("Matrimony is enough problem").

166 *Winnie appears also.* "Winnie Lightner . . . Tells of Daring Double in Warner Bros. Film . . . ," Amsterdam (NY) Evening Recorder, 29 Sept. 1931, 6.

167 *Henry Jenkins, the only scholar.* Henry Jenkins, *What Made Pistachio Nuts?: Early Sound Comedy and the Vaudeville Aesthetic* (New York: Columbia University Press, 1992), 263, 265.

167 *Another scholar.* M. Alison Kibler, *Rank Ladies: Gender and Cultural Hierarchy in American Vaudeville* (Chapel Hill: University of North Carolina Press, 1999), 230n37.

169 *The plot thickens.* "Pre-code" meaning prior to the strict enforcement of the Motion Picture Code beginning in 1934.

170 *Saddled with its storyline.* Motion Picture Herald, 4 July 1931, 31 ("long rounds of applause").

   Del Ruth, like other directors, had almost no say in what became of his pictures once filming was complete. (Thomas Schatz, *The Genius of the System: Hollywood Filmmaking in the Studio Era* [New York: Pantheon Books, 1988], 140.)

170 *To some Hollywood journalists.* Dan Thomas column, Olean (NY) Times, 7 July 1931, 13 ("warbles twice"). Helen Louise Walker, "Musical Pictures Are Here Again," Motion Picture, Nov. 1931), 52 ("Maybe you have felt it coming").

170 *Despite its defects.* Motion Picture Daily, 2 July 1931, 9. Variety, 22 Sept. 1931, 26. Film Daily, 20 Sept. 1931, 10. Photoplay, Sept. 1931, 98. (Madison, WI) Capital Times, 12 Oct. 1931, 12 ("everything gets straightened out"). Kossuth County (Algona, IA) Advance, 8 Oct. 1931, 4. "Hollywood's Standing Circus Supplies the Movies . . . ," Brooklyn Eagle, 26 July 1931, B9.

171 *Mordaunt Hall.* New York Times, 19 Sept. 1931, 10. Los Angeles Times, 26 Sept. 1931, A7. New Yorker, 26 Sept. 1931, 74.

171 *While making* Side Show. "Lightner Recovering from Heart Dilation," Brooklyn Eagle, 12 May 1931, 2. Esther Ralston, *Some Day We'll Laugh: An Autobiography* (Metuchen, NJ: Scarecrow Press, 1985), 123–24, 128, 155–56.

172 *Another personal concern.* Motion Picture Daily, 13 June 1931, 2. Chicago Tribune, 30 June 1931, 17.

172 *Winnie hurried back.* Variety, 13 May, 1931, 43 ("biggest role"). Los Angeles Times, 20 May 1931, A9. Wall Street Journal, 28 July 1931, 3. Los Angeles Times, 9 Sept. 1931, A9. New York Times, 14 Oct. 1931, 31; 16 Nov. 1931, 23.

172 *Warner Bros. had acquired.* Variety, 13 Oct. 1931, 17 ("picked out of the hat").

175 *While fleeting allusions.* Richard Barrios, *Screened Out: Playing Gay in Hollywood from Edison to Stonewall* (New York: Routledge, 2003), 66–68, has an excellent analysis of Watson's Paisley. Film Daily, 29 Dec. 1931, 2, reports the absence of censorship in the United States. The film did not escape unscathed elsewhere, however: In the Canadian provinces of Ontario and Alberta the censors did not object to Paisley, but they did cut Winnie's joke about Madame Du Barry costing $10 a night. (Variety, 29 Mar. 1932, 31.)

175 *Although* Manhattan Parade *was made.* Variety, 8 Dec. 1931, 4 (*Manhattan Parade* is one of six pictures recently produced at an average cost of $225,000). Motion Picture Herald, 5 Sept. 1931, 12 (new contract between Warner Bros. and Technicolor). "A Projectionist Praises Color," ibid., 7 May 1932, 35. Ruth Morris,

"Uncommon Chatter," Variety, 29 Dec. 1931, 163. That Technicolor still required extremely bright lighting is evident in a photograph showing a *Manhattan Parade* set surrounded by huge lamps. (Motion Picture Herald, 26 Dec. 1931, 18.)

176 *While Winnie's newly glamorous appearance.* Jack Burton, *The Blue Book of Hollywood Musicals: Songs from the Sound Tracks and the Stars Who Sang Them Since the Birth of the Talkies a Quarter-Century Ago* (Watkins Glen, NY: Century House, 1953), 45, appears to be the earliest of several secondary works that say the two songs were to have been in the film, although the source of that information is unclear. Both songs were copyrighted in 1931, which is consistent with the claim.

176 *Manhattan Parade premiered.* New York Times, 25 Dec. 1931, 32. Los Angeles Times, 25 Dec. 1931, A9.

177 *There were mixed reactions.* Variety, 29 Dec. 1931, 167.

177 *Even before.* Variety, 1 Dec. 1931, 3; 22 Dec. 1931, 2. Photoplay, Feb. 1932, 94 ("Salaries are being cut").

177 *The decision by Warner Bros.* Variety, 22 Dec. 1931, 2 ("castle in the air").

178 *Hollywood columnist Robbin Coons.* "Hollywood Sights and Sounds," Niagara Falls Gazette, 29 Dec. 1931, 8.

CHAPTER 11: BEST FRIENDS FOREVER

180 *With Young serving.* A reviewer of the film wondered "how girls on salesladies' salaries can live and dress so well." It was a good question. The studio apartment in which Winnie and Young resided had its own kitchenette and bathroom, which made it luxurious by 1930s standards, even if the two women did have to share the only bed. (Syracuse [NY] Journal, 2 April 1932, 11.)

181 *Although the filming.* Martin Dickstein, "Slow Motion" column, Brooklyn Eagle, 20 Mar. 1932, E4.

181 Play-Girl *premiered.* Los Angeles Times, 4 Mar. 1932, 15. Variety, 22 Mar. 1932, 13. Film Daily, 20 Mar. 1932, 10. New York Times, 19 Mar. 1932, 11.

182 *One especially perceptive reviewer.* Frederick James Smith, "The Serious Sex," Liberty, 9 April 1932, 26. Board of Review Collection, Kansas State Historical Society <kshs.org>.

Strangely, a Warner Bros. publicity blurb for *Play-Girl* described Winnie's performance not as a muted return to her former feminism, but rather as a sharp departure from it: "Winnie Lightner, famous as the 'tomboy of the talkies,' will be seen in a new role in 'Play Girl.' . . . Though she usually plays hard-boiled, wise-cracking roles . . . Her role [in *Play-Girl*] is warm with pity and tenderness, a new sort of part for Winnie and one in which she revels." (Cohocton [NY] Valley Times-Index, 20 April 1932, 3.)

182 *When she had completed.* Walter Winchell in transcript of "The Lucky Strike Dance Hour" radio program on station WEAF, 16 Feb. 1932 <tobaccodocuments.org>. "Asks Divorce," Chicago Tribune, 17 June 1932, 10.

182 *Considering that Winnie and Holtrey.* Sanford N. Katz, *Family Law in America* (New York: Oxford University Press, 2003), 2, 79, 81n.

183 *There was no chance.* "Winnie Lightner Sued for Rent," Los Angeles Times, 11 July 1935, 3.

183 *Fortunately, Winnie did not require any cooperation.* "Winnie Lightner Granted Divorce," ibid., 24 Nov. 1932, 9 ("foster father and a crowbar"). "Referee Backs Divorce Plea of Winnie Lightner," Philadelphia Inquirer, 18 Nov. 1932, 2 ("going to remain friends"). Variety, 21 June 1932, 40, quotes Walter Winchell column in New York Daily Mirror, 20 June 1932: "George Holtrey, who is countering Winnie Lightner's melting action, isn't a broker, as reported by the rags. He's a stage hand."

184 *Winnie and her son Richard.* "Opens Agency," Hollywood Filmograph, 7 June 1930, 28. "Swimming Champ Sued for Salary," (Massillon, OH) Evening Independent, 18 Dec. 1931, 15. Variety, 22 Mar. 1932, 42. Hollywood Filmograph, 2 April 1932, 9.

186 *The first critical response.* New Movie Magazine, April 1933, 103. Hollywood Reporter, 29 May 1933, 5. New York Times, 29 July 1933, 14. Christian Century, 15 July 1933, 10. Liberty, 22 July 1933, 31.

187 *The critics had little reason to mention.* Jeffrey Spivak, *Buzz: The Life and Art of Busby Berkeley* (Lexington: University Press of Kentucky, 2011), 49, 66–72, 82.

188 *The gamble that the public.* H. Mark Glancy, "Warner Bros. Film Grosses, 1921–51: The William Schaefer Ledger," Historical Journal of Film, Radio, and Television, 15 (Mar. 1995): 55–73 and microfiche supplement.

189 *Soon the women are standing in night court.* The opening scenes of the picture were timely, in that soon after becoming mayor of New York City in January 1934, Fiorello LaGuardia ordered a crackdown on burlesque. Runways were banned, although stripteases continued to be staged until 1937, when burlesque was banished altogether from the city (Rachel Schteir, *Striptease: The Untold History of the Girlie Show* [New York: Oxford University Press, 2004], 156, 175.)

191 *Released in November.* New York Times, 1 Dec. 1933, 23. Photoplay, Feb. 1934, 56. Hollywood Filmograph, 18 Nov. 1933, 2. H. Mark Glancy, "MGM Film Grosses, 1924–1948: The Eddie Mannix Ledger," Historical Journal of Film, Radio and Television, 12 (June 1992) 127–144 and microfiche supplement.

191 *After the release.* Variety, 13 June 1933, 3 (MGM contract). Motion Picture Herald, 24 Feb. 1934, 51 ("our old friend Winnie"). Ibid., 27 Jan 1934, 61 ("Glad to see Winnie").

192 *Cast aside.* "Kelton-Lightner Team," Hollywood Reporter, 12 Mar. 1934, 3. Film Daily, 14 Aug. 1934, 8.

194 *I'll Fix It premiered.* Film Daily, 10 Nov. 1934, 4. Variety, 20 Nov. 1934, 15. Cecilia Agers, "Going Places," ibid., 13 Nov. 1934, 31. New York Times, 12 Nov. 1934, 17.

CHAPTER 12: I NEVER CARED A HANG FOR FAME

196 *Even before the release.* Los Angeles Times, 16 May 1934, 6 ("An orchid to you"). Marian Rhea, "Diary of a Hollywood News Hound," New Movie Magazine, May 1935, 56.

196 *Winnie no doubt regretted.* Marian Rhea, "Handy Hints from Hollywood," Movie Classic, June 1935, 68. "Picture Stars' Homes Aglow," Los Angeles Times, 24 Dec. 1938, A16. Jimmie Fidler column, Appleton (WI) Post-Crescent, 24 Dec. 1938, 15.

197 *Shortly before Santa was kidnapped.* Jimmie Fidler column, Reading (PA) Eagle, 13 Dec. 1937, 14. It is interesting that Fidler still perpetuated the myth that Theo Lightner was Winnie's sister. A year earlier Winnie had informed another columnist that

she was "living in Beverly Hills" and "very happy." She reminisced a bit about her Manhattan childhood before saying, "But if I go on with such memories I won't be so happy." (O. O. McIntyre, "New York Day By Day," Miami [FL] News, 13 Dec. 1936, 6.)

197 *At the time of Fidler's conversation.* Toronto Globe, 9 Nov. 1936, 2 ("washed up"). Marie Dressler's career had flagged between 1922 and 1927, but then she made a remarkable comeback and remained a star until her death in 1934.

197 *Still, even if her Hollywood prospects.* Variety, 9 Oct. 1929, 54 (two-year RKO contract); 31 Sept. 1938, 46 (plays Loew's State in New York City). Margaret Mara column, Brooklyn Eagle, 18 Nov. 1932, 8 ("excellent comedian" but should change name). Suffolk County (NY) News, 8 April 1932, 9 (buys Greenport house). (Southold, NY) Long Island Traveler, 1 July 1937, 3 (Sandy Beach cottage). Variety, 30 Oct. 1935, 55 (quits Toronto).

Fred Lightner's career has been traced through several hundred reports about him in newspapers and in the show-business trade press. Only the most important are cited.

198 *Until the late 1940s.* Variety 14 July 1937, 48 (replaces Jack Benny); 1 Mar. 1939, 50, 54 (on Broadway); 16 Mar. 1938, 43 (nightclubs). Film Daily, 26 Aug. 1935, 12 (Educational Pictures). Life, 5 Mar. 1945, 49–51.

Fred and Roscella played the Palace in 1934, but by then appearing there was just a routine RKO booking rather than a career milestone. At their opening performance the audience was sparse: "Very few drifted in" from the sidewalk to see five live acts and a movie. (Variety, 13 Feb. 1934, 59.)

198 *If Fred's career demonstrates.* Toronto Globe, 9 Nov. 1936, 2 (master of ceremonies). "Saddest Jump," Variety, 13 June 1933, 1.

199 *Fortunately, Fred never had to.* June Havoc, *More Havoc* (New York: Harper & Row, 1980), 162–63, 167–68. Esther Ralston, *Some Day We'll Laugh: An Autobiography* (Metuchen, NJ: Scarecrow Press, 1985), 155–56. Driving her own car, Ralston followed Fred and Roscella all the way across the continent but then got lost in Manhattan.

199 *Even in the glory days.* "Fastest of the Fast Set But with Roy Del Ruth It Is Speed in Production," Variety, 1 Aug. 1933, 2.

200 *Although the critics acclaimed.* Film Daily, 20 July 1948, 6 ("Fred Lightner is outstanding"). Film Bulletin, 2 Aug. 1948, 12 ("scores with a razor-sharp performance"). Modern Screen, Oct. 1948, 18 ("just plain magnificent"). Leonard Lyons column, Philadelphia Inquirer, 29 Aug. 1950, 3 (disc jockey). *Fourteen Hours* full cast list, Turner Classic Movies <tcm.com>. New York Times, 26 June 1953, 15 ("A Night in Venice"). Walter Winchell column, Buffalo (NY) Courier-Express, 14 July 1954, 16 ("clerk at the Taft Hotel"). Brooklyn Eagle, 1 Dec. 1954, 13 (on Broadway).

200 *If there ever was a time.* Richard Lightner recalled this trip in a 24 July 2012 telephone conversation with the author.

201 *Winnie gave birth.* The court case that ruled on Olive's original suit for separate maintenance is quoted and described in detail in the later appeal case: Del Ruth v. Del Ruth, 75 Cal. App. 2nd 638 [Civ. No. 15268, Second Dist., Div. Three. Aug. 1, 1946], Olive Del Ruth, Appellant, v. Thomas Leroy Del Ruth, Respondent <law.justia.com>.

203 *Only he wasn't. Olive appealed.* "Wife Granted Divorce from Film Director," Long Beach (CA) Press Telegram, 7 Aug. 1947, 27.

203 *Although Roy was stuck.* "Roy Del Ruth Weds Former Comedy Star," Los Angeles Times, 16 Aug. 1948, B1.

203 *Only he wasn't. In January 1951.* "Alimony Sought Again," Spokane (WA) Daily Chronicle, 24 Jan. 1951, 8 ("grossly unfair"). "Wants Alimony Reinstated," (Pasco, WA) Tri-City Herald, 25 Jan. 1951, 15 ("ill and emotionally upset"). "Director Sued for Money 'Spent on Actress,'" Victoria (TX) Advocate, 20 Jan. 1952, 3A. "Film Director Sued for Support by Son," Reading (PA) Eagle, 3 Feb. 1952, 10.

204 *That Roy's freedom had come.* Los Angeles Times, 6 June 1952, 19.

204 *That is not to say.* Jimmy Starr column, Cedar Rapids (IA) Gazette, 27 July 1952, 9. Richard Lightner, telephone conversation with the author, 9 Sept. 2012. Thomas Del Ruth interviewed by Karen Herman, Los Angeles, 18 Jan. 2007 <emmytvlegends.org>.

205 *During those lean years.* Thomas Del Ruth recalled the *Tugboat Annie* incident in a telephone conversation with the author, 10 Feb. 2012.

206 *Not long after.* Jimmy Starr, *Barefoot on Barbed Wire: An Autobiography of a Forty-Year Hollywood Balancing Act* (Lanham, MD: Scarecrow Press, 2001), 204–6 (seeking work). Long Beach (CA) Press Telegram, 28 April 1961, C7 (consulted physician).

206 *Winnie lived on quietly.* Jack Haley, *Heart of the Tin Man: The Collected Writings of Jack Haley*, ed. Mitchell Cohen (Beverly Hills, CA: Tinman Publishing, 2000), 82 ("You know who I mean, Jack"), 83 ("Al Jolson-sized talent" [ellipsis changed to em dash]). Harrison Carroll, "In Hollywood" column, New Castle (PA) News, 22 May 1968, 24.

207 *The party was a merry occasion.* Los Angeles Times, 8 Mar. 1971. Haley, *Tin Man*, 83 ("a superstar who thrilled millions").

It would have pleased Winnie to know that her son Thomas was to become one of Hollywood's most distinguished cinematographers. His numerous film credits include *The Breakfast Club* (1985) and *Stand By Me* (1986). He also worked extensively in television, winning two Emmy Awards for his work on *The West Wing* (2000, 2001).

207 *Even when the arrival.* The color was lost in the 1950s when Warner Bros. copied the movies onto black and white safety stock for showing on television, and then discarded the deteriorating nitrate originals. The modern copies are defective in another respect as well. Because there was no sound track on films produced using the Vitaphone sound-on-disk system, their frame images had a ratio of width to height that differed from that of the new stock, but the difference was ignored when the new prints were made. Consequently, the images on the new prints are missing a portion of the original and so sometimes appear poorly composed. (Richard Barrios, *A Song in the Dark: The Birth of the Musical Film* [2nd ed., New York: Oxford University Press, 2010], 10n2.)

208 *Winnie's career casts light.* Illustrated Buffalo (NY) Express, 7 Nov. 1915, 47 ("dainty" "refined songs").

210 *Wild and wonderful Winnie Lightner.* For the original context of this quotation, see above, pp. 119–20.

INDEX